GOD DOESN'T WHISPER

Jim Osman

Foreword by John MacArthur

Editor: Diedre Osman
Cover artwork provided by Josh Comstock:
PeaceHarbor.co

For updates on the ministry of Kootenai Community Church please visit:
TruthOrTerritory.com
KootenaiChurch.org

Website hosting provided by Thomas Leo:
TLCWebHosting.com

ISBN-13: 978-0-9984550-2-0
Kootenai Community Church Publishing

First Edition: August 2020

Bulk copies of this book are available at special pricing. Please contact the author through the contact page at KootenaiChurch.org.

Other Books by Jim Osman

Truth or Territory:
A Biblical Approach to Spiritual Warfare
Also available in audiobook.

Available in Spanish:
Verdad o territorio:
Un acercamiento bíblico a la guerra espiritual

****

Selling the Stairway to Heaven:
Critiquing the Claims of Heaven Tourists

****

The Prosperity of the Wicked:
A Study of Psalm 73

Available in Spanish:
La prosperidad de los impios:
Un estudio del Salmo 73

Dedication

To my wonderful wife without whose encouragement, hard work, and support, this book would not exist. She has made my life, ministry, and books better than they could ever be without her.

Table of Contents

Foreword

Every now and then I meet with people whom I think to be rather weak in the head, who will journey from place to place and will perform follies by the gross under the belief that they are doing the will of God because some silly whim of their diseased brains is imagined to be an inspiration from above.

Is the truth that which I imagine to be revealed to me by some private communication? Am I to fancy that I enjoy some special revelation, and am I to order my life by voices, dreams, and impressions? Brethren, fall not into this common delusion. God's word to us is in Holy Scripture. All the truth that sanctifies men is in God's Word. Do not listen to those who cry, "Lo here!" and "Lo there!"

--Charles Spurgeon (excerpts from "A Well-Ordered Life" a sermon preached 27 June 1869; and "Our Lord's Prayer for His People's Sanctification," a sermon preached 7 March 1886.)

No religious delusion has been more pervasive or brought more confusion into the church than the belief that God routinely speaks to people outside of Scripture. Even some of the sweetest, most well-meaning Christians sometimes try to discern private messages from God through spontaneous thoughts that occur to them, sudden impressions, a voice in their head, vivid dreams, or some other means that they interpret as direct revelation from on high. This is a pernicious type of *mysticism* that has more in common with occult soothsaying than with any biblical principle of discernment. It is, in fact, a highly dangerous way of seeking to hear from God.

Like every other variety of mysticism, the quest for fresh, private revelation is rooted in the false notion that spiritual reality is apprehended by intuition—that truth is found *subjectively,* by introspection or imagination, rather than *objectively,* by reading and correctly interpreting the truth of God's Word. In practice, the mystical approach severely undermines the authority of Scripture, because private revelations that supposedly come directly from the mouth of God to an individual always seem more personal, more specific, fresher, and more timely than messages that were written down in ages past by Old Testament prophets or New Testament apostles. So those who believe God is commonly speaking to them this way will naturally be prone to give greater weight and attention to their own hunches, premonitions, and impressions than they give to the Bible.

If inner voices or extrasensory perception were important means of discerning the will of God, Scripture would command and instruct believers in the practice. But absolutely nothing in Scripture ever encourages Christians to seek guidance through such means. In fact, the law of Moses strictly forbid every practice of that sort. Deuteronomy 18:10 classifies all kinds of divination, fortune-telling, and omen-reading with the custom of ritual child sacrifice. The penalty for prophesying falsely in God's name was death (Deuteronomy 18:20). Claiming to have a message from God when the message is a product of one's own imagination was therefore properly treated as the grossest kind of abomination. It's no wonder Scripture takes such a dim view of casually treating prophecy as a hit-and-miss proposition, given all the evil that the practice has spawned.

The fact that God sometimes (albeit very rarely) spoke through dreams and visions to some of the pivotal characters in Scripture doesn't mean everyone should routinely seek His truth by listening for an inner voice. God once rebuked a false prophet through a donkey (Numbers 22:28-30). Surely no sane person would suggest we should be listening to animals lest we miss a vital message from God. On the other hand, there are indeed charismatic soothsayers who teach people to seek omens and supernatural signs from birds, animals, signs in the sky, and all kinds of random events. It's hard to imagine any religious practice more at odds with the way Christians are supposed to seek truth. Jesus made clear how Christians are supposed to seek truth and holiness, by praying for His people this way: "Sanctify them in the truth; your word is truth" (John 17:17).

But charismatics are not the only ones who have shown a dangerous vulnerability to the whispering voices in their heads. A few years ago a bestselling book made the rounds among more traditional Baptists promoting the idea of listening for private revelations from God. The book's underlying premise was that Christians who are *not* regularly hearing private messages from God are not truly experiencing God as He intends.

That notion is fraught with dangers and diversions that in real life have absolutely no potential for sanctification or spiritual growth. In fact, the idea that God commonly speaks to His people in indistinct whispers *undermines* faith, because while we might occasionally have an intuitive thought that turns out to be remarkably accurate, those "inner promptings" are more frequently wrong than right. And the person who believes God is speaking through such means will eventually have to conclude either (falsely) that the voice of God is unreliable, misleading, and often totally wrong—or (correctly) that those gentle whispers are not the voice of God at all.

Anyone who is confused about this issue and seeking biblical answers will be profoundly thankful for this superb volume by Pastor Jim Osman. He handles the matter candidly, answers the essential questions biblically, and writes with both gentle grace and sharp clarity. I'm very grateful for the work he has done and eager to see this work find a large audience.

I especially love the way Pastor Osman continually points readers back to Scripture, which is the only place we can reliably hear the voice of God. We know, after all, that in the words of the Bible "we have the prophetic word more fully confirmed, to which you will do well to pay attention as to a lamp shining in a dark place, until the day dawns and the morning star rises in your hearts, knowing this first of all, that no prophecy of Scripture comes from someone's own interpretation. For no prophecy was ever produced by the will of man, but men spoke from God as they were carried along by the Holy Spirit." (2 Peter 1:19-21).

John MacArthur
Pastor-Teacher
Grace Community Church
Sun Valley, California

Acknowledgements

Writing acknowledgments for any book is tricky. An author can never possibly thank or acknowledge everyone who has had a hand in its publication. There will always be someone left out and someone who feels left out. I don't intend to omit anyone worthy of inclusion, so if you feel your name deserves a mention in this space, then please write it here: I wish to thank _____. Without your help, I'm not sure I could've ever written this book. I'm glad we got that out of the way.

I must thank a few people who don't know they've influenced me or had any hand in this book. First, Phil Powers, my Fourth Year professor at Millar College of the Bible, was the first used by God to make me question this methodology that undermined my belief in the sufficiency of Scripture. His patient and gracious teaching gave me a love for the truth and a confidence in the Word of God that has never left me. Additionally, Greg Koukl's clear teaching on this subject has had a profound influence on me. Garry Friesen's book, *Decision Making and the Will of God*, was the final nail in the coffin. God used those three men to liberate me from an oppressive life of superstition and experience-driven theology.

The congregation of Kootenai Community Church makes it a joy to shepherd, teach, and write. Their love for the truth is a weekly encouragement. Their commitment to Scripture is an inspiration. Their love for their leaders makes our work a joy and not a burden. The body of Christ at Kootenai is filled with gifted and generous people. More specifically, Thomas Leo provides the hosting for our online resources. Josh Comstock provided the artwork for this book and works hard to maintain the websites that make Kootenai's ministry available online. The elders with whom I serve - Dave Rich, Cornel Rasor, and Jess Whetsel - lighten my workload enough that I can write. Their friendship, fellowship, and faithfulness to their calling continue to humble and encourage me. They are among my dearest friends and it is a joy to serve Christ with them. They are an example to all they lead and serve. I continue to pray that the Lord may grant us many years of fruitful service together. My secretary, Marcia Whetsel, keeps all nonessential distractions off my desk and out of my thinning hair. Her hard work makes mine easier.

Justin Peters (justinpeters.org) has long encouraged me to write this book. In fact, Justin was promoting this book before it was written. He has provided valuable feedback and resources. His friendship continues to be a great blessing. Justin contacted Phil

Johnson who facilitated getting a draft of this book to Pastor John MacArthur who graciously wrote the foreword, in spite of his busy and demanding schedule. I am grateful for that kindness.

A mature church body, gifted leaders, good friends and a hard-working secretary, made this book possible, but my wife's diligent encouragement, skilled editorial work, and unfailing confidence made it a reality. Her careful proofreading is a labor of love for which I could never give sufficient thanks. She is a treasure whose worth is far above jewels (Proverbs 31:10). Her attentive labor has made this book better in every way! If this book bears any fruit for eternity, she will certainly share in its reward.

Though last, it is certainly not least: I thank my God, King, and Savior Jesus Christ. He has lavished on me untold and undeserved blessings. He has saved me, delivered me from error, sanctified me by His Word and secured me everlastingly for His own eternal joy and glory. To Him, the blessed and only Sovereign, the King of kings and the Lord of lords, Who alone possesses immortality and dwells in unapproachable light, be glory both now and forever! Amen. Soli Deo Gloria!

Preface

This was supposed to be my first book. It ended up being my fourth.

In 2014 I decided to write a book as a fundraiser for our church building program. At the time, we were meeting in a school cafeteria for weekly services while we raised money to build a new church building. I suggested to my wife that I take the series of articles I had written for our church newsletter on "Hearing the Voice of God" and turn them into a book. That series of articles was the most downloaded resource on our website (kootenaichurch.org). From the very first mention of it, Diedre was an enthusiastic supporter.

I was writing a series of articles on biblical spiritual warfare and started revising the voice of God articles for publication. However, I found the work of a weekly sermon, a monthly article on spiritual warfare, and a book on yet a third subject was more than my limited intellect could handle. I set aside the voice of God book project to finish the series on spiritual warfare. Before I was done, I decided to turn the articles on spiritual warfare into a book.[1]

I occasionally returned to the articles on the voice of God only to set them aside for other writing projects. When I finally started to revise the articles, I was disappointed in their content and quality. They weren't nearly as good as I remembered them. That started me on a reading, studying, and writing process that has lasted nearly 2 years. This book is a complete rewrite of the original material.

For the longest time, this book didn't have a title. Diedre and I referred to it as "the voice of God book." Then one evening I sat down at the kitchen table to read the mail. My oldest son was sitting at the other end finishing off a bowl of cereal. I picked up the latest catalog from Christian Book Distributors (CBD) and there on the front page was an advertisement for Mark Batterson's newest book, *Whisper: How to Hear the Voice of God.*

"I guess I'm going to have to buy this book too," I said.

My son curiously looked up over his bowl of cereal.

"Here is yet another book claiming to teach us how to hear from God," I said shaking my head in disbelief. "Listen to this description: 'God still speaks today. His voice and guidance wasn't only for the saints and prophets of old, but for followers of Jesus now.

---

[1] Jim Osman, *Truth or Territory: A Biblical Approach to Spiritual Warfare* (Kootenai: Kootenai Community Church Publishing, 2015).

In *Whisper: How to Hear the Voice of God*, author and pastor Mark Batterson shares seven ways that God communicates with His followers, if they'll stop to listen. Through the tools of Scripture, Doors, Dreams, People, Promptings, and Pain, God weaves divine messages of love, encouragement and insight, into our lives every day.'"

"Wait,… people actually believe that?" he asked. "Can I see that?"

I handed him the catalog across the table. "Yes, unfortunately, people believe it. God *doesn't* whisper!" I said emphatically. "Wait! THAT is going to be the title of my book!" I said. "*God Doesn't Whisper.*"

A couple of months later I started writing. I was combing through a file folder filled with articles, book reviews, and notes I have collected on the subject over the years, when I found a three-part series written by Greg Koukl of Stand to Reason titled "Does God Whisper?" I had printed the articles, filed them away for future use, and forgotten the titles. The similarity between the title of this book and the series of articles by Koukl is not an intentional act of plagiarism. If anything, it is a subtle tribute to the influence of Greg's teaching in my life.

In the pages that follow, I have endeavored to give credit where credit is due. I have benefited in profound ways from both Greg Koukl and Garry Friesen's work on this subject. At times I am unsure where their language ends and mine begins. Over the years I have gleaned from their illustrations and borrowed some wording. Both their works and ministries predate mine, so if I have not footnoted something that sounds like it came from one of them, it is either because I have forgotten where I heard it or, because my convictions on this subject run so parallel to theirs, I have accidentally stumbled into the same language.

I intend to convince you that God doesn't whisper. In fact, I'm hoping that you will see that such a notion of God is wholly unworthy of Him. I pray that the Lord will use this book to advance His truth, magnify His name, and encourage His people in His Word. *Soli Deo Gloria!*

Jim Osman
Kootenai, Idaho
June, 2020

Part 1

Introduction

Chapter 1

A Crisis at College

1

This book is a refutation of something I once firmly believed. At one time, I wholeheartedly embraced the practices and theology critiqued in these pages. I believed that Christians could and should learn to hear the voice of God for His guidance in decision-making. I believed the mark of maturity - the measure of spirituality - was a carefully cultivated ability to discern the whispers of God in signs, impressions, and circumstances.

I knew the Scriptures provided no "Jim-specific" instructions. There is no "book of Jim" telling *me*, specifically *me*, where to live, which woman to marry, which career path to choose, which church to attend, or which house to buy. These decisions, and many more, are life-altering. I didn't believe it was possible for a Christian to live obediently unless he could discern God's guidance outside Scripture.

This belief was not derived from a careful study of Scripture. I received this teaching from others. I had a good friend, instrumental in my conversion to Christ, who would describe "putting out a fleece" to discern God's direction for decisions. Other friends described "signs" from God revealing His will in answer to prayer. I was committed to cultivating the ability to hear the voice of God. I could not imagine living a godly, obedient, Christian life apart from it. Early in my walk with Christ, I faced a crisis that caused me to question this theology. I started to examine the "hearing from God" paradigm, putting all my preconceived notions under a microscope.

I asked, "Does the Bible teach that Christians should cultivate the discipline of hearing from God through outward signs or inner voices?" I searched the Scriptures and examined the methods by which, I assumed, God speaks to His people. The answers I found

3

liberated me from what I now regard as a superstitious and burdensome view of divine guidance and private revelation.

What crisis caused such a paradigm shift? A terminal illness? The death of a loved one? A near-death experience? No. It was nothing as traumatic as that. In retrospect, it sounds so insignificant and silly.

SHOULD I STAY OR SHOULD I GO?

After enduring 12 years of torturous misery in the ninth circle of Hell on earth (euphemistically called "public school"), I achieved my life's ambition of graduating high school. I intended to go to a secular university - *after* one year at Millar College of the Bible, a small, non-denominational college in southern Saskatchewan, Canada. When I set foot on the Millar campus, I had no intention of attending more than a year. Full-time ministry was not even on my radar. My one-year commitment to Bible college was only intended to provide me a spiritual foundation so I could pursue my other interests in a God-honoring fashion.

As the first year drew to a close, I was confronted with the most difficult decision I had ever faced. Should I leave Bible college after only one year and pursue my goal of becoming a CPA, or come back for a second year of studies? The stakes were high. Back home I had friends and family pressuring me to "stop all this fooling around at Bible college" and get down to pursuing a career. My friends at college wanted me to return so we could be together for a second year of studies.

This decision would determine the course of the rest of my life. I had earned a one-year certificate in biblical studies, establishing a spiritual and doctrinal foundation. My time had not been wasted. In fact, spiritually speaking, it was paying large dividends. One year of learning created an insatiable hunger for more knowledge. Though I wanted to know more, I could not see myself in any kind of full-time ministry. That seemed to make further study quite unnecessary and possibly foolish. Pastoring a church was not even a consideration at that point. I just wanted to learn.

Committing to a second year at Millar would mean committing to a third as well. There was no middle ground. I would settle for the one-year certificate or commit to the full course and earn a three-year diploma.

It was no small decision for a nineteen-year-old. If I committed to three years of Bible college, I would be putting off my dream of going to a secular university to pursue a degree in accounting. On the other hand, pursuing a degree in accounting would make any Bible instruction beyond one year unnecessary. I would be delaying my goals to satisfy my spiritual curiosities. My whole future hung in the balance!

At the time, I believed that making a wrong decision would result in missing God's will and forever being consigned to a life of "second-best." I only had one shot and I did not want to end up with a "second-best" career, a "second-best" education, or a "second-best" wife. I would be forever haunted by the fact that God had given me one shot at doing His will, and I missed it! What if I botched this, the most fundamental and far-reaching decision of my life thus far? Could God ever trust me with another one? Further, I was hounded by the fear that God would punish me for being disobedient to His will. I cowered under the dread that He might discipline me for failing to recognize the signs and discern His will.

As if that were not complicated enough, the school offered a tuition reduction to those who would commit to return before the end of the current year. Was this a sign from God or good marketing by the school? Was God giving me a sign or was Satan laying a trap to trick me into making the wrong decision? Could this be Satan's ploy to lure me away from God's perfect will under the guise of "wise stewardship"? How was I to know?

Though I was not the only student faced with this choice, it did seem I was the only one who lacked clear direction on the matter. Other students made up their minds rather painlessly. Some knew they were coming back. Others knew they were leaving after only one year. I would hear my classmates say, "The Lord told me that I was supposed to come back next year," or, "The Lord is not leading me to return." I needed that kind of clear direction. I needed the Lord to reveal His will through a specific personal revelation, and that is what I prayed.

"Lord, if You want me to come back for second-year, I need to know. I don't want to make a bad decision. My whole future hangs in the balance. I just need You to speak to me and tell me. I need a sign of some sort. Please give me clear direction, a sign of Your will for me in this situation. I am listening."

I longed to hear God give me some clear direction. I tried to be alert to any hints or signs He might give. I sensed nothing.

"Lord, the end of the school year is approaching fast. I need You to tell me. Send me a message of some sort: a sign, a strong feeling one way or the other. Whisper it, please!"

5

Still nothing. My frustration mounted. Why wasn't the Lord speaking to me? My classmates had heard from God. He was apparently more real to them than He was to me. I was searching for an explanation.

"Perhaps it is because I am such a new believer," I reasoned. My college friends had mostly grown up in Christian homes - attending church all their lives. Unlike most of them, I was only 4 years old in my faith. Perhaps I had not been a believer long enough to learn how to hear God's voice.

Perhaps I just wasn't "spiritual" enough. Doubts began to haunt me which only added to my frustration. Did I have *all* of the Spirit? Why was the Spirit of God so silent toward me, a child of God? Perhaps I didn't walk closely enough with God. I prayed, but maybe I wasn't praying hard enough, often enough, fervently enough, or even long enough. Maybe I wasn't saying the right things or asking the right questions. Maybe I wasn't serving the Lord faithfully enough. What if only the "great servants of God" get to hear directly from Him? Where would that leave me?

Ultimately, I began to doubt if I was a child of God. Why did others "hear from God" but I only got silence in response to my prayers? Why could they pick up on the hints God was dropping while I remained oblivious to His voice? I remembered Jesus promising in John 10:27 that His sheep hear His voice. Others apparently heard it while I did not.

Scripture appeared to be jam-packed with examples of believers who heard God speak: Noah, Abraham, Isaac, Jacob, Moses, Joshua, David, Solomon, Daniel, Peter, Paul, Cornelius, and countless others. Couldn't God break His silence long enough to do for me what He had done for so many others?

I comforted myself with the possibility that maybe I didn't have enough knowledge of the Bible to hear the voice of God. Maybe I needed to be more knowledgeable and mature before John 10:27 would apply to me. I wasn't nearly as well-taught and mature in the faith as many of my classmates. I was light-years behind my classmates. Many of them were raised in the church and some were children of staff at the school. Perhaps my problem was a lack of knowledge.

I decided to give God His "out."

"Lord, if it is Your will for me to return next year, I need a sign. If You want me back then cause my whole second year tuition to be paid in full. Then I will know Your will. That will be a clear sign that would convince friends and family back home that You are

6

supernaturally directing this decision. Please do for me what you did for Gideon. Please give me a sign. Amen."

Days passed. Nothing. Maybe my request was too ambitious. I dialed it back to something more reasonable.

"Ok, Lord, just provide half a year's tuition. Cause someone to pay for the first semester. I will take that as a sign You want me to return."

Days passed. Nothing.

"Lord, if someone sends in money to cover my books for second year, then I will know that it is Your will. Never mind tuition, all I ask for is enough money for books." Suddenly I felt less like Gideon with a fleece and more like Abraham negotiating with God to spare a city.

Still nothing.

I was distraught. I *wanted* to come back for second year, but God wasn't telling me what He wanted me to do! Why was God so silent? Didn't He love me? Wasn't He interested in my future? Didn't He know what was at stake? Couldn't the God who spoke the universe into existence give me a little word, a whisper, a nudge, ... *SOMETHING*? I needed direction - specific guidance - like never before. Why was I unable to hear when all my friends seemed to be getting personal messages? Maybe something was wrong with me!

THE INSIGNIFICANCE OF IT

The crisis at college was monumental to me as a young believer. What I needed from God seemed so simple. I just needed a sign. I wasn't asking for direction in a decision with multiple options. I had it narrowed down to two. That seemed easy enough. I wasn't asking for a burning bush, a pillar of smoke, or any miraculous sign.

I was praying, looking, and listening as best I knew how. I kept my eyes open and tried to discern any kind of hint or suggestion that might be from Him. How hard could it be for the God of all the universe to drop a few breadcrumbs to show the way? Even if I was ignorant and immature in the faith, why would that keep God from communicating clearly with me? Why would my lack of perception create such an insurmountable obstacle to hearing God's voice? Can't He get His message across, even to one who isn't experienced in listening for His voice?

I couldn't believe God lacked ability to communicate when needed. It didn't seem that the problem was with me either. I was certainly hungry enough to hear from God. I couldn't have desired to hear from Him more. I was desperately longing for clear guidance. I micro-analyzed every thought, feeling, intuition, nudging, and prompting that popped into my anxious brain. I examined every event, circumstance, and happening around me, trying to wring out of them some clear indicator of the divine will.

I began to think, "If God doesn't lack the power to speak, and I do not lack the passion to hear, then maybe the problem is with my understanding of how God communicates to His people." Was I expecting God to do something He had not promised? Did I really need a sign or a revelation of some kind to know and do the will of God? Did I need information not revealed in Scripture?

It was widely believed among the student body that we must listen for God and cultivate the discipline of hearing His voice. I assumed all the talk I heard about God leading through still small voices, promptings, and impressions was biblical. I accepted it without misgivings. Mature Christians spoke as if God were whispering directions in their ears. I assumed I was missing out on this intimate relationship due to my lack of piety or maturity.

I figured it was only a matter of time before I would achieve that level of spirituality. Soon, I would also learn the essential discipline of reading signs and hearing the voice of God. Eventually, I would be able to make decisions with the confidence I was guided by God's voice.

THE NON-CHARISMATIC VIEW

This view of hearing God's voice was not unique to one small Bible college in the 1990s. It is the predominant view of modern evangelicalism. I have encountered numerous believers who make decisions based on subjective impressions, signs, or still small voices in their head. I would venture that among "non-charismatic"[1] Christians, more than 80% believe God continues to speak outside Scripture. That may be a wildly conservative estimate.

A Google search for "hearing the voice of God" churns up a subjective slough of teaching from every quarter of Christendom. Amazon offers a robust selection of products specifically designed to prepare you to hear from God and teach you to discern His voice. "Private revelation" is no longer the ugly theological stepchild of the charismatic movement. It has been adopted into evangelicalism and warmly embraced in traditionally non-charismatic churches.

---

[1] I put "non-charismatic" in quotations because though they claim to be non-charismatic, they affirm the cardinal charismatic doctrine of modern revelations.

Those in charismatic and Pentecostal circles affirm ongoing personal revelation. They believe God continues to speak through modern prophets. They affirm that every believer can hear God's voice for themselves. Likewise, those in the Word of Faith (WOF) and New Apostolic Reformation (NAR) movements assert that God gifts apostles and prophets who speak with the same authority, clarity, and accuracy as in Scripture. The NAR movement claims that God is raising up a new generation of apostles with authority and miracle-working power to bring His Kingdom to this earth.[2]

Your local bookstore is likely well stocked with books written by non-charismatic pastors of non-charismatic churches educated in non-charismatic colleges and seminaries, who encourage us to listen for God's voice outside Scripture. Nobody would accuse Charles Stanley of being charismatic, yet he wrote *How to Listen to God*. He has produced volumes of articles, videos, books, and sermons on the subject. Zondervan published *The Power of a Whisper* by Bill Hybels, another non-charismatic pastor. Priscilla Shirer, the daughter of popular preacher Tony Evans, has produced numerous books on hearing the voice of God. Shirer has written *He Speaks to Me* and *Discerning the Voice of God*. Her website promotes a plethora of resources designed to instruct Christians on hearing the voice of God through various means. Priscilla Shirer is a graduate of the non-charismatic Dallas Theological Seminary.

We should expect the Southern Baptist Convention and their affiliated churches and ministries to reject these teachings on private revelation, but Henry Blackaby's book *Experiencing God* has found wide circulation in Baptist circles. Blackaby has single-handedly promoted the practice of listening for the voice of God wider than any other non-charismatic in modern times. That accomplishment is due in no small part to the blitzkrieg-like promotion of his resources by the Southern Baptist Convention, Lifeway Christian Resources, and a myriad of Baptist pastors across the country. Following his footsteps, Beth Moore maintains a ubiquitous presence in cessationist Southern Baptist circles, constantly regaling crowds with her tales of hearing God speak. The infiltration of this theology into non-charismatic circles has been swift and thorough.

---

[2] For an excellent critique of these charismatic movements and their doctrines, check out the ministry of Justin Peters at his website, justinpeters.org. The video series of Justin's seminar *Clouds Without Water* is highly recommended. I would also recommend *Defining Deception* by Costi Hinn and Anthony Wood (Southern California Seminary Press, 2018).

Is this theology biblical? In the pages that follow, I will answer that question. I will interact with the teachings of those who promote the practice and theology of hearing from God. We will compare them with Scripture to see if the Bible teaches that Christians should expect regular personal revelation outside of Scripture.

BACK TO COLLEGE

What about the crisis at college? Did I ever hear the voice of the Shepherd? No. In the end, I did what I most desired to do. I wanted to return and continue my study of Scripture and theology. If you haven't guessed by now, I never pursued a career in accounting. I never attended a secular university. I returned to Millar for a second and third year without any intention of pursuing full-time Christian ministry. After graduating from the third year, I married my beautiful bride, took a year off from school, and then returned for the newly-minted fourth-year internship program.

I made all those decisions - and thousands of others - without nurturing an ability to hear still small voices. I walk with Christ day by day and enjoy sweet fellowship with Him in His Word. I don't listen for whispers. I have learned that *God doesn't whisper*.

Chapter 2

A Conventional Custom

2

Protestants have their own version of "received tradition." Handed down from generation to generation, from teacher to student, the traditions are not easily exorcised from the verbiage of Christian subculture, the life of the church, or the practice of Christians. Old traditions become "orthodoxy" and questioning them becomes "heresy" to passionate devotees.

We are commanded to "examine everything carefully" (1 Thessalonians 5:21), following the example of the Bereans whom Luke commended because they "received the word with great eagerness, examining the Scriptures daily to see whether these things were so" (Acts 17:11). Every believer must conform their thinking, theology, and practice to the teaching of Scripture. This is impossible if we receive as dogma practices that have no foundation in Scripture.

I ask that you, dear reader, be willing to examine a methodology that has become more ingrained in modern evangelicalism than even the teachings of Scripture. It is such a fixture of modern Christian lingo, preaching, and practice, that many believers cannot imagine their Christian life without it.

The practice in question? Hearing the voice of God (HVG).

Before we critique the practice in the chapters that follow, it is necessary to understand the theology as promoted by its advocates.

THE PRACTICE IN GENERAL

Broadly speaking, I am critiquing the teaching that *God speaks outside of Scripture to His people today*. Variously described as "hearing the voice of God," "listening for the voice of God," or "receiving extra-biblical revelation," this teaching encourages Christians to listen for the voice of God outside Scripture.

Advocates of this teaching assert the following:

1. God is a communicating God, therefore He will speak to His people today just as He did in biblical times.

2. God wants and needs to speak to His people to provide direction for daily living.

3. Christians should expect to hear from God.

4. Christians must learn to listen for His still small voice by cultivating the attitude necessary to hear from God.

5. Hearing from God outside Scripture is essential for a personal, living, and intimate relationship with Him.

6. The inability to hear God speak renders the Christian incapable of knowing and obeying God's will.

This is HVG theology in a nutshell.

DO THEY REALLY TEACH THAT?

In the chapters that follow, we will examine these claims in greater detail. Here is a brief glimpse at how these six things are taught by HVG advocates.

1. God is a communicating God, therefore He will speak to His people today just as He did in biblical times.

In his book *How To Listen to God*, Charles Stanley writes:

I believe one of the most valuable lessons we can ever learn is how to listen to God....And, the Bible is explicit, God speaks to us just as powerfully today as in the days in which the Bible was written. His Voice waits to be heard, and having heard it, we are launched into the greatest, most exciting adventure we could ever imagine.[1]

---

[1] Charles Stanley, *How to Listen to God.* (Nashville, Thomas Nelson Publishers), 1985, 8.

Providing a list of reasons to believe God still speaks, Stanley offers, "First and foremost, He loves us just as much as He loved the people of Old and New Testament days."[2]

Southern Baptist author Henry Blackaby writes:

> If anything is clear from a reading of the Bible, this fact is clear: God speaks to His people. He spoke to Adam and Eve in the garden of Eden in Genesis. He spoke to Abraham and the other patriarchs. God spoke to the judges, kings, and prophets. God was in Christ Jesus speaking to the disciples. God spoke to the early church, and God spoke to John on the Isle of Patmos in Revelation. God does speak to His people, and you can anticipate that He will be speaking to you also.[3]

2. God wants and needs to speak to His people to provide direction for daily living.

Stanley also suggests that we "need His definite and deliberate direction for our lives, as did Joshua, Moses, Jacob, or Noah." He writes, "As His children, we need His counsel for effective decision making. Since He wants us to make the right choices, He is still responsible for providing accurate data, and that comes through His speaking to us."[4]

HVG teachers believe that receiving directions from God is essential for daily living. Priscilla Shirer writes, "Creating time, space, and opportunity to hear God is paramount for those of us who desire to sense His Spirit's conviction, to receive His detailed guidance, and to discern His intimate leading."[5] Further she claims, "Our lives are an ever-changing catalog of intricately woven personal inquiries that we each need divine direction to navigate accurately."[6]

Henry Blackaby teaches that moving forward in ministry or service to God without such extrabiblical guidance might lead to disaster: "Your task is to wait until the Master gives you instructions.

---

[2] Ibid., 9.

[3] Henry T. Blackaby, and Claude V. King, *Experiencing God: How to Live the Full Adventure of Knowing and Doing the Will of God* (Nashville: Broadman & Holman Publishers, 1994), 83.

[4] Stanley, *How to Listen to God*, 9.

[5] Priscilla Shirer, *Discerning the Voice of God: How to Recognize When God Is Speaking* (Chicago: Moody Publishers, 2012), 18.

[6] Ibid., 20.

If you start 'doing' before you have a direction from God, more than likely you will be wrong."[7]

3. Christians should expect to hear from God.

HVG advocates teach that Christians should *expect* to hear the voice of God outside Scripture. Dallas Willard says that "God is also with us in a conversational relationship: he [sic] speaks with us individually as it is appropriate - which is only to be expected between persons who know one another, care about each other and are engaged in common enterprises."[8] According to Willard, this personal relationship is a "conversational relationship." He writes, "We can expect (given the revelation of God in Christ) that if God wants us to know something, he [sic] will be both able and willing to communicate it to us *plainly*, as long as we are open and prepared by our experience to hear and obey."[9]

4. Christians must learn to listen for His still small voice by cultivating the attitude necessary to hear from God.

Charles Stanley writes, "I believe one of the most valuable lessons we can ever learn is how to listen to God."[10] Using Eli and Samuel (1 Samuel 3) as an example, Stanley writes, "Eli taught Samuel how to listen to God, and if we are going to be men and women of God today, we must learn how we can hear what God is saying to us."[11] If Stanley were describing the need to learn *Scripture* - its doctrines and principles - one could hardly object. However, Stanley is describing the practice of learning to discern the voice of God *outside of Scripture* in impressions and circumstances.[12]

---

[7] Blackaby and King, *Experiencing God*, 89.

[8] Dallas Willard, *Hearing God: Developing A Conversational Relationship with God* (Downers Grove: IVP Books, 2012), 67–68.

[9] Ibid., 250. I agree that God is able to "plainly" speak. However, plain communication is not the kind of "voice of God" promoted by Willard. There is nothing plain or clear about hunches and vague impressions that need confirmation. Notice the limitation that Willard places on God's ability: ". . . as long as we are open and prepared by our experience to hear and obey." What kind of god is limited by our openness and preparedness? The god of HVG theology is unable to speak clearly or be heard if we are not receptive to his voice.

[10] Stanley, *How to Listen to God*, 8.

[11] Ibid., 80.

[12] Ibid., 10-18. Stanley distinguishes between the way God spoke in the Bible and the way God supposedly speaks today. Under the heading "How God Spoke in Old and New Testament Days," Stanley lists direct revelation, dreams and visions, written words, prophets, circumstances, angels, and the Holy Spirit. Under the heading "How God Speaks Today," Stanley lists four ways: Scripture, the Holy Spirit, other people, and circumstances.

Similarly, Henry Blackaby encourages us to "learn" to hear God. He writes, "He wants to have an intimate relationship with you. He wants you to depend only on Him when you are seeking a word from Him. He wants you to learn to hear His voice and know His will."[13] Blackaby teaches that God "has always been speaking to His people," and "you learn to know the voice of God through an intimate love relationship that He has initiated."[14]

5. Hearing from God outside Scripture is essential for a personal, living, and intimate relationship with Him.

Blackaby teaches that hearing from God is a normal and natural element of God's intimate relationship with us. Says Blackaby:

> An intimate love relationship with God is the key to knowing God's voice, to hearing when God speaks. You come to know His voice as you experience Him in a love relationship. As God speaks and you respond, you will come to the point that you recognize His voice more and more clearly....No substitute, however, exists for the intimate relationship with God.[15]

Later he writes, "The method, however, is not the key to knowing God's voice. You learn to know the voice of God through an intimate love relationship that He has initiated."[16] Blackaby is not speaking of Scripture when he says, "God's revelations are designed to bring you into a love relationship with Him."[17]

Willard teaches that we "can learn through experience the particular quality, spirit and content of God's voice."[18] Such people will, "then distinguish and understand the voice of God; their discernment will not be infallible, but they will discern his [sic] voice as clearly and with as much accuracy as they discern the voice of any other person with whom they are on intimate terms."[19]

No Christian would object to having a living, loving, and intimate relationship with their Lord. What I do object to is the teaching that such a relationship is *impossible* without regular

---

[13] Blackaby and King, *Experiencing God*, 90.

[14] Ibid., 96.

[15] Ibid., 88.

[16] Ibid., 96.

[17] Ibid., 97.

[18] Willard, *Hearing God*, 256.

[19] Ibid.

communications outside of Scripture. The quotations above show how central this nurtured ability is in the thinking of those who promote this view.

Priscilla Shirer says this divine communication is the result of our relationship with God: "Once we have been positionally sanctified, we become a part of God's family, and He will speak to us because of that relationship."[20]

Charles Stanley writes:

> If our relationship with Him is a one-way trip and there is no communication or dialogue between us and the Lord Jesus Christ, then there isn't much fellowship. Fellowship is nil when one person does all the talking and the other does all the listening. God still speaks to us today because He wants to develop a love relationship that involves a two-party conversation.[21]

HVG teachers believe that "two-party conversation" is the heart and soul of the Christian life. Blackaby claims, "One critical point to understanding and experiencing God is knowing clearly when God is speaking. If the Christian does not know when God is speaking, he is in trouble at the heart of his Christian life!"[22]

6. The inability to hear God speak renders the Christian incapable of knowing and obeying God's will.

Blackaby boldly declares, "He still speaks to His people. If you have trouble hearing God speak, you are in trouble at the very heart of your Christian experience."[23] Why would Blackaby suggest such a thing? Simply put, if hearing the voice of God is the mark of an intimate, loving relationship, then not hearing the voice of God indicates a lack of relationship. If an ability to hear His voice indicates maturity and obedience, then not hearing the voice must signal immaturity and disobedience.

THE SPECIFICS OF HVG THEOLOGY

The list of manners and methods by which people believe they hear from God is as specific as any practitioner wishes and as undefined and open-ended as they might need.

---

[20] Priscilla Shirer, He Speaks to Me: Preparing to Hear from God (Chicago: Moody Publishers, 2006), 92.

[21] Stanley, *How to Listen to God*, 9.

[22] Blackaby and King, *Experiencing God*, 83–84.

[23] Ibid., 87.

Charles Stanley lists seven ways God spoke in the Old Testament: direct revelation, dreams, audible voices, prophets, circumstances, angels, and the Holy Spirit.[24] He trims the list a little by offering four principle ways God speaks to believers today: Scripture, the Holy Spirit, other people, and circumstances.[25] Stanley clarifies what he means by God speaking through the Holy Spirit: "When I say the Holy Spirit 'speaks,' I do not mean audibly. Rather, He impresses His will in my spirit or mind, and I hear Him in my inner being."[26] Stanley lists five ways that God gets our attention: a restless spirit, a word from others, blessings, unanswered prayers, and unusual circumstances. These are intended to help us identify His voice.

Not to be outdone, Henry Blackaby offers his own list of four ways God speaks today: through the Bible, prayer, circumstances, and the church.[27]

These lists attempt to anchor the reader to some objective standard of divine revelation while at the same time teaching that God speaks through any and all subjective experiences and circumstances. Most of the books referenced in these pages provide detailed discussions on how to recognize the voice of God through various subjective experiences. HVG authors are alert to the danger that subjective experiences can be misinterpreted and abused. How can you tell if your "impression" is the voice of the Holy Spirit or the distracted musings of your own brain? How do you discern if a circumstance communicates a direction from God or a deception from the enemy? These authors feel compelled to provide entire books designed to help us test our subjective communications and experiences so as to avoid being deceived.

Some authors cast off constraint and advocate listening for the voice of God in *almost anything.* In his book, *The Power of a Whisper,* Bill Hybels describes going through a particularly difficult time at Willow Creek Community Church. In need of encouragement, he "hopped on a boat, headed out on the lake and prepared to hear meaningful words from heaven." Rather than turning to Scripture for encouragement, Hybels listened for a subjective voice from Heaven. He describes his experience that day:

---

[24] Stanley, *How to Listen to God,* 10–12.

[25] Ibid., 13–18.

[26] Ibid., 16.

[27] See Chapters 12-15 of *Experiencing God* by Henry Blackaby and Claude King.

But hour after hour I sat there, hearing nothing but the wind and the waves.

Just as I was ready to haul up the anchor and motor back toward the harbor, I saw a Bud Light beer can float by. I stood there staring at the can, wondering, *Is this a message from God? If so, what could it mean? Am I supposed to drink Bud Light? Am I supposed to tell my congregation not to drink Bud Light? Is there a message inside the can?*[28]

We may chuckle at someone trying to exegete the message of a floating beer can, but once we start looking outside Scripture for God's voice, nothing can be off limits. A floating beer can fits easily into the category of "circumstances" promoted by Stanley and Blackaby. Hybels never doubted that God might be trying to speak to him through the beer can. He only doubted his ability to discern the intended message saying, "I had watched and waited and listened, but apparently God had nothing to say to me that day - or at least I couldn't hear it, despite my best efforts."[29]

John Eldredge teaches us to exegete all kinds of random experiences and signs for hidden messages from God. In his book, *Walking with God*, Eldredge says, "God has been speaking to me through hawks."[30] Eldredge describes numerous occasions in which God spoke to him through the hawks nesting at his ranch. What message did God give through the hawk? "A symbol of My heart," God allegedly said. On another occasion Eldredge received a different message through a hawk. He writes, "I asked him [God] what it meant." God's response: "My love."[31]

Though most would not advocate trying to discern the voice of God in beer cans and hawks, the methods they promote could not, in principle, *exclude* such communications.

THE CONVENTIONAL METHODS

HVG authors promote a fairly standard list of methods for hearing the voice of God and receiving divine guidance for decision-making. In the chapters that follow, I will examine and critique (with

---

[28] Bill Hybels, *The Power of a Whisper: Hearing God, Having the Guts to Respond* (Grand Rapids: Zondervan, 2010), 107.

[29] Ibid., 107-108.

[30] John Eldredge, *Walking with God* (Nashville: Thomas Nelson, 2008), 117.

[31] Ibid., 117-118.

Scripture as our guide) the following practices commonly found in the books and teachings of those who advocate HVG theology.

THE STILL SMALL VOICE – CHAPTER 7

Taken from 1 Kings 19, the "still small voice" is assumed to be anything from an impression upon our hearts, to an inaudible voice heard within, to an actual audible whisper.

SCRIPTURE – CHAPTER 8

Of course, HVG advocates believe God speaks through His Word. They just don't believe that He speaks *only* through His Word. For HVG teachers, Scripture is God's voice when a verse jumps off the page or "comes alive." When you feel a strong impression about a verse or a phrase within a verse, *that* is the voice of God speaking through Scripture.

SIGNS – CHAPTER 9

Nearly anything can be a sign carrying the voice of God. It might be an advertisement on television, a newspaper headline, the shape of a cloud, a word or phrase overheard in conversation, a song lyric on the Classic Rock station, or even a floating beer can.

OPEN AND CLOSED DOORS – CHAPTER 10

This is the voice of God in circumstances. An "open door" is a favorable circumstance or unhindered path. A "closed door" is an unfavorable circumstance - one attended by obstacles, opposition, or difficulty. These circumstances are regarded as divine direction for decision-making.

THE FLEECE – CHAPTER 11

Using Gideon's example (Judges 6-7), HVG advocates promote using "fleeces" to determine God's will. They propose "Gideon-like" tests of circumstances asking God to provide guidance through signs. If X happens, it is a sign that the will of God is option A. If Y happens, they conclude the will of God is option B.

THE INNER PEACE – CHAPTER 12

The inner peace is a subjective feeling of contentment or ease regarding a direction or decision. Colossians 3:15 is cited as proof that a feeling of peace always accompanies any direction God has revealed. Allegedly, God's peace always confirms His voice.

FEELING LED – CHAPTER 13

Sometimes referred to as the "leading of the Holy Spirit," this inwardly perceived sense of direction is sometimes described as being "prompted by the Holy Spirit." Some HVG teachers include "strong feelings," "urges," and "hunches" in this category.

DREAMS – CHAPTER 14

Many believe that our dreams, and in some cases "visions," are a reliable means of hearing from God.

CONFIRMATIONS

These signs, circumstances, and impressions can serve as either the voice of God or as a confirmation of the voice of God. They look for an alignment of signs or signals in order to determine what God is trying to say. HVG teachers look for two or three agreeing indicators all pointing in the same direction. Supposedly, this is the Lord's "confirmation" concerning His voice.

A SUBJECTIVE MESS

Some methods (open and closed doors, fleeces, and signs) would fit under the broad category of "circumstances" mentioned by Henry Blackaby and Charles Stanley. They would consider some methods (dreams, promptings, voices and inner peace) to be "the voice of the Holy Spirit." They would not regard any *one* medium as a sure and reliable source for the voice of God. Each needs to be buttressed by the agreement of at least two or more others. As Blackaby puts it:

> In our day God speaks to us through the Holy Spirit. He uses the Bible, prayer, circumstances, and the church (other believers). No one of these methods of God's speaking is, by itself, a clear indicator of God's directions. *But when God says the same thing through each of these ways you can have confidence to proceed.*[32]

For instance, finding my heart warmed by a passage of Scripture is only the voice of God if I hear a similar "message" through a sign, and/or inner prompting. A still small voice is only reliable if a Scripture passage, a sign, or an open door confirms the message. A message received through a sign must be tested by a fleece or confirmed by an inner peace.

---

[32] Blackaby and King, *Experiencing God*, 35. Emphasis mine.

Is this how God speaks? Does God "whisper" messages in our spiritual ears? Is He trying to get our attention? Is He trying to get a message through to us? Do we really need this complex system of methods to discern His voice?

No, we do not. This methodology is fundamentally flawed and hopelessly subjective. The examination of HVG theology in the light of Scripture will demonstrate that *God doesn't whisper.*

Chapter 3

Don't Change the Channel!

3

Don't write me off just yet!

As precious as this methodology might be, you shouldn't fear a rigorous examination of it. What do you have to lose? If being led by nudgings, voices, and signs is a biblical methodology, then you have nothing to fear from a careful scrutiny of the passages cited to support HVG theology. If it is not biblical, then you have so much more to gain! You will gain an appreciation for God's Word and its sufficiency. You can be set free from a frustrating, confusing, morass of subjective and uncertain "signs" which only obscure the precious Word of God.

There is a lot at stake with this issue. The ramifications of getting this wrong are enormous. On this I can agree with HVG advocates - getting this right *is* at the heart of our Christian life and experience. This issue draws a dividing line across the landscape of Christian theology.

How does God communicate? Has God spoken, once for all, in the pages of inspired Scripture, or does He continue to speak through less reliable means?

Is Scripture sufficient? HVG teachers speak highly of Scripture, affirming that it is in a category by itself. Most would never claim that promptings, impressions, and signs are *equal* in authority to Scripture, however, their practices suggest they do not truly believe Scripture is *sufficient* for the Christian.

Is God trying to communicate? Is it necessary to learn the discipline of "hearing the voice of God"? Do I need to quiet myself, ridding my life of distractions, busyness, and activity so I can listen for His still small voice?

Is hearing from God outside Scripture essential to a loving and intimate relationship with Him? No Christian wants their affections for Christ to feel distant, detached, and dispassionate.

What will happen if I fail to hear God's communications? Do I run the risk of being disobedient to God's will if I cannot discern His whispered instructions? HVG teachers advocate a view of God's will that threatens dire consequences if missed.

There is a lot at stake.

I FEEL YOUR PAIN!

I am sympathetic to how you might feel by this point. We haven't even started a biblical evaluation of HVG theology, and already you might feel attacked at the very heart of your Christian faith. If you have spent years "hearing from God" and seeking His direction from your circumstances, then my critique of those experiences might sound like an aggressive personal attack.

I have felt your pain. For the first few years of my Christian life, I believed that God revealed His will through signs, promptings, and inaudible voices outside Scripture. Although the crisis faced at the end of my first year of college started me on a journey of doubting that paradigm, letting go of my traditions did not come easily.

Initially, I was angry. I felt lied to. I wouldn't say those who taught me HVG theology were being intentionally deceptive. I believe they - like Stanley, Blackaby, and Hybels - were well-meaning. I also believe they were gravely wrong on this issue. Feeling deceived by close friends and classmates, I struggled to make that distinction. How could I not see it? Why wasn't I mature, spiritual, and discerning enough to see through this? I wasn't sure with whom to be more angry - myself or others whom I admired?

I also felt my relationship with God was threatened. If your "conversational intimacy" with God has consisted of trying to hear His whispers, then my claim that *God Doesn't Whisper* would threaten that intimacy. Maybe you're not sure what "intimacy" with God would look like without straining to hear His voice. You might fear being stranded in a one-sided conversation (prayer) with only the Bible as a source for guidance and comfort.

You may have grown to rely upon the practice to such a degree that you wonder how God would be involved in your life without whispers from Heaven. Those tokens of God's love, attention, and personal care are constant reminders that you belong to the Good Shepherd Who gives attention to every detail of your life.

Finally, I felt abandoned. Though I would never have wanted to disparage Scripture in any way, I was not convinced that it was really *all* I needed. What if God speaks in Scripture and Scripture *alone*? Can you live your Christian life with *nothing* but Scripture as your guide? Does the thought of living in this world with only the Word of God terrify you? It is a very real fear that cripples many people. Initially, going through a week without seeking personal divine guidance felt like being stranded on an island without food and water.

BUT WHAT ABOUT. . . ?

As we examine HVG methodology in light of Scripture, you will inevitably start playing the "What About? Game." It sounds like this: "*What about* the times I sensed divine leading, followed it, and it turned out well?"

What about that time you sensed God telling you to make cookies for the neighbor lady? When you delivered the cookies, you found out she had received bad news that morning from the doctor. Obeying that prompting gave you an opportunity to comfort her, pray with her, and share the gospel. If that wasn't God whispering, what was it?

What about that time you decided to take a different route to work only to find out later there had been an accident on your normal route? Was that God speaking to you? If not, then what was it?

What about that time you were leaving the house but felt an overwhelming uneasiness. Uncertain what it was, you felt a need to go back inside where you discovered a pot left on the kitchen stove. It could have caused a fire if you had not heeded the impulses of your heart. What was that, if not the voice of God?

We have all had these experiences, *believer and unbeliever alike.* What do we make of them? Are these the "whispers of God"? Is this divine revelation? If these are not supernatural, divine communications intended to direct our steps moment by moment, then what are these experiences?

I will try to answer these fears, concerns, and questions in due course.

AM I ROBBING YOU?

Have I just described you? Do you fear I am trying to rob you of joy and intimacy with God? That is not my intention! I am not trying to replace a near and personal God with one distant and detached. In fact, the opposite is true. I am trying to replace an unbiblical paradigm with a biblical one.

If God is not whispering to us in our thoughts and impressions, then I am not taking anything from you by pointing that out. Divorcing someone from error does not rob them of anything. It frees them to enjoy the blessings of knowing truth and walking in it.

Imagine you *believe* you have five million dollars in your savings account. Now, for the sake of this illustration, you don't really have it, you just *believe* you do. Further, imagine you are *living* as if it is true. That deeply-held belief gives you tremendous comfort and a sense of well-being. You don't worry about retirement! You don't need to watch your spending. You have planned a luxurious vacation for later this year and have purchased a few expensive Christmas gifts for the family. Convinced you possess a healthy nest egg, you are considering early retirement, expecting to live off the interest.

One day you stop in at your bank to make a sizable withdrawal. After a brief conversation with the teller, the branch manager approaches you with a perplexed look on his face.

"Good morning!" he cheerfully greets you.

"Good morning."

He pauses for a bit and then hesitantly says, "I just need to inform you that the money you requested is not in this account. Were you perhaps thinking of a different account?"

"No," you insist, "this is the only account I have. I have one account and it has five million dollars in it."

Slowly, but with confidence, he hands you a freshly printed statement with your balance on it. It reads $546.37.

"What did you do with my five million dollars?" you ask impatiently.

"It was never there. You don't have five million dollars. This account has never had more than $5,000 in it at any given time," the branch manager gently replies.

Certain you had millions, you were living as if you did. You may feel like the banker took it from you, but he didn't. You never had the small fortune to begin with. He didn't hurt you by pointing that out. He actually did you a favor by divorcing you of a false notion that was putting you in peril. The branch manager is not your enemy for telling you the truth.

If you think you are hearing God's voice in circumstances, that your hunches are heavenly whispers and your random thoughts divine missives, then I hope you will sit down and take a look at the bank statement with me. Together, let's answer this: "Does Scripture teach this?" If Scripture doesn't teach that God is whispering heavenly messages via stray thoughts, then I am not taking anything from you by pointing that out.

Here is my challenge to you: If we don't find the practice of hearing the voice of God taught in Scripture, then are you willing to jettison those beliefs and practices? Are you willing to conform your thinking and theology to what Scripture says? If the biblical texts cited in support of HVG theology do not teach these practices, we have a biblical responsibility to reject what is false, no matter how good it makes us feel.

HOW DARE YOU BBQ MY SACRED COW!

Haddon Robinson once said, "Sacred cows make the best hamburger, but the meat can be hard to swallow."[1] Experience tells me this is true. I have eaten burgers made from my own sacred cows. I once held to a view of spiritual warfare that I later found to be completely unbiblical.[2] Though painful, watching that cow get tossed into the grinder liberated me from bondage to superstition and false doctrine. I have watched my sacred cows of Bible translations, pet doctrines, opinions, politics, and even my favorite sports team go through the grinder. The meat is hard to swallow but it satisfies the hunger.

There are few cows as sacred in modern evangelicalism as the belief that God is speaking to His children outside Scripture through visions, dreams, promptings, impressions, confirmations, signs, an inner peace, and the still small voice. Few cows are as dangerous to our spiritual life and welfare as this one. For 1800 years of church history, this doctrine was treated as aberrant and in some cases heretical. Today it is accepted and promoted as essential to Christian living. Once viewed as an attack on the authority and sufficiency of Scripture, this is now taught from pulpits, in books, and on Christian TV and radio.

This was once my sacred cow. It was painful to watch it go through the grinder, but I wouldn't have it any other way. This particular sacred cow kept me shackled to superstition and muddled in a hopelessly confusing morass of mixed messages. I pray that

---

[1] Garry Friesen and Robin Maxson, *Decision Making and the Will of God* (Sisters: Multnomah, 2004), 6.

[2] For more on this subject, see my book *Truth or Territory: A Biblical Approach to Spiritual Warfare*.

the Lord will use this book to set you free in the very same way. Years later, I am still enjoying the hamburger!

Part 2

The Theology Evaluated

My critique of HVG theology is not merely a disagreement over the use of certain methods and means. Though I do take issue with listening for a still small voice, watching for supernatural signs, and being led by feelings and impressions, behind all those methods are several beliefs regarding the nature of God, the nature of Scripture, and the nature of our relationship to both. We need to examine those beliefs - the presuppositions that lie at the heart of an unbiblical methodology.

In the next section I will address the unbiblical practices. First we need to critically examine the three unbiblical assumptions upon which the HVG methodology is built.

These assumptions are:

1. I *need* to hear from God outside Scripture.
2. I should *expect* to hear from God outside Scripture.
3. I must *learn* to hear from God outside Scripture.

Notice two things about each of those three assumptions.

First, I am critiquing a theology that claims God speaks "apart from Scripture." In a later section, we will see how God speaks to His people in Scripture today as we examine the power and sufficiency of the Word of God. Here I am specifically critiquing the belief that God reveals His will, including specific instructions and directions for daily living, to believers *outside of* and *apart from* the written Word of God.

Second, notice the logical progression of those assumptions. If it is true that I *need* to hear from God apart from Scripture, then it logically follows that God will provide exactly what I *need*. If Scripture is not sufficient to provide the divine instruction, direction, and comfort I *need*, God will provide it outside of Scripture. I should therefore *expect* to receive it. If I can *expect* God to provide extrabiblical revelation, then I need to *learn* how to listen for His voice. Our theology of God will determine our theology of revelation (how God communicates). Our theology of revelation will determine where we seek it, how we listen to it, and how we respond to it.

If God speaks through methods and means outside of Scripture, then we are obligated to submit to it as authoritative. It is, after all, God's Word. We must seek it out, study it to determine its meaning, and faithfully, unflinchingly obey it.

Let's examine these three assumptions and see if we are warranted in believing them.

Chapter 4

Faulty Assumption #1:
I Need to Hear from God
Outside Scripture

4

Every believer longs to experience intimacy with God. Christians yearn to know the redeeming God revealed in Scripture and incarnated in Jesus Christ. We want to learn truth, wisdom, and obedience to God's will. Every believer knows something of the longing expressed by David in Psalm 42:1-2: "As the deer pants for the water brooks, So my soul pants for You, O God. My soul thirsts for God, for the living God; When shall I come and appear before God?" This is a natural desire.

HVG teachers believe that an intimate love relationship with God can *only* be experienced by regularly hearing the voice of God outside Scripture. Therefore, He *needs* to speak to us and we *need* to hear from Him.

In his book *Frequency*, Robert Morris writes:

> So a personal relationship must involve communication - it *must*. Otherwise, how could a person ever have a personal relationship with God? If true dialogue doesn't take place, then it would be a one-sided attempt at communication, with us staring up into the sky, talking to God but hearing nothing in return.[1]

Elaborating on this in a sermon titled "Frequency - I'm a Sheep, Part 1," Morris said to his congregation at Gateway Church in Southlake Texas:

> What is the main difference between a believer in Jesus Christ and a non-believer? . . . It is that a believer has a

---

[1] Robert Morris, *Frequency: Tune in. Hear God* (Nashville: Thomas Nelson, 2016) Kindle edition, 5. Emphasis mine.

personal relationship with Jesus Christ. . . . It's hard for me to believe that that personal relationship does not include communication. And yet there are entire persuasions of theological thought that God doesn't speak anymore and that, to me, is crazy to think that way. . . . So the difference is that we have a personal relationship with Jesus. . . . But if you have a thought that God doesn't speak anymore...I feel so sorry for you; that you have a personal relationship with someone that never speaks to you. I don't know how personal that is.[2]

Charles Stanley says:

If our relationship with Him is a one-way trip and there is no communication or dialogue between us and the Lord Jesus Christ, then there isn't much fellowship. Fellowship is nil when one person does all the talking and the other does all the listening. God still speaks to us today because He wants to develop a love relationship that involves a two-party conversation.[3]

Morris and Stanley are correct to say that relationships require "two-way communication," but they are incorrect to assume it requires communication *outside* of Scripture. They talk as if God has not spoken! Morris says nothing about Scripture as God's Word to us. He describes prayer as "us staring up into the sky, talking to God" and, without a personal whisper from Heaven, we would be "hearing nothing in return." Hasn't God spoken in Scripture? Doesn't it qualify as "hearing something in return"? Not for HVG teachers. The Word of God does not sufficiently meet this need. Why should we think that speaking to God in prayer and hearing Him in Scripture is not a "two-party conversation"?

Henry Blackaby makes much out of the connection between private revelations and a personal relationship with God. One of the "Seven Realities of Experiencing God" offered in his book is the proposition that "God pursues a continuing love relationship with you that is real and personal."[4] At the heart of this "love relationship" is the need to receive a personal word from God. There is no room

---

[2] Morris, Robert. "Frequency – I'm a Sheep, Part 1." Published June 21, 2016. Source: https://www.youtube.com/watch?v=A6VQFe8s76Q

[3] Stanley, *How to Listen to God*, 9.

[4] Blackaby and King, *Experiencing God*, 32.

in Blackaby's theology for a love relationship with God that relies solely on Scripture. Personal revelation from God is essential.[5]

Is it possible for a believer to have an intimate, loving, and personal relationship with God established solely on what He has said in Scripture? Not according to Dallas Willard. In his book *Hearing God*, Willard says, "As with all close personal relationships, God can be counted on to speak to each of us when and as it's appropriate."[6] Willard echoes Stanley and Morris when he writes:

> Being close to God means communicating with him [sic], which is almost always a two-way street. . . . Hearing God's directions is only one dimension of a rich and interactive relationship. Obtaining specific guidance is but one facet of hearing God.[7]

Rick Warren also assumes Scripture is not adequate. In a sermon titled, "Learn How to Recognize God's Voice," Warren said:

> Very few things are more important than this because you can't have a relationship to [sic] God if you can't hear God. If all you do is ever talk to Him in prayer and you never hear God speak to you, that's a one-way relationship. That isn't much of a relationship. God wants to speak to you.[8]

These statements from HVG teachers have two things in common. They all agree that a true, intimate, loving relationship with God requires communication from God. And they all agree that Scripture is not sufficient to meet that need.

FEELINGS, NOTHING MORE THAN FEELINGS

For HVG teachers, it is not enough to read of God's love in Scripture or to see it manifested at the cross. We must be made to "feel loved," and nothing can assure us of God's love quite like receiving personal whispers.

---

[5] Blackaby boldly asserts, "If you have trouble hearing God speak, you are in trouble at the very heart of your Christian experience" (*Experiencing God*, 87). The close connection that Blackaby makes between the "love relationship" and receiving personal revelations is evident when he says, "You come to know His voice as you experience Him in a love relationship. As God speaks and you respond, you will come to the point that you recognize His voice more and more clearly. Some people try to bypass the love relationship. . . . No substitute, however, exists for the intimate relationship with God" (*Experiencing God*, 88).

[6] Willard, *Hearing God*, 12.

[7] Ibid. 9.

[8] Warren, Rick. "Learn How to Recognize God's Voice." Published Oct. 7, 2014. Source: https://www.youtube.com/watch?v=-827QmRDjUA

Priscilla Shirer teaches, "The foundation of our faith is on sweet fellowship with God, who clearly, biblically, wants our relationship with Him to be both intimate and interactive."[9] She believes subjective revelations through whispers and impressions are an essential way we enjoy an "intimate and interactive" relationship with God. She writes, "I mean, come on, do you really think He loved you enough to die for you, but not enough to talk to you?"[10] Given that she promotes private revelations in her books, it wouldn't be unfair to say she means something akin to this: "Do you really think God loved you enough to die for you and then just leave you with the Bible?!" When she speaks of God talking, she is not referring to Scripture. She is speaking of revelation outside Scripture - inner impressions, promptings, and feelings that she calls "the voice of God." She is describing extra-biblical revelation.

What about Scripture? To be fair, Shirer does not exclude Scripture from her list of ways God speaks. It is included as one of many sources of divine revelation, though an inferior one. It is not personal, intimate, and private. It is not fresh, modern, and specific to the individual. When Shirer and others do "hear from God in Scripture," the message they receive is consistently something that would have been unrecognizable to the author or original audience.[11] For Shirer, the Divine Deposit of 66 books, supernaturally written, divinely preserved, and faithfully translated, is not sufficient evidence of God's love. In practice, when it comes to knowing and feeling God's love, she, along with the other HVG teachers, acts as if the Bible doesn't exist. Why should we believe the love of God is most powerfully communicated through vague whispers and cryptic impressions and not through inspired Scripture?

Echoing Shirer, Charles Stanley teaches that God speaks to us today because "He loves us just as much as He loved the people of the Old and New Testament days."[12] I believe God loves us, but why should I assume that personal knowledge of God's love necessitates continuing private revelations? Does Scripture not sufficiently inform me of God's love? HVG teachers read of God's

---

[9] Shirer, Discerning the Voice of God, 10-11.

[10] Ibid., 11.

[11] See Chapter 8, "The Verse Jumped off the Page."

[12] Stanley, How to Listen to God, 9.

love in Scripture, but that is not enough to convince them. They need private whispers.

MILLIONS OF IMPORTANT DECISIONS

HVG teachers must assume God *needs* to speak to us before they can claim that He *will*. If the Bible provides all I need for life and godliness (2 Peter 1:3), then there is no *need* to hear from God outside Scripture, tune into "God's frequency," or listen for His still small voice.

Yet HVG teachers insist that God *needs* to speak to us in order to provide specific and timely counsel for decision-making. We are faced with dozens of potentially life-altering decisions that the Bible does not specifically address: whom to marry (Janet or Sue), which job to choose (Phoenix or Portland), or which house to buy (three bedrooms or four). HVG teachers claim it is necessary that God provide specific instructions to reveal His specific will for my life, thus enabling me to make the right decision.

As Robert Morris writes, "We need to hear God's voice in so many areas of our lives - our jobs, our families, our friendships, our health, our areas of service, our futures. The only way we can walk in certainty is by hearing God."[13] Morris is not talking about reading Scripture. He is talking about "hearing His voice" *outside* of Scripture. He writes:

> As a senior pastor, I absolutely need to hear from God. There's no way I can fulfill the responsibility of leading a church unless God is leading me. My intellect won't cut it. My seminary studies won't cut it. My talent or personality won't cut it. And I certainly don't have good looks to depend on. The only way I can lead a church is by having a daily, personal, intimate walk with God. I need to listen to God and hear God. He leads. I follow.[14]

The Bible has plenty to say about our jobs, families, friendships, health, service, and futures. Yet, according to Morris, the Bible does not provide sufficient direction for a senior pastor! If Morris believed that the Bible was sufficient, he wouldn't *need* to "hear" anything else. Morris would say the Bible has plenty to say, "generally speaking," about these various areas of our lives. However, the Bible doesn't provide the detailed and specific personal instruction that Morris believes is *necessary* for pastoring

---

[13] Morris, *Frequency*, 6.

[14] Ibid. 7.

a church. For instance, the Bible does not tell us whether to go to two services or build a new building. It does not reveal how many or which missionaries to support, or how many youth pastors to hire. According to Morris, these decisions, and thousands more, cannot be made on the basis of what is revealed in Scripture alone. We need something more.

Henry Blackaby teaches that the needs of our churches, our communities and our world are not sufficiently addressed in Scripture. In *Experiencing God,* He writes:

> You need to know what God has on His agenda for your church, community, and nation at this time in history. Then you and your church can adjust your lives to God, so that He can move you into the mainstream of His activity before it is too late. Though God likely will not give you a detailed schedule, He will let you know one step at a time how you and your church need to respond to what He is doing.[15]

To meet this pressing need, Blackaby teaches that circumstantial signs and confirmations can be "read" in order to discern God's will. The implication is clear: without special, specific, and direct divine revelation through subjective means, Christians would be in the dark concerning most of God's will for them, their church, and their community. Scripture does not sufficiently reveal God's agenda. Without subjective whispers as our guide, we cannot "adjust our lives to God" and get involved in His activity. Scripture is insufficient to properly equip us for good works and service in this world. We need something more.

Since "our lives are an ever-changing catalog of intricately woven personal inquiries that we each need divine direction to navigate accurately,"[16] God *needs* to give us direction! How could we possibly plan a day's activities, a vacation, a grocery list, or even a wardrobe selection without divine help?! Don't think for a moment I am ridiculing this teaching by misrepresenting it. Charles Stanley suggests that God had to give him special direction on purchasing a Thanksgiving turkey, telling him, "Go to this store and buy the turkey now." Stanley says direct communication was necessary for him to buy the right turkey at the right place because he was short

---

[15] Blackaby and King, *Experiencing God,* 68.

[16] Shirer, *Discerning the Voice of God,* 20.

on time.[17] According to Stanley, God has also provided specific directions on other purchases, including a car.

This is consistent with how HVG advocates view our need to hear God's voice outside of Scripture. Stanley says:

> We need His definite and deliberate direction for our lives, as did Joshua, Moses, Jacob, or Noah. As His children, we need His counsel for effective decision making. Since He wants us to make the right choices, He is still responsible for providing accurate data, and that comes through His speaking to us.[18]

Clearly HVG teachers believe that hearing the voice of God is necessary to fulfill the will of God in both big decisions and small. If this is true, then the consequences for not hearing God's voice are both monumental and eternal!

FOR WANT OF A NAIL

We are faced daily with a myriad of decisions not directly or explicitly addressed in Scripture. They range from the petty, to the pressing, to the profound. A petty decision might be which shirt to wear on Monday, what to eat for lunch, or whether to take the elevator or the stairs to the second floor. Pressing decisions might be the timing of our vacation, which airline tickets to purchase, or whether my child should go to the sleepover at a friend's house. Profound decisions include whom to marry, which career to pursue, or which college to attend.

We are far more likely to pray about which person to marry than we are about which shirt to wear. But how can we know for sure that a petty decision is really petty? How do we know it isn't actually one of the most consequential decisions you will ever make? Why is it that we insist on hearing from God on the profound decisions, but we don't seem at all interested in hearing His voice on the petty decisions? We can't know, apart from hindsight, if a small and inconsequential decision is really small and inconsequential.

This truth is aptly illustrated by the old proverb about a kingdom falling due to a missing horseshoe nail. Known as "For Want of a Nail," the proverb goes something like this:

---

[17] Stanley's retelling of this story in answer to a viewer's question regarding hearing from God can be found in this YouTube video posted on the In Touch Ministries YouTube channel: https://www.youtube.com/watch?v=V4ocm31RJ7g.

[18] Stanley, *How to Listen to God*, 9.

For want of a nail the shoe was lost.
For want of a shoe the horse was lost.
For want of a horse the rider was lost.
For want of a rider the message was lost.
For want of a message the battle was lost.
For want of a battle the kingdom was lost.
And all for the want of a horseshoe nail.[19]

The proverb teaches that there can be unforeseen consequences from seemingly small and inconsequential happenings. No one would predict that a kingdom would fall simply because a farrier lacked a single horseshoe nail, yet hindsight might show that the otherwise insignificant event could actually have monumental consequences. In light of such an outcome, the "insignificant event" turns out to be a history-altering detail.

I made one decision when I was 13 that would forever change the course of my life. I decided to go to a neighbor's house to see his collection of *The Hardy Boy Mysteries* books. I was an avid fan and reader of the series and my sister informed me that a man living a couple of doors down owned the complete set of hardbacks.

I walked over to view the collection. That was the beginning of a friendship that resulted in me attending Sunday school and then youth group at Kootenai Community Church. A couple of years later, the church paid for me to attend the local Bible camp[20] where the gospel message came to me "in power and in the Holy Spirit and with full conviction" (1 Thessalonians 1:5). The Lord turned me from my sin and granted me the faith to trust Christ (Philippians 1:29; Ephesians 2:8-9). Later, my friend attended Millar College of the Bible where I went to a large weekend youth event in February of 1989. There I met a girl with whom I became infatuated. She was planning to attend Millar College in the fall of 1990, so naturally, I decided to attend as well. Though she ended all potential for a relationship prior to my arrival at school, I went to Millar anyway, intent on winning her back. I didn't. However, I did meet another lovely young lady who became my wife and the mother of our four children.

What if I hadn't decided to go look at that *Hardy Boys* book collection? I might not have ever gone to church, then camp, then college. I might have stayed in Sandpoint and pursued other life

---

[19] Though the precise origin of the proverb is unknown, it is found in a number of different forms beginning as early as the 13th century. https://en.wikipedia.org/wiki/For_Want_of_a_ Nail.

[20] Cocolalla Lake Bible Camp (http://clbcamp.org/index.html).

choices. I might have met a different woman, married *her* instead, and I would have different children with different names! My present children wouldn't even exist![21]

Without Bible college, I wouldn't have been asked to pastor Kootenai Community Church. Consequently, someone else would be the pastor and I would never have given my life to preaching and writing. I wouldn't have written this book, and you wouldn't be reading it - all because I decided *not* to go look at a *Hardy Boys* book collection sometime in the mid 1980s.[22]

HVG advocates cannot consistently live out this theology. Do they pray each morning about which pair of socks to wear? Do they wait to hear divine revelation concerning what to eat for breakfast, how big the serving should be, or how many cups of coffee to drink? Do they get God's will on which shirt to wear every morning?

You might object: "Certainly, the job I decide to take will have far more profound consequences than which shirt I wear?" Really? How can you know that the shirt you wear today is not a *Hardy-Boys*-book-level decision?

For a thought experiment, imagine the following:

Say I choose to wear my red polo with "Kootenai Community Church" and an emblem of the cross embroidered on the front. I go to Walmart and while standing in line, the person in front of me notices my shirt. He asks me a question about the church which leads to a discussion of spiritual things. The discussion results in him coming to our church where he hears the gospel and gets saved.

Was my decision to wear that particular shirt a petty decision? What if I had chosen the plain brown polo hanging right next to it? None of that would have happened and he would still be lost! To paraphrase the earlier proverb: "For want of a polo, a soul was lost."

Should I stand in front of my closet tomorrow and wait for a word from the Lord? Do I need His direction for that decision? Must

---

[21] Greg Koukl from Stand to Reason (str.org) is fond of taking this absurd illustration even further. As he explains, this would mean that my current wife would have had to marry the wrong man (since she never met me because of my bad choice) and she would have the wrong children as well. Like ripples of water from a stone tossed into a calm pond, the horrible effects of God's people missing God's best for them would spread for generations to multiplied thousands. God might never be able to correct it, and all because I made a single wrong choice!

[22] As one who affirms whole-heartedly a robust doctrine of the sovereignty of God, I don't believe that contrary scenarios like the one I have just proposed are, in fact, possible. I don't believe it was possible that I should miss salvation or marry the wrong woman and have the wrong children.

I consult others for godly counsel, check the shirt selection against the Word of God, wait for God to send a confirming sign or speak through a still small voice? Why does this decision, which might prove to be quite consequential, not require the complex system of divining God's will promoted by HVG teachers?

What if the *key decision* I made that day was not which shirt to wear, but which checkout line to enter. Never have I sought divine guidance or the voice of God concerning which checkout line to use, yet it could prove to be as significant a decision as which college to attend. What if that encounter in the checkout line didn't have anything to do with the shirt I wore or which line I stood in? What if the encounter was the result of turning left upon entering the store instead of turning right? In fact, it could have been the result of a hundred cascading decisions all made prior to entering the store, many of which might have appeared completely unrelated to each other.

How do I know when I should wait to hear from God and when I shouldn't? HVG teachers are very selective in what they say are the "big decisions" requiring divine guidance. If their approach to hearing from God concerning decision-making is correct, they need to apply it consistently. They should acknowledge that there is no such thing as an "unimportant decision." They should apply their methodology just as thoroughly when deciding between orange chicken and chow mein as when deciding which car to buy.

Even Charles Stanley, who claims God told him where to go buy a turkey, did not consult God on which brand of turkey to buy, which specific turkey, which checkout line to use, whether to purchase anything else, use cash or credit, or choose paper or plastic bags. Why should we believe his choice of a store needed to be the subject of God's special revelation but his selection of a payment method did not?

THE CHICKEN AND EGG DILEMMA

HVG advocates face a genuine "chicken and egg dilemma." On the one hand they claim that in order to hear God's voice, we must first cultivate a loving and intimate relationship with Him. Without this loving and intimate relationship, we can never grow in our ability to hear Him, discern His voice, and distinguish it from impostors. Priscilla Shirer says, "Our ability to recognize God's voice hinges on having an intimate relationship with Him."[23] In the same chapter, she writes:

> Christians are the Lord's sheep. He is our Shepherd. As we grow in the Lord, we begin to learn how to recognize His voice and understand His messages. A lamb is less capable of distinguishing His [sic] shepherd's voice than a sheep is. Lambs learn as they get to know their shepherd and practice responding to his voice. This skill comes over time as the two build a relationship.[24]

According to Shirer, the ability to hear God *must be preceded* by an intimate relationship with Him. Later she writes:

> When we get into an intimate relationship with Him through His Word, we become acquainted with His character, language, and tone of voice. This enables us to recognize His voice and, by the power of the Holy Spirit, to discern the voices of strangers (John 10:5).[25]

In order to hear the voice of God, we have to first cultivate an intimate, loving relationship with Him. Yet, as noted earlier in this chapter, HVG advocates believe that a relationship with God devoid of "hearing His voice" is no *real* relationship at all. They disparage such Bible-centered relationships as a one-way street - a barren, silent, one-sided fellowship. They teach that we must cultivate a loving and intimate relationship with God through His Word in order to hear from Him, and yet, we need to hear from Him to have a real relationship with Him.

HVG advocates teach that we must have a relationship with Him in order to hear Him, but we can't have a relationship with Him unless we hear Him. So which is it?

This irreconcilable contradiction is seen in Henry Blackaby's writings on the subject. Blackaby teaches that having an intimate love relationship with God is necessary in order to hear His voice. He writes:

> An intimate love relationship with God is the key to knowing God's voice, to hearing when God speaks. You come to know His voice as you experience Him in a love relationship. As God speaks and you respond, you will come to the point that you recognize His voice more and

---

[23] Shirer, *He Speaks to Me*, 162.

[24] Ibid., 163.

[25] Ibid., 164.

more clearly. Some people try to bypass the love relationship. Some look for a miraculous sign or try to depend on a "formula" or set of steps to discover God's will. No substitute, however, exists for the intimate relationship with God.[26]

And yet, on the previous page he writes, "He still speaks to His people. *If you have trouble hearing God speak, you are in trouble at the very heart of your Christian experience.*"[27] According to Blackaby, we can't have a real, genuine, intimate relationship with God apart from hearing His voice and yet, such a relationship is required to hear His voice. Either hearing the voice of God is the *cause* of the love relationship or it is the *result* of the love relationship, but it can't be both.

BUT WHAT ABOUT…THE BIBLE?

HVG teachers *assume* Scripture is not sufficient truth from God. If they believed in the sufficiency of Scripture, they would never suggest that we *need* more. I understand this characterization sounds harsh, but given the way they speak of God's communication and how they continually seek voices outside Scripture, I believe it is a fair and accurate one. Though they view Scripture as a *necessary* component for Christian living, they do not believe Scripture is God's all-sufficient provision for life and godliness.

They view Scripture as a necessary tool given by God to teach us how to hear His voice in our thoughts. I believe Scripture itself is the living Word of God. It doesn't help me hear God's voice elsewhere - it is God's voice. It is His Word.

They act as if God has not spoken in Scripture. Robert Morris characterizes a life lived without the "voice of God" as "talking to God but hearing nothing in return."[28] Those are the words of someone who does not view Scripture as the voice of God. How could he say that 66 books written by the Holy Spirit over the course of centuries for the benefit and blessing of His people is "nothing in return"?

They do not believe Scripture is sufficient for a loving, personal, and intimate relationship with God. This is why they promote

---

[26] Blackaby and King, *Experiencing God*, 88.

[27] Ibid., 87. Emphasis mine.

[28] Morris, *Frequency*, 6.

listening for God's voice through promptings, visions, dreams, impressions, and signs. For them, a Christian left with Scripture and Scripture alone is "in trouble at the very heart of [their] Christian experience,"[29] isolated from communications of God's love, care, and direction.

They do not believe Scripture is a sufficient revelation of the nature and character of God. Charles Stanley boldly declares, "I believe the most important reason God is still talking today is that He wants us to know Him. *If God has stopped talking, then I doubt we will ever discover what He is really like.*"[30] That is not someone who believes Scripture is sufficient revelation of the nature of God. Stanley teaches that without continuing revelation, we would be left without vital information regarding the nature of God. This is an absurd assault upon the sufficiency of Scripture. It's an affront to the Word of God to say that real knowledge of God comes through inner promptings, subjective voices, and circumstantial signs – like the kind that instructs you where to buy a Thanksgiving turkey. It's preposterous to claim that modern revelation is necessary to "discover what He is really like." The greatest revelation of God's nature is found in Scripture and in the incarnation of Jesus Christ. It is not whispered to us through feelings, impressions, and still small voices.

Though the teachers I am critiquing wouldn't openly verbally deny the sufficiency of Scripture, they do deny it in practice. Their advocacy for extra-biblical revelation is, in fact, a back-handed denial of this cardinal doctrine.

Scripture is all we need!

God has written down His will for us. He has preserved it for us. He has put it in our language, given us the capacity to read it, to know it, and to understand it. I can meditate upon it at great length. It doesn't change. It is not subject to my feelings, my emotions, or my mood swings. I don't have to wonder if I am hearing God's Word or being deceived by a hundred other "voices." His Word is contained in Scripture and authenticated by signs and wonders. It is as "living and powerful" today as the day it was written (Hebrews 4:12).

The ultimate, perfect, and final revelation of God is found in the person of Christ. He is revealed in the pages of Holy Scripture. If

---

[29] Blackaby and King, *Experiencing God*, 87. Emphasis mine.

[30] Stanley, *How to Listen to God*, 9-10. Emphasis mine.

you think you need something more, you have an inadequate appreciation of Scripture. You have a low view of the Bible.

What reason do you have for not believing it is sufficient? Why would you think any of the methods promoted by HVG teachers are necessary for your life and godliness? Do you really *need* to hear from God outside of Scripture? Only if Scripture isn't sufficient.

Chapter 5

Faulty Assumption #2: I Should Expect to Hear from God Outside Scripture

5

A cardinal doctrine of Christianity is the belief that God has revealed Himself to mankind according to His own will. Christians believe in a personal, transcendent God Who has taken the initiative to reveal Himself to us.

If God hadn't revealed Himself to us in the person of Christ and in Scripture, our knowledge of Him would be limited to that revealed in creation. Even then, our understanding would be skewed and unreliable since sin has marred God's creation, placing it under a curse (Romans 8:18-22). We observe a fallen creation that doesn't look or function as originally created. Further, all our observations are tainted by our own sin, moral darkness, and fallen intellect. The revelation in creation is sufficient to hold us accountable for our sin (Romans 1:18-21) but not sufficient to redeem us from God's justice.

According to Hebrews 1:1-2, the greatest and final revelation of God's nature and will is Jesus Christ: "God, after He spoke long ago to the fathers in the prophets in many portions and in many ways, in these last days has spoken to us in His Son, whom He appointed heir of all things, through whom also He made the world." The zenith of God's revelation is the person of Christ. The Old Testament anticipated that revelation and the New Testament explains it. Biblical Christianity affirms that the 66 books of our Bible contained in the Old and New Testaments is the full, inspired, inerrant, infallible, authoritative, and perfect Word of the Living God. We believe God has spoken and preserved His Word for us by His providential working through history.

Further, no Christian would argue that God *cannot* communicate with men. We believe God is sovereign and can do

51

whatever He pleases (Psalm 115:3; Daniel 4:34-35). Throughout biblical history, God communicated clearly to men and women and used human instruments to record that communication, preserving it to the blessing and benefit of His people for centuries to come.

No believer who loves Scripture would ever suggest that God *cannot* speak or that He *has not* spoken. The question that concerns us here is: "Has He promised to speak to me *today* outside of Scripture?"

AS THEN, SO NOW

HVG advocates teach that God is speaking today, *just as He did in biblical times*. Charles Stanley writes, "We might ask, 'Why would God still want to talk to us today? Hasn't He said enough from Genesis to Revelation?' There are several compelling reasons why God still has His lines of communication open with His people."[1] Stanley offers these four reasons for his claim:

> First and foremost, He loves us just as much as He loved the people of Old and New Testament days . . . . The second reason God still speaks today is that we need His definite and deliberate direction for our lives, as did Joshua, Moses, Jacob, or Noah . . . . A third reason God speaks today is that He knows we need the comfort and assurance just as much as did the believers of old . . . . I believe the most important reason God is still talking today is that He wants us to know Him.[2]

In three of the four reasons for believing God still speaks, Stanley references God's activity with believers of old including Joshua, Moses, Jacob, or Noah. He suggests we need God to speak today just as believers in biblical times needed God to speak to them. He is assuming the information God revealed to them is not sufficient for us. It doesn't communicate His love for us or provide us comfort and assurance.

He writes, "Throughout Scripture we have the promise that God will indeed speak to us, but if we come to Him doubting His ability to speak, we will have a difficult time listening."[3] Those who do not

---

[1] Stanley, *How to Listen to God*, 9. Notice the language of sufficiency unwittingly employed by Stanley: "Hasn't He said enough from Genesis to Revelation?" Though some may object to my repeated claim that HVG teachers deny the sufficiency of Scripture, their own language betrays their true theology. Stanley's answer shows that he does not believe it is enough. Consistently, HVG teachers say that we need something more.

[2] Ibid.

[3] Ibid., 80.

embrace this paradigm of "hearing from God" do not doubt God's *ability* to speak. We simply deny that God does so through the highly subjective, unreliable, and spurious methods Stanley promotes. He assumes that God's revelation in the past constitutes a promise of revelation in the present.

Following suit, Henry Blackaby writes, "The testimony of the Bible from Genesis to Revelation is that God speaks to His people. In our day God speaks to us through the Holy Spirit."[4] Blackaby assumes that since God provided the Scriptures (Genesis-Revelation) by speaking to His people *then*, He is still doing so *today* through the Holy Spirit. He writes:

> If anything is clear from a reading of the Bible, this fact is clear: God speaks to His people. He spoke to Adam and Eve in the garden of Eden in Genesis. He spoke to Abraham and the other patriarchs. God spoke to the judges, kings, and prophets. God was in Christ Jesus speaking to the disciples. God spoke to the early church, and God spoke to John on the Isle of Patmos in Revelation. God does speak to His people, and *you can anticipate that He will be speaking to you also.*[5]

The HVG argument is not made from Bible passages that clearly teach God is always speaking. There is no passage in Scripture that promises that if God spoke to Moses He will speak to me. HVG advocates assume that if God revealed truth in the past He must reveal truth today in the same ways. They assume that God must deal with His people today in the *same way* He dealt with the saints of old.[6]

When they read the Bible, they do not see a perfect, sufficient, and complete revelation of divine truth. Instead, they see a historical record of ways God has communicated in times past. It serves as a template for discerning God's voice in the present - an example of all the ways we should expect to hear God speak today.

Mark Batterson abuses the text of Hebrews 1:1 to make this very point. He selectively quotes only a portion of the opening sentence of Hebrews: "God spoke to our ancestors . . . at many

---

[4] Blackaby and King, *Experiencing God*, 35.

[5] Ibid., 83. Emphasis mine.

[6] I understand that many HVG advocates quote various verses of Scripture to support their claim that God is speaking today. I will deal with those in future chapters. In this section, I am only dealing with the presuppositions that lie behind their uses of the Scriptures.

times and in various ways."[7] He then recounts a number of "strange and mysterious ways" in which God spoke: the burning bush, signs and wonders, an illness, a disembodied hand writing on a Babylonian palace wall, and Balaam's donkey.

Batterson then writes, "Let me be absolutely clear about one thing. After highlighting the various ways in which God speaks, the writer of Hebrews zeros in on God's greatest revelation: Jesus Christ. He is the full and final revelation of God."[8] So far, so good! But Batterson does not stop there. In the very next paragraph he writes, "Does God still speak in 'various ways'? I believe He does. I believe God speaks in the *same ways* now as He did then, but now we have the distinct advantage of having Scripture as our sounding board."[9]

Did you notice the blatant contradiction? "He [Jesus Christ] is the full and **final** revelation of God," and, "I believe God speaks in the **same ways now** as He did then . . . ." If Jesus is the final revelation of God, then God is not speaking the same way now as He did then. Either Jesus is the final revelation or God continues to speak today. If God continues to speak today, then Jesus wasn't the final revelation. Batterson can't have it both ways.

For HVG advocates, the "strange and mysterious ways" God spoke in the past serve as examples of how He speaks today. Do they really believe God will speak through a talking donkey, a hand writing messages on walls, and burning bushes? If God is speaking through those same means, why do we not have video evidence of these things regularly taking place among us today?[10]

Further, notice how Batterson described Scripture as "our sounding board." In the very same section, he writes:

---

[7] Mark Batterson, *Whisper: How to Hear the Voice of God* (New York: Crown Publishing Group, 2017), 54.

[8] Ibid., 55.

[9] Ibid. Emphasis mine. Notice that the passage explicitly says these means of God speaking characterized the times of the prophets "long ago." The "long ago" of the passage is set in stark contrast to "these last days" in which God's revelation is given in Christ. The author of Hebrews says these "many portions" and "many ways" belonged to the period of revelation "long ago." Mark Batterson claims "God speaks in the same ways now as He did then." He directly contradicts the very passage he quotes.

[10] See Numbers 22:22-30, Exodus 3:1-9, and Daniel 5:1-28. Some may contend that I am pressing their teaching to the point of absurdity. I am merely taking their teaching to its logical conclusion. I am simply asking HVG teachers to be consistent. They teach that God is speaking the same today as He did then, using the very same methods and means. They teach that Scripture is an example of the various means God still uses. I doubt that any of these teachers have ever expected the audible voice of God from a talking donkey. The fact that they don't is proof positive that they don't believe it's the same today as in Bible times.

To believe that God speaks *only* through the Bible is to handcuff the God of the Bible as the Bible has revealed Him to us. Yes, Scripture provides our checks and balances. And God will never say anything that is contrary to His good, pleasing, and perfect will as revealed in Scripture.[11]

For HVG teachers, the value of Scripture lies in its use to check God's personal voice to us. We go to Scripture and see if our own personal revelations match the pattern of God's past revelations. The "sounding board" serves either to confirm what I sense God has whispered or to help me know when I am getting it wrong.

Batterson claims that we have an advantage the saints of old didn't. We have Scripture as a "sounding board" by which we can test God's voice. But how do we know the "sounding board" is right? How do we know the saints of old got it right if they didn't have a "sounding board" by which to check God's voice to them?

Don't miss the hopelessly subjective theological mess created by HVG teachers at this point. On the one hand they claim that God speaks in the same way today as He did in Bible times with no difference in the manner, frequency, or quality. On the other hand, they tell us that *we need* the Bible as a "sounding board" against which we can "check" the whispers of God. If the saints of old did not need a "sounding board" when they received the whispers of God, why do we need one to double check the exact same kind of whispers? How do we know they got it right without a "sounding board"? According to Batterson, they were at a disadvantage. How do we know Scripture is accurate, authoritative, and infallible, if they received the *same kinds* of whispers we do, but wrote it down without a "sounding board"?

The only resolution to this confusing contradiction is for HVG teachers to admit one of the following:

1. God *cannot speak* today with the same accuracy, clarity, and authority as He did in Bible times. He was able to give clear, precise revelation long ago without the need of a "sounding board." However, for some reason, He is no longer able to do so.

2. God *does not* speak today with the same accuracy, clarity, and authority as He did in Bible times. He has changed the manner and clarity with which He speaks. Today's voice is an inferior,

---

[11] Batterson, *Whisper*, 55.

unclear, and easily misunderstood message that needs to be checked by an outside standard – the "sounding board."

3. There is no real guarantee that Scripture is any more inspired and trustworthy than my latest random thought.[12]

Regardless of which option they choose, they are forced to admit that this foundational assumption of the HVG paradigm is false. Either they must deny that Scripture is unique or they must deny that God is speaking in the same way today as long ago.

COMMUNICATION AND RELATIONSHIP

HVG advocates teach that since God is a "communicating God," He is always speaking. In his book *The Power of a Whisper*, Bill Hybels writes in a chapter titled 'Our Communicating God," "Throughout history God has spoken. . . . In short, our God is a communicating God. Always has been, and always will be."[13] He cites Elijah, David, Moses, and other examples of God's communication, assuring us that God is *always* communicating with His people.

For Hybels, Willard, and Blackaby, God's communications are an essential element of a loving relationship. Hybels quotes Willard when he says, "People are meant to live in an ongoing relationship with God, speaking and being spoken to."[14] For Willard, personal and direct communication with God outside of Scripture is so necessary that he wonders "How could there be a personal relationship, a personal walk with God - or with anyone else -

---

[12] Dallas Willard teaches this very thing in his book *Hearing God*. In a chapter titled "The Word of God and the Rule of God," Willard teaches that the subjective voice of God we receive is of the same nature as the written Word of God: "The Bible is *one* of the results of God's speaking." He redefines "infallibility" in such a way as to deny the biblical doctrine. He denies that the text alone is infallible saying, "It is infallible in this way precisely because God never leaves it alone." In other words, it is only to be regarded as "infallible" when God uses it for redemptive and communicative purposes. Concerning the inerrancy of Scripture, Willard writes, "The inerrancy of the original texts is rendered effective for the purposes of redemption only as that text, through its present-day derivatives, is constantly held within the eternal living Word." With Willard, the Bible is not an objectively infallible and inerrant revelation but can only be considered such as God might use it to communicate His voice to us in the present. Of course, He might use a multitude of other means as well, all of which in the moment become infallible and inerrant communications to us. After describing many kinds of revelations, Willard says, "But *all* of these are God's *words*, as is also his [sic] speaking that we hear when we *individually hear God*" (185).

[13] Hybels, *The Power of a Whisper*, 41.

[14] Ibid., 59; Willard, *Hearing God*, 18.

without individualized communication?"[15] He claims that "God is also with us in a conversational relationship: he [sic] speaks with us individually as it is appropriate - which is only to be *expected* between persons who know one another, care about each other and are engaged in common enterprises."[16] Such regular communications are to be "expected."

These authors cannot picture a relationship with God devoid of personal, individual revelation *outside of Scripture*. Robert Morris teaches that God's voice "arises intrinsically as part of a genuine and ongoing relationship with God."[17] Priscilla Shirer says, "Once we have been positionally sanctified, we become a part of God's family, and *He will speak to us because of that relationship*."[18] They claim that, like any loving and intimate relationship, our relationship with God requires constant two-way communication.

Notice the assumption behind this teaching, namely that God has not spoken to us sufficiently in the Scriptures. Something more is necessary. HVG teachers fail to understand that Scripture and prayer constitute a two-way relationship. We speak to God in prayer. He speaks to us in Scripture. In prayer we offer to God our requests, our praise, and our adoration. We express to Him the affections of our hearts, the lamentations over our sins, and the exultations of our joy. When we read Scripture, we can hear God speak, through the written Word, of His love for us, His redemptive purposes, and His steadfast promises. In Scripture, God describes to us His sovereign will for all of creation, and His individual will for us His people.[19] THAT is two-way communication.

PROOF TEXT TO THE RESCUE!

John 10:4: "When he puts forth all his own, he goes ahead of them, and the sheep follow him because *they know his voice*."

John 10:27: "My sheep *hear My voice*, and I know them, and they follow Me."

HVG teachers cite Scripture in their attempt to prove God has promised to speak to us today outside of Scripture. The most cited

---

15 Willard, *Hearing God*, 26. Emphasis original.

16 Ibid., 67–68. Emphasis mine.

17 Morris, *Frequency*, xviii.

18 Shirer, *He Speaks to Me*, 92. Emphasis mine.

19 Though Scripture does not tell us specifically which thing to choose in all the various decisions we face, God has revealed all that is necessary for God-glorifying decision-making. See Chapter 17.

text is John 10. Nearly every advocate of this theology appeals to Jesus' words in the Good Shepherd Discourse.

Henry Blackaby cites John 10 several times. In an ironically-titled chapter, "God Speaks Through the Bible," he writes:

> Jesus compared the relationship He has with His followers to the relationship a shepherd has with his sheep. He said, "He who enters by the door is the shepherd of the sheep. . . . The sheep hear his voice. . . . The sheep follow him, for they know his voice" (John 10:2-4). In just this way, when God speaks to you, you will recognize His voice and follow Him.[20]

Borrowing the language from Jesus' discourse, Blackaby draws this conclusion: "With the Scripture as our guide, we know God can speak in unique ways to individuals. His people will hear and recognize His voice."[21] Notice that for Blackaby, Scripture is not itself the voice of God. Rather, it is a *guide* to hearing and knowing the voice of God when it comes in private, individualized ways *outside Scripture.*

Further, Blackaby cites John 10 to teach this: "Is it important to know when the Holy Spirit is speaking to you? Yes! How do you know what the Holy Spirit is saying? I cannot give you a formula. I can tell you that you will know His voice when He speaks (John 10:4)."[22]

Charles Stanley writes:

> Our problem is not that we doubt God's ability and desire to communicate, but we are all too easily stumped as to how to identify His Voice. Since we are His sheep and His sheep "know His voice" (John 10:4), there must be some perceptible clues as to the nature of His conversation.[23]

In a chapter titled "Identifying the Voice of God," Stanley claims:

> Jesus made it clear in John 10:27 that the believer's normal experience is to hear God accurately. "My sheep hear My voice, and I know them, and they follow me." . . . The natural walk of Spirit-filled, committed believers is such that when God speaks, we can identify His Voice.[24]

---

[20] Blackaby and King, *Experiencing God,* 102.

[21] Ibid., 103.

[22] Ibid., 111.

[23] Stanley, *How to Listen to God,* 48.

[24] Ibid., 50.

Robert Morris, identifies John 10 as "one of the foundational Bible passages that describe this type of close relationship with God."[25] He writes, "John 10 underscores this truth for us: God wants us to live by hearing His voice."[26] Morris argues that our ability to hear God is not "primarily a behavior. It's a reflection of our identity."[27] He makes much of the fact that Jesus identifies us as His own sheep. According to Morris, *all* those who belong to Jesus are able to hear His voice by virtue of the fact that we are His sheep. He refers to this as our "innate ability" saying, "Sheep are born as sheep. They're born with the innate ability to hear a shepherd. It's woven into the very sequence of their DNA."[28]

According to Morris, John 10 teaches us how the "Great Shepherd" provides daily personal guidance for each sheep. Morris writes, "Who is Jesus? Jesus is our Good Shepherd. And what are we? We're sheep. And how does the Good Shepherd guide His sheep? By His voice. That's how we're to live: by listening to Jesus' voice. We're to depend on hearing His voice regularly and clearly."[29] According to Morris, John 10 is Jesus' promise to regularly speak to you outside Scripture: "He declares that He Himself is the Good Shepherd, and He *promises* that His sheep hear His voice."[30]

Priscilla Shirer leans on John 10 saying, "Christians are the Lord's sheep. He is our Shepherd. As we grow in the Lord, we begin to learn how to recognize His voice and understand His messages."[31] According to Shirer, this is Jesus' promise to us:

Jesus, speaking to His disciples in John 10:27, assured them - and us - of this *promise*: 'My sheep hear My voice.' No if's. [sic] No buts. No exceptions. No escape clauses. If you're His child - if you're one of His sheep - the certainty of God speaking to you is as sure as the chair you're sitting in.[32]

---

[25] Morris, *Frequency*, 6.

[26] Ibid.

[27] Ibid.

[28] Ibid., 10.

[29] Ibid., 9.

[30] Ibid., 10.

[31] Shirer, *He Speaks to Me*, 163. Joyce Meyer makes the same claim while equating the voice of the Shepherd with an "inner peace." See Joyce Meyer, *How To Hear From God: Learn to Know His Voice and Make Right Decisions* (New York: Faith Words, 2003), 94.

[32] Shirer, *Discerning the Voice of God*, 33–34. Emphasis mine.

Joyce Meyer uses John 10 to support her teaching that when God gives personal revelations we will "just know" whether it is from Him or not. She writes, "So people ask, 'How can I be sure I am hearing from God?' The Word says that we just *know* His voice from others."[33] She claims the believer has an innate ability to "just know" whether it is God speaking or a deceiving spirit.

John 10 is a key passage for HVG advocates. We can summarize their teaching on John 10 as:

1. Jesus has promised to speak to His sheep.

2. We should *expect* regular communications from the Shepherd in impressions, promptings, and feelings.

3. All Christians possess an ability to hear and recognize the Shepherd's voice.[34]

But, is this *really* what John 10 is about? Was Jesus describing continuous, personalized communications outside of Scripture for daily living and guidance?[35]

JOHN 10: THE CONTEXT

Four verses in John 10 are pressed into service to support this teaching:[36]

10:3: "To him the doorkeeper opens, and *the sheep hear his voice*, and he calls his own sheep by name and leads them out."

10:4: "When he puts forth all his own, he goes ahead of them, and the sheep follow him *because they know his voice*."

10:16: "I have other sheep, which are not of this fold; I must bring them also, and *they will hear My voice*; and they will become one flock with one shepherd."

---

[33] Meyer, *How to Hear From God*, 236.

[34] They teach that though we have the innate ability to discern His voice, it is still a skill that must be learned. Entire books are written to teach us how we can become better at "hearing."

[35] During our weekly Sunday morning worship services, I preached a 7-year-long series of messages on the Gospel of John. A thorough exposition of all these relevant passages and their context is available at our church website: kootenaichurch.org.

[36] The fact that partial phrases from these four verses are so commonly cited in HVG books without any reference to or explanation of their context, is an indication that something is amiss. This typically signals an abuse of a passage and a misrepresentation of an author's intended meaning.

10:27: "*My sheep hear My voice*, and I know them, and they follow Me."

Jesus promised that those who belong to Him will hear His voice and follow Him. He also promised that His sheep will not follow after the voice of strangers.

10:5: "A stranger they simply will not follow, but will flee from him, because they *do not know the voice of strangers*."
10:8: "All who came before Me are thieves and robbers, but the *sheep did not hear them*."

Though often overlooked, verse 6 is key to understanding the intended meaning of the Good Shepherd Discourse: "This figure of speech Jesus spoke to them, but they did not understand what those things were which He had been saying to them" (10:6). John explicitly says that Jesus' description of "hearing His voice" and "knowing His voice," is a *figure of speech*. Those to whom He was speaking *did not understand* what He was saying. There is an obvious irony in the fact that those to whom Jesus was speaking concerning "hearing His voice" did not understand what He was saying.

Who are "they" and "them" of verse six? Who were the people to whom this discourse was addressed? To answer that, we have to move back in the text, beyond the artificial chapter division into the events of Chapter 9; into the conversation at the end of that chapter.

In John 9, Jesus healed a man who had been born blind (9:1-7). That undeniable miracle caught the attention of the Pharisees who interviewed the man. The once-blind man recounted the basic details of his encounter with Jesus (9:13-17). The Pharisees refused to believe the man's testimony and doubted that he had actually been blind and received sight (9:18). They interviewed the man's parents. Afraid that they might be put out of the synagogue, his parents refused to confirm any details which might anger the Pharisees. They only affirmed that the man was their son and that he had been born blind (9:18-23).

Unsatisfied with that answer, the Pharisees called the man back a second time to question him. The Pharisees were intent on discrediting his claims in order to discredit the miracle Jesus had performed. Though the man was neither a debater nor theologian, he held his own before the Pharisees with remarkable poise,

61

sticking with the undeniable facts: "One thing I do know, that though I was blind, now I see." Finding no way to discredit the man or the miracle, the Pharisees "put him out" of the synagogue (9:24-34).

Jesus heard what the Pharisees had done and sought out the man whom He had healed. Jesus revealed that He was the divine Son of Man, prompting the once-blind man to confess his newfound faith saying, "Lord, I believe." He worshipped Jesus (9:38). The man had not only received physical sight, but spiritual sight as well. He believed in Jesus and worshiped Him.

In the very next verse (9:39), Jesus interpreted the lesson of His own miracle stating, "For judgment I came into this world, so that those who do not see may see, and that those who see may become blind." It is obvious that Jesus was not speaking in physical terms but describing the spiritual truth the miracle was intended to teach.

The Old Testament predicted that the Messiah would bring light to those in darkness causing them to see. Those spiritually benighted would receive the light of truth.[37] The miracle of giving physical sight to the blind was a picture of a greater spiritual reality, namely, that spiritual eyes were opened and those in darkness came into the light.

On others, His coming had the opposite effect. Those who claimed to have spiritual sight were shown to be blind. This is what Jesus meant when He answered the Pharisees in the closing verses of Chapter 9: "Those of the Pharisees who were with Him heard these things and said to Him, 'We are not blind too, are we?' Jesus said to them, 'If you were blind, you would have no sin; but since you say, "We see," your sin remains'" (vv. 40-41).

They understood Jesus was not speaking of physical sight. They professed themselves to be clear-sighted, but they were spiritually blind. They were blind to their own blindness. Since they would not admit their need for sight by acknowledging their own blindness, they would remain in darkness. This was God's judgment on them.

The miracle was a vivid illustration of Jesus' teaching. The man was blind both physically and spiritually. Jesus gave him physical sight and in doing so, opened his spiritual eyes as well. In contrast, the Pharisees, who refused to admit their own spiritual blindness, responded to the miracle with unrepentant unbelief, all while claiming, "We see" (v. 41).

---

[37] Isaiah 9:2; 29:18; 32:3; 35:5; 42:7; Luke 7:18-23.

Chapter 9 closes with words of reproof directed at unbelieving Pharisees for their unwillingness to admit their own spiritual blindness. Chapter 10 is the continuation of Jesus' words to the Pharisees. The Good Shepherd Discourse was delivered to the same unbelieving Pharisees mentioned in 9:40. This is one of the most interesting things about the Good Shepherd Discourse: it was not addressed to His sheep. Presumably, there were sheep (true believers) there to hear it including the man born blind and the disciples. However, it was not addressed to them. These words were addressed to the Pharisees, the unbelieving and false shepherds of Israel.

Knowing the context is essential to understanding the metaphor. The man born blind had come to understand that Jesus was the Son of Man - God in the flesh. He had embraced Christ and His unambiguous claims of deity. He had believed on Jesus as the Son of Man and worshiped Him. He was a *sheep*. The false shepherds of Israel, the religious leaders charged with caring for the flock of God, had excommunicated him. They had reviled and slandered him by putting him out of the synagogue. In this discourse, the True Shepherd addressed the false shepherds for their treatment of this man.

UNDERSTANDING THE METAPHOR

To him the doorkeeper opens, and the sheep hear his voice, and he calls his own sheep by name and leads them out. When he puts forth all his own, he goes ahead of them, and the sheep follow him because they *know his voice*. A stranger they simply will not follow, but will flee from him, because they do not know the voice of strangers. (John 10:3–5)

In the shepherding regions of the Judean countryside, each village had a fold where the sheep spent the night. Individual shepherds would graze their sheep during the day. At night they would bring the sheep back to the communal fold where sheep from many different flocks would spend the night together. As they approached the door, the shepherd would stop and inspect each sheep before putting it into the communal fold.

The sheep fold was a pen with high walls and one door. This walled enclosure provided shelter from the elements and protection from predators. One man, a hired hand, spent the night with the sheep. This made it possible for one person to guard multiple flocks of sheep overnight.

In the morning, the shepherd would arrive to gather his sheep. The doorkeeper would open the door and the shepherd would call his sheep. The sheep, recognizing his voice, would follow him out the door to pasture. The sheep that did not belong to him would remain inside the fold since they would not come to the voice of a stranger. Only *his* sheep would come because they recognized his voice. In this way, the shepherd could quickly and efficiently separate his sheep from all others. This is the cultural background behind the metaphor Jesus used in verses 3-5.

The imagery was lost on the Pharisees. John notes, "This figure of speech Jesus spoke to them, but they *did not understand* what those things were which He had been saying to them." That editorial statement is the key to a proper interpretation of Jesus' words. The language is a "figure of speech." Jesus was not speaking of a literal voice or of literal hearing. If He were, John would not say that it was a "figure of speech." If the "hearing" in the passage is a figure of speech, then it doesn't refer to actual "hearing."

John notes that the Pharisees did not understand that which Jesus was describing. Jesus explained the figure of speech in greater detail in John 10:7–18:

> So Jesus said to them again, "Truly, truly, I say to you, I am the door of the sheep. All who came before Me are thieves and robbers, but the sheep *did not hear them*. I am the door; if anyone enters through Me, he will be saved, and will go in and out and find pasture. The thief comes only to steal and kill and destroy; I came that they may have life, and have it abundantly. I am the good shepherd; the good shepherd lays down His life for the sheep. He who is a hired hand, and not a shepherd, who is not the owner of the sheep, sees the wolf coming, and leaves the sheep and flees, and the wolf snatches them and scatters them. He flees because he is a hired hand and is not concerned about the sheep. I am the good shepherd, and I know My own and My own know Me, even as the Father knows Me and I know the Father; and I lay down My life for the sheep. I have other sheep, which are not of this fold; I must bring them also, and *they will hear My voice*; and they will become one flock with one shepherd. For this reason the Father loves Me, because I lay down My life so that I may take it again. No one has taken it away from Me, but I lay it down on My own initiative. I have authority to lay

it down, and I have authority to take it up again. This commandment I received from My Father."

Jesus used the analogy to teach that He is both the door to the sheep (10:7) and the Shepherd of the sheep (10:11). Unlike thieves and robbers, Jesus comes to give life to His sheep (10:9-10). He is not a hireling who runs from danger, but lays down His life for them (10:11, 15, 17, 18). He is the Good Shepherd, committed to gathering in His sheep, saving them, and securing them everlastingly.

Here is the crux of the issue: what does it mean to hear His voice?

When read in context, it is difficult to miss the salvific point of the metaphor. Jesus was not describing the ability of believers to hear the whispers of the Shepherd in their daily lives through impressions and nudges. He was describing His work of bringing His sheep to salvation. He mentions giving them eternal life (10:10) and laying down His life for them (10:17-18).

Later in this same passage, at the time of the Feast of Dedication, Jesus used the same language and analogy, to confront the same hostile Jews with their unbelief. John 10:25-30 says:

> Jesus answered them, "I told you, and you do not believe; the works that I do in My Father's name, these testify of Me. But you do not believe because you are not of My sheep. *My sheep hear My voice*, and I know them, and they *follow Me*; and I give *eternal life* to them, and they will *never perish*; and no one will snatch them out of My hand. My Father, who has given them to Me, is greater than all; and no one is able to snatch them out of the Father's hand. I and the Father are one."

HVG proponents quote verse 27 to prove that Jesus promises to speak personally to all His sheep. Even a cursory look at the immediate context shows that the verse in question has nothing to do with that. In this passage, hearing His voice *results* in salvation. His sheep hear His voice and they follow Him and He gives them *eternal life*. Further, because they are His, He secures them so that "they will never perish; and no one will snatch them out of [His] hand." Jesus was describing the individual salvation of His sheep, not individual revelation through whispers and impressions. Hearing His voice is a figure of speech (10:6) for heeding the divine summons that draws the elect to Christ for salvation. In other Scripture passages, this is referred to as "the call."[38]

As with the passage earlier in the chapter, Jesus was not addressing believers, but the unbelieving Jews who had gathered around Him in the portico to question Him. That they were not believers is indicated by Jesus' words in verse 26: "But you do not believe because you are not of my sheep."

Jesus was explaining their unbelief. They did not believe on Him *because* they did not belong to Him. If they belonged to Him, they would hear His voice and believe. If they belonged to Him (i.e. were His sheep), He would give them eternal life, and secure them eternally. His sheep are secure because the Father gave them to the Son. They are the people for whom the Son would lay down His life.[39]

Sheep hearing the Shepherd's voice is a figure of speech Jesus used to describe His saving call to those the Father had given to Him (His sheep). This saving call infallibly brings about the salvation and security of all His sheep. In the words of the analogy, "they hear His voice" and not the "voice of strangers." Those who belong to the Son hear Him when He calls them to salvation. Belonging to Him precedes being called to Him as the metaphor makes clear. It is because His sheep belong to Him (given to Him by the Father) that they hear His voice, come to Him, and receive eternal life. The Pharisees did not believe (hear His voice and come to Him) because they did not belong to Him. They had not been given to Him by the Father (10:26). This was Jesus' explanation of their persistent unbelief.

GETTING IT BACKWARDS

HVG theology says salvation results in hearing the Shepherd's voice. John 10 teaches that hearing the Shepherd's voice results in salvation. HVG theology says salvation gives the ability to hear the

---

[38] See also Romans 1:7; 8:28–30; 9:24; 1 Corinthians 1:2, 22–24; Galatians 1:6, 15; Ephesians 4:1-4; 2 Thessalonians 2:13–14; 2 Timothy 1:9; 1 Peter 5:10; 2 Peter 1:3. Those who come to the Son do so not by their own power but because they are called. The Shepherd of the sheep calls the sheep to Himself. Consequently, we are referred to as "the called." Nowhere in Scripture are unbelievers referred to in this way.

[39] This same truth is taught in numerous passages of John's Gospel, but most thoroughly in Chapters 6, 10, & 17 where the electing purposes of the Father are secured by the obedient sacrifice of the Son. In all three chapters, the Lord Jesus speaks of a specific people who belong to Him as a gift from the Father. These same people are infallibly saved and secured by the work of the Son on their behalf.

Shepherd's voice. John 10 teaches that hearing his voice gives us salvation.

HVG theology says we will hear the voice of the Shepherd if we cultivate an intimate love relationship with Him. John 10 teaches that we hear the voice of the Shepherd because we belong to Him as a gift from the Father.

HVG theology says we hear His voice after salvation. John 10 teaches that we hear His voice prior to salvation.

HVG theology says salvation makes us His sheep. John 10 teaches that we are His sheep before salvation because we were given to Him by the Father.

HVG theology claims that John 10 is Jesus' promise to speak to His people outside Scripture. John 10 is actually Jesus' promise to save, sanctify, and secure His sheep forever.

HVG advocates claim that Jesus promised we will receive personal, private revelation on a regular, even daily, basis. John 10 teaches that Jesus promised that those chosen by the Father (Ephesians 1:4) and given to the Son will most certainly respond to His gospel call with belief resulting in eternal life.

John 10 has NOTHING to do with receiving personalized private revelations. It has nothing to do with hearing Jesus whisper a message to you. It isn't describing an innate or cultivated ability to pick up a frequency of divine whispers, nudgings, and promptings. It isn't describing a conversational walk with Jesus as He whispers directives into our spiritual ears through feelings and impressions. Jesus was talking about salvation, the work of gathering His sheep to Himself (10:16), saving and securing them in spite of the spiritual threat of false shepherds, robbers, and hirelings.

HVG teachers don't just get a couple of details of the text wrong, they turn the meaning entirely on its head. They get it backwards! They take something the text explicitly says is a "figure of speech" and turn it into a literal description of literal communication. Only the most egregious twisting of Jesus' words could result in the perverse interpretation of the text promoted by HVG advocates. Their teaching on John 10 is an inexcusable abuse of the Scriptures by people who should know better!

They write entire books teaching us how to discern the meaning of a whispered impression but they cannot discern the clear meaning of a written text! They think they can discern the meaning of God's whispers in signs, impressions, and inner promptings, but they cannot accurately discern the plain meaning of the inspired Word. If they cannot rightly interpret a passage as objectively clear and straightforward as John 10, why should we trust them to teach us how to interpret our vague, subjective, and unclear impressions?

AN UNBEARABLE BURDEN

When Scripture is twisted, misinterpreted, and misapplied, it wreaks havoc in the spiritual life of the believer. John 10 is no exception. Undiscerning Christians are taught that Jesus has *promised* to speak to them and that hearing Him is an *innate* ability they possess by virtue of being a Christian. As Shirer states, "If you're His child - if you're one of His sheep - the certainty of God speaking to you is as sure as the chair you're sitting in."[40]

For many Christians this never materializes. They do not receive the promised whispers. Their attempts to divine the signs, read their circumstances, and interpret their feelings only result in frustrated confusion and uncertainty. Though their hesitation to trust impressions and experiences is, in fact, a more spiritually mature instinct than listening for whispers, they are made to feel as if they are, at best, immature, second class believers and, at worst, not believers at all.

This abuse of John 10 places an unbearable burden on the shoulders of the untaught believer. They are made to question their spirituality, maturity, and salvation all because of this unbiblical teaching. New believers need to be taught that God speaks in Scripture and Scripture alone. They should not be taught to look outside of Scripture for God's revelation for He has not promised to provide that.

---

[40] Shirer, *Discerning the Voice of God*, 34.

False Assumption #2: I Should Expect to Hear from God

Chapter 6

Faulty Assumption #3:
I Must Learn to Hear from God Outside Scripture

6

You can tell a lot about a book by its title. Just as the title of this book reveals my position on this issue, so those written by HVG teachers reveal their theological hand. They aren't hiding the ball when it comes to what they believe and teach.

Some books defend the non-cessationist belief that divine revelation is as necessary and common today as in Bible times, if not more so. For instance, Jack Deere's *Surprised By The Power of the Spirit* [1] and its sequel, *Surprised By The Voice of God* are intended as a theological answer to John MacArthur's *Charismatic Chaos.*[2] Deere tries to present a theological and exegetical case for his belief that God still speaks, as the subtitle to *Surprised by the Voice of God* indicates: *How God Speaks Today Through Prophecies, Dreams, and Visions.*

Other books claim to provide the secret that will enable us to hear the voice of God. For instance, NAR author "Apostle" John Eckhardt wrote *God Still Speaks: How to Hear and Receive Revelation from God for Your Family, Church, and Community*, and Cindy Jacobs offers *The Voice of God: How to Hear and Speak Words from God.* Joyce Meyer promises to teach us *How to Hear from God: Learn to Know His Voice and Make Right Decisions.*

At the risk of sounding repetitive, I must point out that many of the authors I reference here are not from New Apostolic

---

[1] See the Bibliography at the end of this book for more details on these various books.

[2] John MacArthur is well known in evangelical circles for his commitment to and defense of the cessationsist perspective on revelatory and sign gifts. MacArthur believes the supernatural sign gifts operated in the early church but, having accomplished their divinely determined purpose, are no longer given by the Holy Spirit after the end of the apostolic era.

Reformation, Word of Faith, or Charismatic circles. Even some from inside the non-charismatic camp teach that we can learn to hear God's voice. Priscilla Shirer wrote at least two different books to help us learn to hear God: *He Speaks to Me: Preparing to Hear from God* and *Discerning the Voice of God: How to Recognize when God Is Speaking*. Mark Batterson promises to teach us *How to Hear the Voice of God* in his book *Whisper*.

HVG advocates promise to teach the willing reader how to recognize the whispered communiques of the Shepherd. They assure us this ability to hear God's voice can be *learned*.

But can it? Their promise to teach us how to hear God's voice begs the question that is before us, namely, "Is God speaking to us through these means?" If God isn't speaking, then no instruction can teach us how to hear Him. If He isn't speaking, He can't be heard; therefore, any attempt to "learn" to hear His voice is misguided.

A LEARNED SKILL?

HVG teachers believe God is speaking and we must learn to hear Him. They use the language of "learning to hear God," "learning to recognize His voice," and growing in our ability to "discern God's voice." Their detailed formulas and complex methods allegedly tune us into God's frequency.[3] They believe this is essential for life and ministry.

Charles Stanley says, "I believe one of the most valuable lessons we can ever learn is how to listen to God. . . . And, the Bible is explicit, God speaks to us just as powerfully today as in the days in which the Bible was written. His voice waits to be heard."[4] Contrary to his claim, there isn't a single example in Scripture of someone learning to hear God's voice. Not one. If God's voice is so "powerful," why do we need to be taught how to hear it? What kind of "powerful" voice is stymied because someone hasn't learned to listen for it? Where do we read that His voice "waits to be heard"?

Stanley cites Samuel (1 Samuel 3:4-10) as an example of someone who needed to learn to hear God. He says, "Eli taught Samuel how to listen to God, and if we are going to be men and women of God today, we must learn how we can hear what God is

---

[3] The methods proposed by these authors are critiqued in later chapters.

[4] Stanley, *How to Listen to God*, 8.

saying to us."[5] Allegedly, Samuel's "first assignment from God necessitated that he learn how to hear God's voice."[6]

The story of Samuel doesn't teach this at all! Samuel had no problem hearing the voice of God. The Lord spoke to him saying, "Samuel!" and Samuel arose and went to Eli thinking Eli had called for him. In fact, all three times the Lord spoke to Samuel in this way (vv. 4, 6, 8), Samuel heard His voice. He didn't need to be taught how to hear God! He had no reason to assume God was speaking since "word from the LORD was rare in those days, visions were infrequent" (v. 1). Ironically, in order to prove how powerfully and frequently God still speaks, Stanley cites a passage that describes how *infrequently* God spoke in Bible times! Stanley conveniently leaves that contextual detail out of his citation of the passage.

Samuel had no problem hearing God or understanding what He said. He didn't realize the voice he *clearly heard* and *understood* was, in fact, God. He thought it was Eli.

Stanley isn't alone in misusing this passage. Priscilla Shirer based her book *He Speaks to Me* on the story of Samuel, using him as a model of preparing to hear from God.[7] Misinterpreting the shepherd/sheep analogy from John 10, she writes:

Christians are the Lord's sheep. He is our Shepherd. As we grow in the Lord, we begin to *learn* how to recognize His voice and understand His messages. A lamb is less capable of distinguishing His shepherd's voice than a sheep is. Lambs *learn* as they get to know their shepherd and practice responding to his voice. This skill comes over time as the two build a relationship.[8]

In another book on the same subject, Shirer writes:

Remember, learning to hear God's voice is a process, a learning experience, a discipline that involves active elements like prayer, meditation, worship, and *listening*. Just as any relationship grows stronger and more intimate as you spend more time getting to know a person, so your relationship with God - your ability to discern His voice and

---

[5] Ibid., 80.

[6] Ibid., 79.

[7] Shirer, *He Speaks to Me*. She cites six qualities that "positioned" Samuel to hear from God; a simple relationship, a single-minded worship, a set-apart holiness, a still attentiveness, a sold-out hunger, and a servant spirit.

[8] Shirer, *He Speaks to Me*, 163. Emphasis mine.

to pick it out of the crowd - will grow keener and more developed as you spend more time with Him.[9]

Ironically, the example of Samuel, which she spends the entire book citing, proves just the opposite. Samuel didn't need to learn how to hear God's voice. He heard God speak without ever learning how. We read nothing about "a process, a learning experience, a discipline" in the example of Samuel.

Henry Blackaby claims God "wants you to *learn* to hear His voice and know His will"[10] and that you "*learn* to know the voice of God through an intimate love relationship that He has initiated."[11]

Dallas Willard teaches that hearing from God is part of a "two-way communication between us and God" and that such communication must be learned.[12] He claims that "*learning* to hear God is much more about becoming comfortable in a continuing conversation"[13] and that "*learning* how to hear God is to be sought *only as part of a certain kind of life*."[14]

For HVG advocates, the learning doesn't stop there. We must also learn how to understand Him,[15] how to pick His voice out from among others,[16] how to seek confirmation that it is actually Him speaking,[17] how to avoid being deceived,[18] how to receive a peace about His voice,[19] and how to distinguish between His voice and our own thoughts.[20]

---

[9] Shirer, *Discerning the Voice of God*, 34–35.

[10] Blackaby and King, *Experiencing God*, 90. Emphasis mine.

[11] Ibid., 96. Emphasis mine.

[12] Willard, *Hearing God*, 10.

[13] Ibid. Emphasis mine.

[14] Ibid., 39. Emphasis mine.

[15] Shirer, *He Speaks to Me*, 86–87.

[16] Ibid., 164.

[17] Shirer, *Discerning the Voice of God*, 48.

[18] Stanley, *How to Listen to God*, 50. Stanley devotes a chapter in his book to teaching people how to avoid being deceived while trying to identify God's voice.

[19] Joyce Meyer, *How to Hear from God: Learn to Know His Voice and Make Right Decisions*, (New York: Faith Words, 2003), 81. Meyer makes much of this "internal peace," devoting an entire chapter to instructions on how to be guided by it. I will deal with the question of whether or not God speaks to us through an "inner peace" in Chapter 12.

[20] Willard, *Hearing God*, 114. In Chapter 5, Willard dives head-first into a subjective swamp of confusion by trying to teach us how to mine our own thoughts for the voice of God while not identifying our own thoughts as the voice of God. While trying to defend the notion that God speaks through a still small voice, Willard leaves us with only subjective impressions stamped with the "not-so-certain seal" of divine authority. He says on page 135 that God "will help us learn to distinguish when a thought is ours alone and when it is also his [sic]."

You will search the Scriptures in vain for these elaborate instructions because no one in Scripture ever needed to be taught how to hear God - Samuel included.

THE WAYS WE LEARN

How do we learn this supposedly essential discipline? Is there a book of the Bible to which we can turn or a model we can follow? Is there a secret formula to acquire this vital skill? No.

While promising to teach us how this skill can be learned, HVG advocates are careful to avoid any claims of a formula for hearing from God. They can't turn to the Scriptures for teaching on this subject since there isn't a single example of God trying to be heard. The Bible doesn't teach that this skill can be learned nor that one must learn it in order to hear God.[21]

Without any model or pattern provided in Scripture, HVG teachers can only offer us "trial and error" combined with lots of experience. Jack Deere claims we are able to "learn the language of the Holy Spirit" by trial and error. "Only those who are willing to try and fail will ever become proficient at understanding which impressions come from God and which arise merely from their own soul."[22] He excuses what he calls the "humiliating failures" of "prophet" Rick Joyner with this glib dismissal: "You know, we are learning as much from our failures as our successes."[23] Deere writes, "You can't learn a natural language or the language of the Holy Spirit apart from trial and error."[24]

The consequences of this are disastrous. When one claims to receive divine revelation, they are laying claim to the authority of "God said . . ." To err with such a claim is to misrepresent God by putting words in His mouth. That is serious business!

Bill Johnson of Bethel Church in Redding California, runs the Bethel School of Supernatural Ministry. He says:

> Every year we tell our students that they cannot graduate unless they have taken risk and failed in their efforts to try to learn to operate in their ability to hear God and encourage others with His voice. . . . Sometimes they get

---

[21] The passages typically pressed into service to support this notion (e.g. John 10; 1 Samuel 3) either have nothing to do with what these authors claim or they are grossly misinterpreted and abused.

[22] Jack Deere, *Surprised by the Voice of God: How God Speaks Today Through Prophecies, Dreams, and Visions* (Grand Rapids: Zondervan Publishing House, 1996), 170.

[23] Ibid., 170.

[24] Ibid., 171.

it right, and sometimes they get it wrong. But the point is, they tried. This would be unfair if we didn't at the same time create a safe place to fail so that they can learn how to recognize the Voice of God for themselves.[25]

In HVG theology, experience is the best teacher. Charles Stanley believes we "are often hindered from hearing God because of our inexperience."[26] Citing John 10:27, he says Jesus made it clear "that the believer's normal experience is to hear God accurately."[27] How can we distinguish God's voice from others? Stanley answers, "Mature Christians have had experience in listening to God, and they can distinguish between God's Voice and another's. For others, especially young Christians, it is a bit more of a problem."[28]

Priscilla Shirer says, "Learning to hear God's voice is a process, a learning experience."[29]

How do they suggest we learn to hear the voice? Experience. Experience is necessary to learn how, and yet, you can only get that experience by trial and error. Experience is necessary to avoid being deceived, and it is only by being deceived and making humiliating mistakes that we can get the necessary experience.

If only there were a "more sure Word" from God; a certain, sufficient, and unchanging revelation of His will to which we could turn for guidance. If only there were something we were certain came from God so we wouldn't have to rely upon subjective experiences, feelings, and "trial and error." If only.

WHERE IS THAT, EXACTLY?

Which passage teaches that we must learn to listen for God's voice? Where does the Bible say His voice is difficult to hear, challenging to discern, and waiting to be heard?[30] You won't find it. Yet, without any biblical precedent, either by explicit teaching or example, HVG teachers claim God's voice is so easily eclipsed by the noise of our daily lives and so quietly whispered in the recesses of our distracted minds, that we are in danger of missing it.

---

[25] Cindy Jacobs, *The Voice of God: How to Here and Speak Words from God* (Minneapolis: Baker Publishing Group, 2016), 16.

[26] Stanley, *How to Listen to God*, 133.

[27] Ibid., 50.

[28] Ibid.

[29] Shirer, *Discerning the Voice of God*, 34.

[30] Stanley, *How to Listen to God*, 8.

HVG advocates need to demonstrate two things in Scripture.

First, they must provide some examples of God *trying* to speak without being heard; examples of times when the intended recipient of God's voice was unable to hear Him. They claim God is speaking in the same way today as He did in Bible times, so it should not be difficult to find myriads of such examples. If this happens all the time today, it must have happened all the time back then. They should be able to cite dozens upon dozens of instances where God's ability to communicate was hampered by man's inability to hear Him.

They claim this is happening to us every day. In his book *Frequency*, Robert Morris writes, "We need to tune in to the frequency of heaven and hear the voice of God,"[31] and, "God is speaking all the time, but the only ones who hear are those who tune in to the right frequency through humility and obedience."[32] Apparently the voice of God is like a radio station that is *always* broadcasting. We merely need to tune to the appropriate frequency to pick up the heavenly messages constantly coming our way. It should be easy to show in Scripture a multitude of examples of God speaking, only to be frustrated because the intended recipient of that communication wasn't adequately tuned in. We need *one* example of *one* individual who didn't hear God because they hadn't learned how to hear His voice. There isn't a single example in all of Scripture of someone learning this discipline or needing to do so.[33]

Second, they must point to passages of Scripture that teach believers how to receive these whispers. There is abundant teaching on a wide variety of issues essential to our sanctification and maturity. We have teaching on how to handle persecution (1 Peter), how to relate to a spouse (Ephesians 5), how to mortify sin (Romans 6), how to raise and discipline children (Proverbs), and how to handle conflict and treat masters and/or slaves (Colossians

---

[31] Morris, *Frequency*, 124.

[32] Ibid, 132.

[33] At this point, HVG advocates might claim there are lots of examples in Scripture of God reproving the Israelites because they would not or did not listen to Him. These examples, and there are dozens of them, are not at all the same thing we are talking about here. They differ on several counts. First, those were rebellious, hard-hearted, unbelieving Jews, not genuine, soft-hearted, and obedient believers. Second, the "word" which they did not hear or heed was not some private revelation given through their thoughts, signs, or a "still small voice." It was revelation given through a God-ordained prophet like Isaiah, Ezekiel, or Jeremiah. Third, the Jews both heard and understood the Word of God through the prophets. They refused to believe it. Their issue was not that they did not tune in to the right "frequency," but that they met the clear Word of God with unrepentant unbelief. Fourth, they were not chastised because they did not know how to hear God's voice, but rather, because having heard and understood it, they refused to obey it.

3). We are given detailed instructions on how to structure a church (1 Timothy 3), how to exercise church discipline (Matthew 18), the roles of women in ministry (1 Timothy 2, 1 Corinthians 11), and dozens of other vital topics. Where is the passage that teaches us how to hear from God?[34] Where does an apostle instruct us on this ability so essential to our church, our community, and our nation?[35] Where is that chapter - that clear passage - that describes this essential practice without which we are "in trouble at the very heart of our Christian life"?[36]

Scripture nowhere commands believers to expect, listen for, or learn to hear the voice of God for themselves. The ability to hear God is nowhere taught in Scripture. Priscilla Shirer laments that "deliberately listening for God's voice seems to be a lost art these days."[37] The advice she offers in this vein is completely without biblical support: "If we want to hear Him speak, however, we must also learn to pray without words. To listen for His voice."[38] She teaches that we "must 'listen' for God if we want to hear Him speak to us."[39] Despite her insistence that "*listening to God is a purposeful activity* that we are supposed to start doing,"[40] you won't find any such counsel in the pages of Scripture. Neither Jesus, nor the apostles, nor any author of the Old Testament ever encouraged this activity among the people of God.

The reason for this is simple: *If God is not speaking, no amount of learning can bestow the ability to hear Him. If God is speaking, then no amount of distraction will keep you from hearing Him.*[41] You cannot learn to hear something that is not being said. You cannot

---

[34] They can't cite John 10 since that passage has nothing to do with the practice they are defending. There are a few passages of Scripture pressed into service to support their various practices. I will deal with those passages and practices in the next section.

[35] Blackaby and King, *Experiencing God*, 68.

[36] Ibid., 83-84.

[37] Shirer, *Discerning the Voice of God*, 23.

[38] Ibid., 25.

[39] Ibid. Seeking to prove her point from Scripture, Shirer quotes Isaiah 55:3: "Incline your ear and come to Me. Listen, that you may live." The verse has nothing to do with individual people listening for private revelations. This verse is God's command through the prophet, imploring the nation of Israel to heed His words that they might turn from their sin and live. The verse is about listening to the revealed Word of God, not an impression whispered within our inner thoughts. Frankly, this kind of serial abuse of Scripture is inexcusable, but it is the stock in trade of HVG advocates.

[40] Ibid.

[41] This clear and simple construct is not original with me. I believe the first time I ever heard this expressed was by Greg Koukl of Stand to Reason (str.org) on a podcast during one of his regular weekly radio programs.

miss something that God intends for you to hear. Therefore, the teaching that you must learn how to hear God's voice is utter nonsense.

THE APOSTOLIC TEACHING

Not only are there no examples in Scripture of people being encouraged to listen for the voice of God, but we actually have examples to the contrary.

As Paul sat in a Roman prison awaiting execution (2 Timothy 4:6-8), he didn't direct Timothy to private revelations, still small voices, and inner impressions. He directed Timothy to the written Word of God. Paul reminded him of the "sacred writings" and their divinely inspired nature (2 Timothy 3:14-17). He instructed Timothy to "preach the Word" not "listen for His voice."

Likewise, Peter, knowing his death to be imminent (2 Peter 1:12-15), directed his readers to the written Word of God. That Word, provided through apostles and prophets, he described as "the prophetic word made more sure" (v. 19). Peter counted the written Word as "more sure" than even the most elaborate and glorious of experiences (vv. 16-18).

What most concerned the apostles in their dying days wasn't that "deliberately listening for God's voice seems to be a lost art these days," but that the centrality of the inspired, inerrant, written Word of the living God might be eclipsed. Sadly, I would suggest that in the writings of those who teach others to listen for the voice of God, the fear of the apostles has been realized. HVG teachers allow the clear Word of the living God to be obscured by subjective impressions, uncertain whispers, and unreliable experiences.

Further, it must be an omission of epic proportions that none of the apostles ever thought this discipline was necessary for those who serve as elders[42] in the church. There are two lists of qualifications given in the pastoral epistles (1 Timothy 3:1-7; Titus 1:5-9). Paul doesn't mention the "ability to hear God speak" or "discern the voice of God" or "hear God for himself" in either of these passages. Given the teaching of HVG proponents, we might at least expect to find that elders must be "able to hear God clearly."

---

[42] Scripture makes no distinction in the office of "pastor" or "elder." These two English words are used of the same office in Scripture. An elder is a pastor and a pastor is an elder. Therefore, the qualifications given for an elder in Scripture are the qualifications for an "overseer" (1 Timothy 3:1-7) or pastor (Ephesians 4:11). Besides the passage referenced here in this section, see Acts 20:17-35 and 1 Peter 5:1-5. I highly recommend Alexander Strauch's excellent book, *Biblical Eldership* (Littleton: Lewis and Roth Publishers, 1995) on this subject.

Blackaby says that if a Christian "does not know when God is speaking, he is in trouble at the heart of his Christian life!"[43]

If this is the mark of a vibrant and mature faith, why isn't it a qualification for eldership? If God is giving essential directions for our churches through quiet whispers and subtle impressions, why isn't it required of those who lead the church to be "able to hear God clearly"? We would expect those who are most mature and able to handle the shepherding of others would themselves have cultivated the ability to discern the voice of the Shepherd. How could they teach others this *vital* discipline if they have not mastered it themselves? No such requirement is mentioned. If this ability to hear God is as essential as HVG teachers claim, then this inexcusable oversight by the Holy Spirit is nothing short of gross negligence!

Contrary to the claims of HVG advocates, Scripture doesn't teach that the mark of maturity is an ability to tune into God's "frequency" and enjoy "two-way conversation." Christian maturity isn't the ability to read signs and exegete impressions. Believers are never encouraged to listen for the voice of God outside Scripture. The work of the Holy Spirit is to illumine the objective, written Word of God, not provide "words from God" through vague impressions and random thoughts.

THE CONTRARY EXAMPLES

If the position I am advocating is true, then we would expect to find that when God speaks, He has no problem being heard. We would expect to see examples of both believers and unbelievers hearing God without ever having to learn how to hear His voice. This is *exactly* what we find!

When God spoke to Moses (Exodus 3-4), He didn't need special instruction on how to tune in to God's frequency. Joshua (Joshua 1) didn't need to learn how to hear God's voice to receive God's messages. Noah didn't need years of experience in misreading God's voice - making humiliating mistakes through trial and error - before he was able to accurately hear God.

HVG advocates claim God is speaking today in the same way He did in Bible times. Yet the way in which they claim that God speaks bears no resemblance to what we read in Scripture. No prophet was required to spend years learning to hear God. There are no believers in Scripture who had difficulty hearing God. The

---

[43] Blackaby and King, *Experiencing God*, 83–84.

reason for this is simple - when God wants to speak, He speaks. No one ever had to learn to hear God because hearing Him is not something that needs to be learned! God doesn't whisper! He doesn't stutter. He doesn't have trouble being heard. He doesn't struggle to communicate. He doesn't *try* to get His messages through.

Scripture also gives examples of pagan, rebellious, hard-hearted unbelievers hearing God without years of trial and error.

Before God called Abraham out of Ur of the Caldeans, he and his family were idol worshipers (Joshua 24:2). When God gave instructions and promises to Abraham, Abraham had no difficulty hearing God and understanding the message (Genesis 12:1-4). He didn't need to learn how to hear from God. Abraham was a pagan idolater with no years of experience in discerning the "still small voice." God spoke and Abraham heard clearly without years of learning by trial and error.

Did Saul of Tarsus need to learn how to listen to the voice of the Shepherd before Christ spoke to him on the road to Damascus (Acts 9:1-19)?[44] Later in Acts, Paul spoke of his conversion experience (Acts 22:3-21) and how Jesus spoke to him shortly after his conversion (vv. 17-21). Saul, a persecutor of the Church, didn't need to learn how to "listen" or tune into God's "frequency" to hear the Shepherd. With no previous experience, while an enemy of God, Saul of Tarsus heard God without any problem. Then as a new believer, without years of practice, experience, and trial and error, he was able to hear God when God spoke.

God was able to speak to Cornelius, who wasn't a born-again believer. Yes, Cornelius was one who "feared God," but he was not saved (Acts 10:1-8). He was an unbeliever and he didn't need to learn how to hear God speak. Nebuchadnezzar never learned to listen for God's voice (Daniel 4:31-32) and he heard God.

Abraham, Nebuchadnezzar, Saul of Tarsus, and Cornelius all prove that God is heard when He wills to be heard. No special skill is necessary to hear Him. Why were these unbelievers able to hear God, but modern believers can't without the special instruction and training provided by HVG teachers? Why do believers need years of practice, experience, and trial and error, to be able to hear God while an unbeliever like Abraham or Saul didn't?

---

[44] The account of the conversion of Saul of Tarsus (later called Paul, the Apostle) is detailed 3 times in Acts (Acts 9:1-19; 22:3-21; 26:9-18).

Remember the HVG claim: God is speaking today "*just like in Bible times.*" "God hasn't changed!" they claim. "He hasn't gone mute. The Bible is full of examples of God speaking and He does it the same today!"

The Bible gives plenty of examples of God speaking to men and women. However, it doesn't give any examples of God speaking quietly on a frequency that can only be heard by those who have cultivated a special ability. The examples of Scripture prove the opposite of what HVG teachers claim. God doesn't whisper His Word. When God speaks, He is heard. There are no examples of God speaking and not being heard. There are no examples of someone learning to hear Him.

Nobody needs to learn to hear God. If God is not speaking, you will not hear Him no matter what disciplines of solitude you cultivate. If He were to speak, then you could not miss Him. He never *tries* to speak. *God doesn't whisper.*

Part 3

A Methodology Critiqued

Imagine a familiar Bible story in modern evangelical lingo. It might go something like this:

Moses' life as a shepherd was very busy. Working for his father-in-law, Jethro, required sleepless nights of watching sheep and long days cutting wool. That life left little time for Moses to quiet himself and listen for God's voice. He longed to hear God's voice speak fresh words for him. Just as God had spoken to so many others before him (Job, Noah, and Abraham), he knew God would give him personal direction as well.

Moses needed to get alone and tune into God's frequency so he could discern the quiet whispers of His voice. He went out into the wilderness of Midian near the mount of Horeb to listen for God's still small voice. One day while sitting alone in quiet solitude listening intently to his own thoughts for God's voice, an idea popped into his head: "I should stop tending sheep." Could this be God's whisper?!

"Lord, is that you? Are you telling me to stop tending sheep?" Moses prayed.

He listened intently, but the only sound he heard was the bleating of the nearby flock. The silence caused him to doubt if he had actually heard God or it if was some other "voice." Moses was new to hearing God's whispers. He hadn't quite learned how to tune in to the Great Shepherd's voice. It was still a work in progress, but Moses. . .

Wait! There it was again. He felt a very strong impression that he was to give up shepherding and follow God into "some other endeavor." He wasn't sure yet what "some other endeavor" meant. The impressions were still vague and unclear, but he couldn't get the words "some other endeavor" out of his mind.

"Lord, is that you? Are you telling me that? What do you want me to do, Lord?"

Moses sat in silence as he strained to hear God. He had definitely felt two distinct whispers to his heart about giving up his work as a shepherd, but what else would he do? The only other thing he had known was life as a prince in Egypt, growing up in Pharaoh's house and enjoying the delights of the good life. His thoughts went back to his time in Egypt where his fellow Jews were still in bondage. If he ever thought the shepherding life was hard, he would always console himself with the fact he was not a slave in Egypt.

Moses remembered the promise God made to his forefathers through Joseph: "God will surely take care of you and bring you up from this land to the land which He promised on oath to Abraham, to Isaac and to Jacob."[1]

Moses felt the Lord speak to his heart in a quiet whisper, "YOU deliver them!"

"Oh, that can't be the Lord speaking," thought Moses. "He wouldn't tell me to do something as crazy as *that!*" Then he remembered the seemingly absurd things God had told others to do. He told Noah to build an ark and Abraham to sacrifice his son! "Maybe God *is* in the business of giving outlandish directions," he thought.

"Lord, are you telling me to go to Egypt and deliver the Israelites? Is that what you are saying, Lord? I feel this strong impression and I think it might be you."

Silence.

Moses decided to watch for providential signs that might confirm God's words to him. A few days later, he returned home with the flock. He entered his tent and greeted his wife Zipporah. Turning around he noticed a new tapestry hanging on the wall. "Where did you buy that?" Moses asked.

Zipporah replied, "I bought that 4 days ago from some Egyptian merchants down in the marketplace."

"Did you say, '*Egyptian* merchants'?" Moses asked.

Four days ago! That was precisely the day that Moses felt the Lord speak to His heart and say, "You deliver them!" Surely this was no coincidence. It must be a sign!

Moses prayed, "Lord, if this sign is from You, will you please make it clear? Give me another indicator if it is Your will for me to return to Egypt and deliver the children of Israel."

Moses and Zipporah discussed the tapestry, the impressions, and what they might mean. He couldn't get Egypt out of his mind as he drifted off to sleep that night. During the night, Moses dreamed of his days in Pharaoh's house eating at Pharaoh's table. Oh, how he longed in his dream to go *back to Egypt.*

He awoke and wondered if God had given him the dream to confirm the whispers he heard in the wilderness. Moses told Zipporah of the dream. She said, "If this prompting is from God, then He will confirm His whispers with a peace in your heart. Do you have a peace or do you feel a check in your spirit?"

"I don't know," said Moses. "I am new to the practice of listening for God's voice. I am sure God is speaking, but I am not very

---

[1] Genesis 50:24-25.

experienced at hearing His voice. I think He might be trying to tell me something, but I am struggling to make sure I get it right."

"Perhaps we should put out a fleece," suggested Zipporah.

"A fleece!" exclaimed Moses. "Of course! That would settle it once and for all."

Moses prayed, "Lord, I need one last sign. If you want me to continue tending sheep, then I pray that when I go to the marketplace tomorrow, the Egyptian merchants will still be there. If, when I arrive, they have already gone *back to Egypt*, then I will know You want me to go *back to Egypt* as well. By this, I shall know your clear direction for me."

Moses arrived at the marketplace the next day to find the Egyptian merchants had returned to Egypt. Seeing how the Lord had confirmed his earlier impressions, Moses felt a peace in his heart that this was the message God had been trying to give him all along. He sensed God was getting thematic with him.

Later that night, as Moses was sitting quietly in his tent reading the scroll of Job, he read these words: "Can you bind the *chains* of the Pleiades, Or loose the cords of Orion?"[2] The word "chains" jumped off the parchment! It came alive to Moses as he sensed the Lord say to him, "My people are in chains in Egypt!" He claimed the verse for himself! The Lord had confirmed to Moses that he would loose the chains of bondage from the Israelites and bring God's people out of Egypt.

****

Does the preceding story bear any resemblance to Moses' encounter with the Lord recorded in Exodus 3-4? Does it bear *any* resemblance to *any* account of God speaking *anywhere* in Scripture?

HVG proponents say this is what "hearing God's voice" is like. They claim this is how God speaks to us today - just as He did to the saints of old. They claim that all these means and methods (and many more) are vehicles through which God tenderly whispers to us. The voice of God is heard through inner impressions, providential signs, and words jumping off the pages of Scripture with meanings never imagined by their authors. They say God's whispers can be verified through confirmations, inner peace, and fleeces. Though these are the methods employed by HVG

---

[2] Job 38:31.

teachers, none of them bear any resemblance to what we find in Scripture.

In this section, I will examine the various practices promoted by HVG teachers and the passages they cite. We will see if God is speaking today *just as He did* to the saints of old.[3]

---

[3] Please see Chapters 4, 5, and 6.

Chapter 7

I Heard the Still Small Voice

7

It is nearly impossible to read a book on hearing God's voice without finding references to Elijah and the "still small voice" (1 Kings 19:12).[1] No description of divine communication in Scripture more closely resembles the model promoted by HVG teachers than the phrase "still small voice." The wording has been so successfully hijacked and inserted into modern vernacular that most Christians probably believe it describes God's normal means of communicating with His people. This one incident in 1 Kings 19 has become an interpretive paradigm into which all of divine revelation gets squeezed.

The idiom is used not of external, audible divine messages (like the word "voice" would suggest), but of the impressions, thoughts, and inner promptings widely regarded as the voice of the Holy Spirit. Elijah is the model and the "still small voice" the pattern for modern divine revelation. Don't take my word for it. Listen to the HVG teachers themselves.

HVG ON THE STILL SMALL VOICE

Dallas Willard claims the still small voice is one of many ways God speaks to us: "And from among the individual's experiences of hearing God, the 'still, small voice' has a vastly greater role than anything else."[2] To define "still small voice" Willard cites 1 Kings 19

---

[1] "Still small voice" is the translation provided by the King James Version. As we will see later, there are other ways of translating the phrase.

[2] Willard, *Hearing God*, 115. This quote comes from a chapter titled, "The Still, Small Voice and Its Rivals." Willard attempts to defend the "overall importance" of the written Word and Jesus Christ suggesting they cannot be compared to other means of communication. I point this out to fairly represent Willard. He tries, unsuccessfully, I believe, to defend the

and then comments on the "unremarkable, inconspicuous, unassuming and perhaps not immediately noticed"[3] nature of this means of communication.

He claims that "the still, small voice - or the interior or inner voice, as it is also called - is the preferred and most valuable form of individual communication for God's purposes."[4] This is demonstrably untrue. It is never called "the interior or inner voice." It is called a "still small voice" in 1 Kings 19. Willard calls this an "internal voice" but *Scripture never does.*

Robert Morris mentions the "gentle whisper"[5] of 1 Kings 19:12 and wonders "if that was the same as what we'd call today an impression on our hearts. God impressed what He wanted to say upon Elijah's heart. We don't know for certain which method God chose to use. But maybe a still small voice is tantamount to the prompting of the Holy Spirit."[6]

Beth Moore abused the language of 1 Kings when she tweeted on July 2, 2018: "There's a time to give up & a time to keep trying. Sometimes the time to keep trying feels a whole lot like time to give up. The only difference is the still small voice of the Holy Spirit within you saying, 'try again.'"[7] A study of the passage will show the still small voice was not "within" Elijah.

Mark Batterson makes much of the "gentle whisper" of 1 Kings 19:12, noting the ESV translates it "a low whisper"[8] and the NASB "a gentle blowing."[9] Batterson claims, "God has an outside voice, and He's not afraid to use it. But when God wants to be heard, when what He has to say is too important to miss, He often speaks in a whisper just above the absolute threshold of hearing."[10]

Batterson claims this is how God draws us near to Himself:

---

uniqueness of Scripture; a distinction impossible to maintain once we say God still speaks through all these various means.

[3] Ibid.

[4] Ibid., 118.

[5] *The Holy Bible: New International Version.* (1984). (1 Ki 19:11–13). Grand Rapids, MI: Zondervan.

[6] Morris, *Frequency*, 33.

[7] https://twitter.com/bethmoorelpm/status/1013765999143849985.

[8] *The Holy Bible: English Standard Version.* (2016). (1 Ki 19:11–13). Wheaton, IL: Crossway Bibles.

[9] *New American Standard Bible: 1995 Update.* (1995). (1 Ki 19:11–12). La Habra, CA: The Lockman Foundation.

[10] Batterson, *Whisper*, 9.

When someone speaks in a whisper, you have to get very close to hear. In fact, you have to put your ear near the person's mouth. . . . That's why He speaks in a whisper. He wants to be as close to us as is divinely possible! He loves us, likes us, that much.[11]

How important is the still small voice? Batterson claims:

Nothing has the potential to change your life like the whisper of God. Nothing will determine your destiny more than your ability to hear His still small voice. . . .

That's how you see and seize divine appointments.

That's how God-sized dreams are birthed.

That's how miracles happen.[12]

Batterson spends a good portion of his book citing examples of God's "whispered" instructions for his life and ministry. He warns against missing whispers: "So how do we make sure we don't miss those God-ordained opportunities? We have to turn up the volume on the still small voice of God and make sure He's the loudest voice in our lives."[13] Do you remember Elijah saying something like that? Of course not!

I HAD A THOUGHT!

The majority of HVG teachers cite Elijah as the quintessential example of hearing "divine whispers."[14] A couple of examples serve to make this point.

In her book, *Discerning the Voice of God*, Priscilla Shirer encourages her readers to ask, "What persistent, internal stirrings have I sensed? And how is He corroborating this message in other

---

[11] Ibid., 9-10.

[12] Ibid., 11–12.

[13] Ibid., 167.

[14] Some who promote the use of revelatory gifts in the church refrain from using Elijah as an example, steering clear of citing 1 Kings 19. Sam Storms (*Practicing the Power*) tries to make the case for the continuation of revelatory gifts (prophecy and words of knowledge), but does not cite Elijah. The same can be said of Jack Deere, who, though he mentions events in the life of Elijah, does not mention the still small voice in either of his two books on the Charismatic gifts (*Surprised by the Power of the Spirit* and *Surprised by the Voice of God*). Theologian Wayne Grudem is open to the kind of guidance I am critiquing, but in the section of his systematic theology dealing with this topic, he does not cite Elijah (*Systematic Theology*). Storms, Grudem, and Deere have attempted a more exegetical and theologically serious approach to this subject than the authors cited here. Misuse of the reference to the still small voice seems relegated to books targeting a more undiscerning audience.

external ways?"[15] She claims God is "unrelenting"[16] in His attempts to get our attention through impressions saying, "He will consistently bombard your thoughts and your heart with His message until you're convinced of its authenticity."[17] Allegedly, one indication these thoughts are from God is the sheer tenacity with which we are bombarded by them: "He knows we don't always get good reception, depending on where we are located or where our head is. . . . *Persistent, internal inklings matched by external confirmation is often the way God directs believers into His will.*"[18]

She later writes:

> I often know *God is speaking when a thought occurs to me* that surprises me, maybe makes me a little uncomfortable, and I know it's something I can't do in my own power. When I take a thought like that to the Lord in prayer, when I consult the Word and even godly counsel, and my Holy Spirit-led conscience will not let me rest until I move forward with it, *I assume this is God speaking.*[19]

Not every thought is assumed to be the voice of God, just the persistent, uncomfortable, and surprising ones. As an example, she says that while doing her morning quiet time, "The name of an old friend dropped into my mind," and then the thought, "Call her. She needs you."[20] Upon calling, she discovered her friend needed assistance handling some family and work duties. Shirer claims these thoughts were the voice of the Holy Spirit.

Bill Hybel's book, *The Power of a Whisper*, contains numerous examples of people acting on inner promptings assumed to be the voice of God. Hybels encourages his readers to listen for and obey promptings. He refers to thoughts, feelings, and impressions as "inaudible" or "low volume" whispers saying, "Without a hint of exaggeration, I can boldly declare that God's low-volume whispers have saved me from a life of sure boredom and self-destruction. They have redirected my path, rescued me from temptation and reenergized me during some of my deepest moments of despair."[21]

---

[15] Shirer, *Discerning the Voice of God*, 78.

[16] Ibid., 79.

[17] Ibid., 80–81.

[18] Ibid., 81–82.

[19] Ibid., 125. Emphasis mine.

[20] Ibid., 143–44.

[21] Hybels, *The Power of a Whisper*, 17.

The Psalmist promises that Scripture will do these things for the child of God.[22] Hybles credits them to "inaudible whispers."

Batterson suggests the more sudden a thought occurs, the more likely it is of divine origin. One day while walking past a graffiti-covered building on Capitol Hill, a thought popped into his head: "*This crack house would make a great coffeehouse.*" He then claims, "That thought came out of nowhere, which sometimes indicates something supernatural."[23] Batterson believes our thoughts are vehicles of God's revelation because God "dwells in the synapses of the brain and speaks to us at the level of thoughts, ideas, and dreams."[24]

Dallas Willard directs his readers to their thoughts as a source of divine revelation: "That brings us to the two most important ways in which God speaks to us: (1) in conjunction with the language of human beings, and (2) through the inner voice of our own thoughts."[25]

HVG advocates equate thoughts, impressions, ideas, nudgings, promptings, and feelings with the still small voice of 1 Kings 19. Certainly, if this is the "preferred and most valuable" way God speaks to his people, it should be evident in the text.

TO THE CONTEXT!

The context of 1 Kings 19:12 will reveal the reason God spoke to Elijah in this manner at Horeb. The two chapters preceding the still small voice set the stage for his encounter.

Elijah burst on the scene during the reign of Ahab (1 Kings 17). Nothing is mentioned of his history, upbringing, or calling as a prophet, yet immediately he spoke for God. Chapter 17 begins with Elijah predicting a drought. Chapter 18 closes with rain in answer to Elijah's prayer.

These two chapters contain four significant miraculous events. First, the Lord directed Elijah to the brook Cherith, east of Jordan, where he was supernaturally provided bread and meat by ravens twice a day (17:3-7). Second, the Lord sent Elijah to a widow's

---

[22] The Psalmist says that God's Word redirects our path (Psalm 119:21, 33-38, 97-104, 128, 163, 176), rescues us from temptation (Psalm 119:9-11, 110-112, 133, 158, 165, 176), and re-energizes us during our deepest moments of despair (Psalm 119:25-28, 50-53, 81-88, 143, 145-147).

[23] Batterson, *Whisper*, 14.

[24] Ibid.,119.

[25] Willard, *Hearing God*, 125. This is from a chapter titled "The Still, Small Voice and Its Rivals."

home in Zarephath where He miraculously provided oil and flour for many days (17:8-16). Third, Elijah raised the widow's son from the dead (17:17-24). Fourth, and probably most memorable, Elijah challenged the 450 prophets of Baal on Mount Carmel, where God rained down fire on a water-soaked burnt offering. The prophets of Baal were seized and killed (18:20-40). During that short period of time, God displayed His providential care, goodness, and power – all for Elijah's benefit. Elijah confronted and conquered the largest idolatrous false religion of his day. This was a public rebuke of wicked King Ahab and his bloodthirsty wife, Jezebel.

When Jezebel threatened Elijah's life, he ran. After seeing the supernatural displays of God's power, he despaired of life (19:4, 10, 14), believing he was the last worshiper of Yahweh in Israel. Graciously, the Lord gave His beloved prophet rest and food (delivered by an angel - 19:5-8). Elijah made a 40-day journey to Horeb, where his encounter with God included the sound of the still small voice.

This brief overview allows us to make three notable observations.

First, the miracles surrounding the dramatic confrontation with the prophets of Baal and the end of the drought involved natural elements used in a supernatural way.[26] God answered Elijah's prayer with fire that consumed the burnt offering (1 Kings 18:38). After killing the prophets, Elijah prayed for rain. God answered "with clouds and wind, and there was a heavy shower" (1 Kings 18:45). God manifestly displayed His power through fire, wind, and rain.

Second, after working supernaturally through natural elements to defeat the prophets of Baal, God had *not* moved to either convert or destroy wicked Queen Jezebel. Elijah feared her threats (19:2). Though God had previously supernaturally provided for and protected Elijah, He appeared uninterested in the latest threat. While the royal family was hunting Elijah, no miraculous deliverances were forthcoming. God was silent.

Third, the record of Elijah's prophetic ministry thus far is filled with direct, clear communications from God, *none of which* are characterized as a still small voice. God spoke to Elijah numerous times before he heard the sound of the still small voice. These are introduced with the phrases, "The word of the Lord came to him

---

[26] For these first two observations I am indebted to Dan Phillips (https://bibchr.blogspot.com/) for a paper entitled "Thoughts on 1 Kings 19" provided upon request to a mutual friend, Justin Peters (https://justinpeters.org/).

saying,..." and, "For thus says the Lord God of Israel,..."[27] Twice, an angel spoke to Elijah (19:5, 7). If God's communication with Elijah is the pattern for us, why is the still small voice the model and not the clear, direct, and unmistakable communication that characterized the rest of his ministry? Clearly, it was not the norm in the life of Elijah.

NOW, THE STILL SMALL VOICE

Now we can examine the encounter with the Lord at Horeb accompanied by the sound of the still small voice.

> Then he came there to a cave and lodged there; and behold, the word of the Lord came to him, and He said to him, "What are you doing here, Elijah?" He said, "I have been very zealous for the Lord, the God of hosts; for the sons of Israel have forsaken Your covenant, torn down Your altars and killed Your prophets with the sword. And I alone am left; and they seek my life, to take it away. (1 Kings 19:9-10)

First, notice how God's communication to Elijah is characterized: "*And behold, the word of the LORD came to him, and He said to him...*" (v. 9). The question the Lord asked did not come in a still small voice. He spoke directly to him and he had no problem hearing. God's Word to him was clear and unmistakable. The text doesn't say Elijah had to draw near in a special way to hear an "inaudible whisper." This clear voice of God is not characterized as an "impression," "thought," or a "nudge." Elijah did not check the voice against the written Word, consult with godly counsel, or confirm it with providential signs. In other words, none of the nonsense commonly attached to the still small voice by modern HVG advocates is present in the text.

Second, notice that Elijah felt alone and threatened. For at least 40 days Elijah had been a wanted and hunted man. Yet, in spite of the threats against him, the Lord had done *nothing supernatural* to remove the threat of Jezebel's evil plans.

> So He said, "Go forth and stand on the mountain before the Lord." And behold, the Lord was passing by! And a great and strong wind was rending the mountains and breaking in pieces the rocks before the Lord; but the Lord was not in the wind. And after the wind an earthquake, but

---

[27] 1 Kings 17:2-4, 8-9, 14; 18:1; 19:9, 11.

the Lord was not in the earthquake. After the earthquake a fire, but the Lord was not in the fire; and after the fire a sound of a gentle blowing. (1 Kings 19:11-12)

A clear word from God instructed Elijah to stand on the mountain before the Lord. As with previous communications, Elijah had no difficulty hearing. This was not a whisper. Elijah did not tune into God's frequency. There isn't a hint that God had to "bombard" his thoughts and heart with His message until Elijah was "convinced of its authenticity."[28]

Third, notice that this supernatural display used natural elements to wreak havoc. A mighty wind broke apart the rocks. An earthquake shook the ground in the cave where Elijah stood. In some way, a fire burned outside. Two of these three supernatural displays were marks of previous "deliverances" wrought by the hand of God. The fire had consumed the altar on Mount Carmel (18:38) and wind had accompanied the subsequent rainstorm (18:45). Yet we are told "the Lord was not in" them. This is a significant detail given that "wind, earthquake, and fire are all natural phenomena that often heralded God's presence or appearance."[29]

Though the Lord sent the wind, earthquake, and fire on this occasion, they weren't the means of the Lord's revelation to Elijah, as on previous occasions. The Lord didn't reveal Himself through these dramatic displays. Instead, the Lord's revelation was accompanied by the "sound of a gentle blowing" (v. 12, NASB).

The Hebrew phrase translated "a sound of a gentle blowing" in the NASB is translated "a still small voice" in the KJV, NKJV, RSV, and ASV. It is a fairly odd phrase without biblical precedent. That fact alone should discourage those who wish to turn this into a model for us. This event was so unique that the language used to describe it is used *nowhere else* in Scripture. It is dangerous to build doctrine from an unclear phrase used only once in Scripture. How can this possibly serve as a model for hearing God's voice?

There is a wide variety of possible translations for this phrase, as the following list indicates:

---

[28] Shirer, *Discerning the Voice of God,* 80–81.

[29] See Exodus 19:16–18; Deuteronomy 5:23–26; Judges 5:4–5; 2 Samuel 22:8–16; Psalms 18:7–15; 68:8; Hebrews 12:18. Richard D. Patterson and Hermann J. Austel, "1, 2 Kings," in *The Expositor's Bible Commentary: 1 Samuel–2 Kings (Revised Edition)*, ed. Tremper Longman III and David E. Garland, vol. 3 (Grand Rapids, MI: Zondervan, 2009), 783.

KJV, NKJV, RSV, ASV: a still small voice
ESV: the sound of a low whisper[30]
CSB: a voice, a soft whisper
NASB: a sound of a gentle blowing
NIV: a gentle whisper
LEB, NLT: the sound of a gentle whisper
ROT: the voice of a gentle whisper
NET: a soft whisper
NRS: a sound of sheer silence
NJB: a light murmuring sound
NAB: a light silent sound
DBY: a soft gentle voice
GWN: a quiet, whispering voice
LXX: φωνὴ αὔρας λεπτῆς, κἀκεῖ κύριος [sound of a light breeze - and there was the Lord!][31]

This is obviously a challenging phrase to translate! The phenomenon being described is anything but clear. However, we can be certain of this: it wasn't a "persistent internal inkling," an "inner voice," or an "internal stirring." It was external to Elijah, which the next verses make abundantly clear! Interestingly, the next verses are seldom mentioned in connection with HVG teaching on the still small voice.

> When Elijah heard it, he wrapped his face in his mantle and went out and stood in the entrance of the cave. And behold, a voice came to him and said, "What are you doing here, Elijah?" Then he said, "I have been very zealous for the Lord, the God of hosts; for the sons of Israel have forsaken Your covenant, torn down Your altars and killed Your prophets with the sword. And I alone am left; and they seek my life, to take it away." (1 Kings 19:13-14)

He went out and stood at the entrance of the cave to hear a voice coming from *outside* the cave. If the still small voice were an

---

[30] The ESV provides a note offering an alternate translation: "a sound, a thin silence." *The Holy Bible: English Standard Version.* (2016). (1 Ki 19:11–13). Wheaton, IL: Crossway Bibles.

[31] A treatment of this phrase in the journal *Vetus Testamentum* from 1975 by J. Lust offers an entirely different understanding of the phrase. He writes, "The philological analysis of 1 Kings xix 12 [19:12] as well as the study of the context and the traditions involved suggest a translation of $qôl\ d^e m\ \cdot m\ \ d\ q$ [קוֹל דְּמָמָה דַקָּה] differing from the commonly accepted one. We propose to read: 'a roaring and thunderous voice.'" See Lust, J. "A Gentle Breeze or a Roaring Thunderous Sound? Elijah at Horeb: 1 Kings XIX 12." *Vetus Testamentum* 25, no. 1 (1975): 110-15. doi:10.2307/1517376. Obviously, this is quite different than how the phrase is typically understood, especially by HVG advocates.

internal nudging, impression, or thought, he wouldn't have needed to go to the mouth of the cave to hear it. He could have stayed inside the cave and listened to his own thoughts. Elijah heard a voice outside the cave, not inside his head. It is obvious from even a casual reading that what Elijah heard ("still small voice" or "a sound of a gentle blowing"), wasn't an internal prompting whispered in the synapses of His brain.

Once Elijah made his way to the mouth of the cave, "a voice came to him and said . . . " The language of Scripture is clear. Elijah heard the voice of God in an audible, clear, and unmistakable way. It was not an impression or thought. God spoke audibly and clearly.

LESSONS FROM ELIJAH

The "sound of a gentle blowing" was not God's attempt to whisper impressions into Elijah's consciousness. There is no indication the still small voice was intended as a pattern for God's communication with us. What then is the lesson of this unique and mysterious incident? I would suggest at least two.

First, even a prophet like Elijah was not to expect miraculous and supernatural deliverance from his problems. He was discouraged by Jezebel's threat which seemed an insurmountable burden. His repeated lament (19:10, 14) indicates that he sought, and maybe even expected, a supernatural deliverance. When miraculous deliverance wasn't forthcoming, Elijah despaired of life (19:4). The Lord's encouragement to Elijah wasn't in dramatic manifestations of power (wind, earthquake, and fire), but in the reminder that there still remained 7,000 in Israel who hadn't bowed the knee to Baal (19:18). In other words, Elijah didn't need miraculous deliverance by flashy displays of power, but to hear of God's faithful believing remnant.

Second, this reminded Elijah that the work of God's faithful people is seldom accomplished by big and flashy displays of power. God was not in the loud and explosive displays. God works in silence, behind the scenes, in the unnoticed corners of the world. There, God's work is done as His remnant labors faithfully. The "gentle blowing" or "still silence" is an apt description of most of God's work in this world. It passes virtually unnoticed. The flashy and miraculous displays like earthquakes, fires, and cataclysmic winds, aren't necessary for God's continuous preservation of His faithful remnant.

IT DOESN'T FIT THE TEXT

Would you say the use of this passage by HVG advocates is faithful to the teaching of the text? It is true that the words "still small voice" describe an indistinct and uncertain sound that preceded God's clear communication with *one* of His prophets on *one* occasion. Even at that, the words are a questionable translation at best. This passage is misused as proof God speaks to us in inaudible voices perceptible only in our thoughts.

Dallas Willard says:

> In the still, small voice of God we are given a message that bears the stamp of his [sic] personality quite clearly and in a way we will learn to recognize. But, in contrast with other cases, the *medium* through which the message comes is diminished almost to the vanishing point, taking the form of thoughts that are our thoughts, though these thoughts are not *from* us.[32]

That is quite a rhetorical sleight of hand! He took a passage that mentions an external, audible sound and turned it into a description of your thoughts, which he then claims come from God. There is quite literally *nothing* in the description of the "sound of a gentle blowing" that would justify that teaching. There is no indication it was a thought in Elijah's mind. If the Holy Spirit had wanted us to understand this as a "thought," He could have inspired the biblical author to describe it that way.

Though Willard claims "we will learn to recognize it," he can point to no place in the narrative of Elijah that even remotely suggests this. Elijah didn't need to "learn to recognize it." In fact, we don't ever read of any one person "learning to recognize God's voice." Scripture doesn't teach this. The biblical record is clear: everyone to whom God spoke heard and understood Him – Elijah included.

Willard says, "The still, small voice - or the interior or inner voice, as it is also called - is the preferred and most valuable form of individual communication for God's purposes."[33] Actually, it is *not* also called "the interior or inner voice." Not ever. Scripture doesn't call it that. Scripture never refers to our thoughts as God's "still small voice." Scripture never describes the voice of God as "an inner voice" or the "interior voice." This is false teaching invented by Dallas Willard and baptized in biblical-sounding verbiage.

---

[32] Willard, *Hearing God*, 115.

[33] Ibid., 118.

Further, if this is "the preferred and most valuable form" of communication, why do we find it in *one* place describing *one* unique encounter with *one* prophet? Why don't we read of God using this method with Noah, Moses, or Paul? If this were God's preferred means of communication, we should expect to see it everywhere we look in Scripture. Are we to believe this method is so "valuable" and "preferred" that it is only mentioned once, and even there, the translation of its description is uncertain at best?

Willard claims, "It is important to bear in mind that you may not be very aware of hearing the voice; it need not force itself to the front of your thoughts. . . . So when you hear God's voice, you do not automatically know it is God's voice."[34] Does that sound like 1 Kings 17-19? Was Elijah unaware he was hearing the voice? The text says Elijah was able to discern God was not in the wind, earthquake, and fire. The sound of the breeze was quite different. It wasn't *through* the gentle blowing but *after* the gentle blowing that Elijah stepped out and heard God speak.

I am not trying to pick on Dallas Willard, but he makes more out of the still small voice than almost any other author. As you can see, what he teaches is completely unbiblical and dangerous.

MAKING MODELS OUT OF MOLEHILLS

Are we justified in taking Elijah's experience as a model for our own?

HVG teachers are selective in their choice of "models" for hearing God's voice. Why is the still small voice of Chapter 19 considered normative and not the numerous clear revelations in Chapters 17 and 18? Previous to the incident at the mouth of the cave, "the Word of the Lord" came to Elijah in a clear, unmistakable way many times, yet those references are ignored in favor of an obscure reference to "gently blowing wind" or "thin silence". Why? Because HVG teachers can make this "light silent sound" into whatever fits their fancy. They invent a method of hearing God and project it onto the still small voice. This creates a veneer of biblical precedent for their teaching.

Elijah twice had an encounter with an angel shortly before he heard the "sound of gentle blowing," and only heard the "gentle blowing" *once.* Why is the gentle blowing considered normative while angelic visitations are not? Angelic visits were twice as common for Elijah as the still small voice.

---

[34] Ibid.

ELIJAH WAS UNIQUE

Why isn't Elijah a model for producing food during a drought? Why isn't he a model for demonstrating the falsehood of Jehovah's Witnesses when they come to your door? HVG teachers don't suggest you build an altar and rain down fire from Heaven to prove their god is false. They don't promote Elijah as a model for handling false prophets, namely, killing 450 at a time. Why don't they teach that *those* events from the life of Elijah are a pattern for today?

They probably regard Elijah as a man uniquely gifted and used by God. "Those supernatural events are unique to Elijah's special role as God's prophet," they might say. "We can't expect those things to be normative for everyone." Yes, exactly. And so it is with the revelation he received. He was a *prophet* who heard God speak. It is special pleading to say that the revelations he received by "the Word of the Lord" were not unique but rather normative. There is no justification for saying Elijah is a model for us. Scripture doesn't promise us similar experiences. In fact, we find just the opposite. Elijah was a unique man, with a unique place in the plan and purposes of God.

Is God telling Charles Stanley to buy a turkey, Mark Batterson to start a coffee shop, and Priscilla Shirer to call a friend, the *exact same kind* of communication God gave to His prophets? Is it really identical in both kind and quality? If not, then they can't claim that modern "whispers from Heaven" are the *same thing* God did in the Bible. The jig is up! HVG teachers need to admit that what they are promoting is nothing like the revelation we find in Scripture.

SUMMARY

HVG teachers claim the still small voice is the way God speaks to His people today. Allegedly, Elijah is the prime example of this "preferred and most valuable" means of hearing God. Yet, nothing of what they teach is found in 1 Kings 19. Elijah didn't have trouble hearing God. He wasn't uncertain Who spoke. He didn't tune in to God's frequency. He didn't struggle to receive a whisper amid the cacophony of distractions. He didn't learn how to hear God's voice.

Everything HVG teachers claim to be part of hearing the still small voice is not mentioned in the passage. All the details mentioned in the text, are the opposite of what HVG teachers say we should expect when we hear the still small voice for ourselves.

Chapter 8

The Verse Jumped off the Page

8

"The Lord gave me the name for our baby," he said with a smile.[1]

"Come again?" I replied with obvious skepticism.

"The Lord told me this morning what we should name the new baby."

I continued to eat my lunch, waiting for an explanation from across the table. Though good friends, we had many discussions like this. He would claim to receive divine guidance, I would challenge him, and we would have a vigorous discussion about extra-biblical revelations.

It was not uncommon to hear him claim, "The Holy Spirit told me. . .," or, "The Lord led me. . . ." On this occasion: "The Lord gave me the name for our baby."

"What is the name and how did the Lord tell you?" I asked without hiding my skepticism. He was accustomed to my less than enthusiastic responses.

"I was reading Joshua 18 this morning and the name 'Benjamin' jumped off the page. I felt the Holy Spirit speak to my heart and tell me that we should name our baby Benjamin. As I kept reading, the name kept coming up. The Lord was confirming it to me."

"That's interesting." I said.

"You don't believe the Lord spoke to me like that, do you?" he challenged.

"No."

"Don't you believe the Lord still speaks to His people?"

---

[1] Though this conversation really did take place, I have changed some of the names and details to protect the innocent.

"Oh, I believe the Lord speaks to His people. He does so in and through His written Word," I said trying to clarify a common misunderstanding of my position.

"Oh!" he said, apparently thinking I had just conceded his point. "This *was* in Scripture. I was reading the Bible when the Spirit used His Word to give me a personal word from the text. So you *do* believe God told me what to name my son?"

"No, because I don't believe the meaning of that passage is 'You should name your son Benjamin.' That is not why the passage was written or what the Holy Spirit had in mind when He inspired it." I responded.

"So, you don't believe the Holy Spirit can give me a personal word for my situation out of the passage I am reading?" he asked.

"I don't believe the Holy Spirit will reveal meanings in the passage that it never had. I don't believe He intends for us to find personal messages unrelated to the author's intended meaning."

He was not convinced. "How would you explain what happened then? Why did the name 'Benjamin' jump off the page? Why did I feel it impressed upon my heart?"

"Well," I explained, "I know you and your wife are thinking and praying about what to name your son. Today you were reading through your Bible and you ran across a very appropriate name: Benjamin. It is a nice name. You had not considered it until this morning, but when you read it, the name had a nice ring to it. The same thing could have happened reading a newspaper, phone book, or book of baby names. You feel drawn to the name 'Benjamin.' That's great. I just don't think you can claim it is the voice of God."

****

John was interested in Becky, a young lady attending the church singles' group. They talked a couple of times and she seemed open to a friendship. Last Sunday they chatted at the water fountain in the foyer before the service. John was thinking of asking her out. That evening while reading through Genesis, John came across Genesis 24:16: "The girl was very beautiful, a virgin, and no man had had relations with her; and she went down to the spring and filled her jar and came up."

There it was - right before him! A beautiful girl who came to get a drink. This was just like what he experienced earlier that day at church. John wondered if this was the Lord's way of revealing that Becky was "the one."

Excitedly, he read further and found these words: "Bowed low and worshiped," and, "The Lord has guided me in the way" (vv. 26-27). Just like the man in the story, John had worshiped the Lord after meeting Becky at the water fountain. The girl mentioned in Genesis was named Rebekah. The girl of John's interest was named Becky. "This can't be a coincidence!" John thought. "Certainly, the Lord is in this!" Then he saw those words again, "*The Lord has guided me in the way*." They jumped off the page at John, coming alive like never before. He sensed the Lord was speaking a fresh word from Scripture.

****

Has this happened to you? Have you felt like a word, phrase, or verse jumped off the page of your Bible while reading over your morning coffee? I have. Are these examples of "hearing the voice of God"? HVG teachers would say that these two scenarios are examples of the voice of God. While I believe God speaks in Scripture, the issue here is: *How* does God speak to us in Scripture?

THE HVG VIEW OF THE BIBLE

HVG teachers believe the Bible is the Word of God and should be included in any list of ways in which God speaks to us. They encourage believers to read Scripture regularly because, in the HVG paradigm, Scripture has two functions. First, God may speak when a verse of Scripture comes alive and jumps off the page at us. Second, Scripture helps us recognize when God speaks to us through other means.

According to Priscilla Shirer, "Very often His authoritative voice arrives in conjunction with or wrapped in the context of Scripture."[2] Scripture is a "context" for God's Word, the wrapping for His authoritative voice. What does this "context of Scripture" look like? In the very next paragraph Shirer writes:

This, again, is another reason why staying deeply in God's Word is so vital to discerning His voice. The more Scripture you hide in your heart, . . . the more opportunity you give the Holy Spirit to bring it quickly to mind, punctuated at a specific moment with a personalized message for you. You see, the Bible not only provides the boundaries within

---

[2] Shirer, *Discerning the Voice of God*, 146-147.

which everything He says will fall, it is the chief mechanism through which God will speak.[3]

For Shirer, Scripture isn't by itself God's message to you. It's the context - the wrapping - in which God's "personalized message for you" comes. It's a mechanism *through which* God may speak. Just as the Postal Service is the mechanism through which a personal letter comes, so Scripture is a way God can deliver a message to you. For HVG teachers, Scripture isn't the message, it's the delivery mechanism for a message. The personal message is whatever "comes alive to you." To quote Shirer:

> When God's Word leaps off the page and *grips* you - I mean *stuns* you as though you were awakened from sleep by a thunderclap - don't rush ahead with your Bible reading. Stop right there. Lock on to those words that have already locked eyes with your soul. This isn't some random occurrence or coincidence. It is God Himself speaking through His Word. It is the living Word of God at work.[4]

Shirer quotes Ann Graham Lotz: "When He speaks, it's in a language of our personal lives, through a verse or passage of Scripture that just seems to leap up off the page with our name on it."[5]

HVG teachers value Scripture, not because it is God's Word, but because we *might* hear God speak if something "leaps off the page and grips" us.

Shirer writes:

> Therefore, the more acquainted you become with the Word, the more accurately you'll be able to hear from Him. The Bible provides the framework into which His messages to you will come. Anything the Spirit says will fall within the boundaries of what has already been written."[6]

---

[3] Ibid., 147.

[4] Ibid., 149.

[5] Ibid., 93.

[6] Ibid., 128. By "fall within the boundaries," she means that your personal revelation will never contradict Scripture or direct you to disobey Scripture. Most HVG teachers are quick to offer this caveat. This serves as the "check" against fanciful revelations. She calls Scripture God's "general revelation" and contrasts that with a "specific message clearly tied to the circumstances you're currently facing" (Ibid., 149). She provides an example of a time when God spoke to her "in such a way that [she] could hardly help but hear Him, by bringing a short verse of Scripture to life" (Ibid., 145). It is not until the verse comes to life that she regards Scripture as the voice of God.

The language she uses is intentional and represents well the view of HVG teachers: "The Bible provides the *framework* into which *His messages* to you will come." Scripture is not the voice of God, but it can potentially *convey* the voice of God when it comes alive, jumps off the page, or grips you personally. In HVG theology, one could read Scripture and not hear the voice of God. You would hear the framework, mechanism, and context in which the voice of God *might* come, but not actually hear the voice of God. The message you receive when something grips you is God's voice, not the text itself. This is a very subtle distinction and though difficult to see at first, it is significant.

Mark Batterson speaks highly of Scripture when he describes it as "the final authority," "inspired,"[7] and "God-breathed,"[8] but then undermines Scripture when he teaches us to read the Bible so we can "learn to discern God's voice."[9] Batterson writes:

> There is a very subtle form of idolatry called bibliolatry. It involves treating the Bible as an end in itself instead of a means to an end. The goal of Bible knowledge isn't just Bible knowledge. . . . The goal is learning to recognize and respond to your heavenly Father's voice so you can grow in intimacy with Him.[10]

"The end" of Bible reading is being able to hear the voice of God through the various means Batterson promotes in his book. The Bible helps us discern the voice when (or if) it comes. For HVG teachers, the Bible is not the voice of God but an inspired book that teaches you how to hear the voice of God. The Bible is not the message, but it helps us discern the message when God sends it. *That* is how HVG teachers view Scripture.

BLACKABY AND THE BIBLE

In a chapter titled "God Speaks Through the Bible," Blackaby affirms that Scripture is God's Word. However, like other HVG teachers who offer this nod to orthodoxy, Blackaby immediately undermines it with this description of Scripture:

> The Bible describes God's complete revelation of Himself to humanity. It is a record of God's dealings with humanity

---

[7] Batterson, *Whisper*, 64.

[8] Ibid., 65.

[9] Ibid., 66.

[10] Ibid., 67.

and His words to them. God speaks to you through the Bible. Have you ever been reading the Bible when suddenly you are gripped by a fresh new understanding of the passage? That was God speaking![11]

Blackaby makes a subtle distinction unnoticed by most readers. It is incorrect and demeaning to Scripture to say "the Bible describes God's complete revelation of Himself to humanity." Scripture *is* God's complete revelation of Himself to humanity. This is not picking nits! "My wife" and a "description of my wife" are *not the same thing,* just as "God's revelation" and a "description of God's revelation" are not the same thing.

Notice his second statement: "It is a record of God's dealing with humanity and His words to them." A *record* of God's dealings? A *record* of His words? Scripture is not a "record" of things God has said. It *is* what God has said. For Blackaby, the value of Scripture is not that it is the very Word of God, but that it *models* for us what the Word of God will sound like when we hear it outside Scripture.

According to Blackaby, "When suddenly you are gripped by a *fresh new understanding* of the passage . . . . That was God speaking! . . . When you come to understand the *spiritual meaning* and application of a Scripture passage, God's Spirit has been at work."[12] This language is similar to Shirer when she describes a passage "jumping off the page."

Blackaby's reference to "spiritual truth" and "spiritual meaning" is significant. Only when the text leaps off the page with a "fresh new understanding" or new "spiritual meaning and application" has the Spirit of God spoken. Apparently reading through the book of Leviticus and understanding the passage in the way intended by the author does not constitute an "encounter with God."

In another chapter, "God Speaks Through Circumstances," Blackaby provides a telling example of his approach to Scripture.

> Earlier I told you about our daughter Carrie's bout with cancer. That was a difficult circumstance for our whole family. The doctors prepared us for six or eight months of chemotherapy plus radiation. We knew God loved us. We prayed, "What are you proposing to do in this experience that we need to adjust ourselves to?"

---

[11] Blackaby and King, *Experiencing God,* 103.

[12] Ibid. Emphasis mine.

As we prayed, a Scripture promise came that we believed was from God. Not only did we receive the promise, but we received letters and calls from many people who quoted the same Scripture. The verse reads, "This sickness is not unto death, but for the glory of God, that the Son of God may be glorified through it" (John 11:4).

Our sense that God was speaking to us grew stronger as the Bible, prayer, and the testimony of other believers began to line up and say the same thing.[13]

The passage Blackaby cited has nothing to do with the sickness of his daughter. It is not a promise, but a description of one particular sickness of one particular man, Lazarus. Jesus didn't provide a "promise" anyone may claim. He was describing the sickness of Lazarus which resulted in death for the explicit purpose of demonstrating His resurrection power (John 11:25-26). After Lazarus died from the sickness described in 11:4, Jesus raised him from the dead.

The meaning of John 11:4 is this: the sickness of Lazarus would glorify God when Jesus raised him from the dead. According to Blackaby, the meaning of John 11:4 is this: God promised that his daughter Carrie wouldn't die from her cancer. Blackaby turned a *description* of one man's sickness into a *promise of* his daughter's healing. He took words from the pages of Scripture, divorced them from their original context, and gave them a meaning completely unrelated to the intent of the author. He claimed them as a promise for himself. Worse yet, he took solace in the same abuse of that passage by others. Then he laid the blame for this abuse of Scripture at the feet of the Holy Spirit saying, "The Holy Spirit took the Word of God and revealed to us God's perspective on the end result of that circumstance."[14]

This is what he means by "spiritual meaning." Blackaby saw a "spiritual meaning" ("spiritual application") in the passage - a "fresh new understanding" unrelated to the text itself. This fresh insight constitutes "an encounter with God." The Holy Spirit's alleged promise came wrapped in words found in John 11 but it had nothing to do with the meaning of John 11.

Without any sense of self awareness, Blackaby writes, "Don't just look for a Scripture that seems to say what you selfishly want

---

[13] Ibid., 119–20.

[14] Ibid., 120.

to do, and then claim it is God's will. That is very dangerous. Don't do it."[15] This is precisely what Blackaby did with John 11:4. He imported a meaning foreign to the text and claimed it as the Holy Spirit's promise.

What about people whose loved ones died of their sickness after they claimed that same promise? They may genuinely feel they heard God speak in the same way. When their circumstances end in tragedy rather than triumph, they can only conclude that God didn't keep His Word to them. That it worked out fine in the case of his daughter doesn't in any way validate Blackaby's misuse of Scripture.

WILLARD ON THE WORD

Dallas Willard is far more mystical and borderline pagan in his approach to the voice of God. Willard expands the definition of "word of God" to something so broad and indiscriminate, that it includes nearly everything. He claims: "God *created*, God *rules* and God *redeems* through his [sic] word. God's creating, God's ruling and God's redeeming *is* his [sic] word."[16] That is a clever rhetorical trick that turns all of God's activities into "his Word." In another place, Willard claims that God's speaking is "spiritual power." "The word as *a person's speaking* is therefore to be understood as a spiritual power - whether of ourselves, of God or of some other personal agency and whether for evil or for good."[17]

If God's speaking is a spiritual power, then any expression of "spiritual power" can be understood as "the word of God." Willard claims:

> The *word of God,* when no further qualification is added, is his [sic] speaking, his [sic] communicating. . . .
>
> All expressions of God's mind are "words" of God. This is true whether the specific means are *external* to the human mind (as in natural phenomenon [Ps 19:1-4], other human beings, the incarnate Christ [the Logos] or the Bible) or *internal* to the human mind (in our own thoughts, intentions and feelings).[18]

---

[15] Ibid., 112. Blackaby warns against claiming warrant for blatant violation of Scripture's moral commands, but his abuse of Scripture in this way is no less egregious as it entails claiming God has said something He never said.

[16] Willard, *Hearing God,* 156.

[17] Ibid., 159.

[18] Ibid.

Willard defines "God's Word" so broadly that it includes nearly everything that has existed or happened! He includes Christ, natural phenomena, other people, the Bible, human thoughts, intentions, feelings, God's creative work, ruling providence, and redemption. Since he equates all the works of God with the Word of God, Willard claims God is always speaking, using words, and exuding that "word force" of His activity. God's Word, as he understands it, is like an energy force that vibrates through all of reality, manifesting itself in an almost infinite number of ways.

Consequently, Willard doesn't equate Scripture with the Word of God. After teaching that the "word of God" isn't the same thing as Scripture, he asks, "Finally, how are we to understand the relationship of the Bible to this word of God?"[19]

He answers:

> The Bible is *one* of the results of God's speaking. It is the *unique* written Word of God. It is inerrant in its original form and infallible in all of its forms for the purpose of guiding us into a life-saving relationship with God in his [sic] kingdom . . . . So far it is clear that, *while the Bible is the written Word of God, the word of God is not simply the Bible.*[20]

While he affirms the Bible is the *written* Word of God, he can't say the Bible contains *all* of the Word of God. It's only one form of God's Word – albeit a written one. Willard claims the Bible is "one of the results of God speaking." Given his definition of "God speaking," nearly anything could be described as "one of the results" of God speaking: my angina, my neighbor's barking dog, or inclement weather.

Willard wants to plant his flag in orthodoxy by using "inerrant" and "infallible" in his description of Scripture, but that description is without meaning in his theology. These words are a dog whistle to Bible-believing Christians intended to hide the heterodox theology of HVG teachers behind the language of orthodoxy. Why should we regard Scripture as "unique" if it is "just one of the results of God's speaking"? What makes it unique? What makes Scripture inerrant and my thoughts not inerrant if they are both God speaking? How can Scripture be infallible and my dreams fallible if both are *equally* examples of God speaking? You can't claim inspiration for one of

---

[19] Ibid., 184.

[20] Ibid., 185.

God's Words (Scripture), but not another (impressions). HVG advocates can't answer this!

The only way the doctrines of inspiration, inerrancy, and infallibility can mean anything is if Scripture *alone* is the Word of God. In a theology where God speaks outside Scripture, the ground beneath these doctrines erodes away to nothing. Scripture is unique because it *alone* is the Word of God. HVG teachers claim that their impressions, nudgings, voices, circumstances, signs, fleeces, visions, dreams, and whispers are *also* God's Word, but not infallible, inerrant, or inspired. This distinction is meaningless and biblically untenable.

When God speaks, He speaks inerrantly. It cannot be otherwise. Everything God says is without error because God cannot lie (Titus 1:2). God cannot speak an "uninspired" word.[21] He cannot speak a fallible or errant word because He is an infallible God who cannot and does not err.[22] These are true of Scripture not because it is in written form, or because it is old, or because it was written by apostles. These are qualities possessed by Scripture by virtue of its Source. If Scripture comes from God, it *must,* by necessity, possess these qualities. Any revelation, voice of God, or word from God must also possess these qualities. If Scripture is just one of many ways the voice of God is heard, then there is no rational or biblical basis for believing it is "unique" or "special."

THE FORTUNE COOKIE BIBLE

The HVG approach to hearing the voice of God results in horrible abuses of the biblical text as the example of Blackaby's use of John 11:4 demonstrates. This is unavoidable since it encourages people to find their own "personal message" or "spiritual meaning" in a passage without regard to the actual meaning of the text. Instead of trying to understand the author's intended meaning from the context of a verse, the Christian, hungry for a "personal word from God," will seek from the text a "fresh understanding." Individual

---

[21] The word translated "inspired" in most English translations (2 Timothy 3:16) comes from the Greek word θεόπνευστος - *theopneustos* (God-breathed) and describes the writings of Scripture. Inspired writings are the product of "men moved by the Holy Spirit" who spoke for God (2 Peter 1:21).

[22] According to MacArthur and Mayhue, "Historically, inerrancy and infallibility have been inseparably linked" (MacArthur and Mayhue, *Biblical Doctrine*, 109). Inerrancy means "without error" and is used of the original autographs of Scripture. Infallibility describes Scripture's inability to mislead or affirm falsehood. Because Scripture is infallible, it *cannot* fail to accomplish its divinely intended purpose.

words, phrases, and even numbers get twisted into a pretzel of personal revelation.

This view of Scripture doesn't encourage an exegetical approach to Bible study and application. It fosters a gnostic, mystical approach of pursing personalized messages not found in the text. It turns the Bible into a collection of "fortune cookie" maxims interpreted according to the whims of prevailing circumstances.

I could provide examples of this from all the authors I have critiqued to this point,[23] but none have mastered the art of Scripture manipulation quite like Robert Morris. He provides numerous examples of this Scripture-twisting approach.

Morris claims God told him to pastor a church when he was 30 years old. When offered the opportunity to become a senior pastor, he devoted himself to "seeking the Lord's face and hearing His voice" on the matter. While worshiping and praying, Morris claims, "I distinctly felt the Holy Spirit impressing me to read Luke 3. That passage kept coming back to mind, Luke 3, Luke 3, Luke 3."[24] Morris read Luke 3 and came to verse 23: "Now Jesus Himself began His ministry at about 30 years of age." Morris then says, "This was the confirmation I was looking for. A peace that passes understanding came over me. The confirmation was felt deep in my heart."[25]

The number "30" jumped off the page at Morris. He took this as God's voice confirming he should go into ministry at the age of 30. If Morris had seen the number "30" on paper from inside a fortune cookie, he could have divined the same message. I would suggest that if you are as likely to hear God's voice in a fortune cookie as in Scripture, you have a low view of Scripture.

On another occasion, Morris was considering moving closer to a recent church plant. Allegedly, God gave him direction in the following bizarre way:

> We were sitting in church one Sunday right about that time and worshiping the Lord, and I felt a distinct impression to read Genesis 35:1 - but to read it out of Debbie's Bible. That was strange. I knew what Genesis 35:1 said in my

---

[23] The abuse of Scripture in this manner by those in the HVG movement is pandemic. Personal messages divined from words and phrases isolated from their context is the stock in trade of the HVG movement.

[24] Morris, *Frequency*, 43.

[25] Ibid.

Bible. I opened it again and read the verse out of my New King James Version: "Then God said to Jacob, 'Arise, go up to Bethel and dwell there; and make an altar there to God.'"

God had impressed the verse on my heart earlier as a word about starting a church. He wanted me to go somewhere, dwell somewhere, and make an altar to the Lord there. Fine. I was doing that. But why did I feel this distinct nudge to read this verse out of Debbie's Bible? She was using the New Living Translation. I set down my Bible, opened hers, and read the verse again: "Then God said to Jacob, 'Get ready and move to Bethel and settle there. Build an altar there to . . . God.'"

Move to Bethel.

That was the changed word God wanted me to see. Not simply *dwell* there, but *move* there.[26]

Morris lifted one particular word from one particular translation from its context and took it as a "word from God" for his situation. The meaning of that command from God to Jacob is *irrelevant* to the message Morris received. He saw the word "move" and took it as the voice of God to him. With this manner of conjuring the voice of God from words in the Bible, the actual meaning of any given passage may have *nothing at all* to do with whatever personal "message" is gleaned from it.[27]

The Bible is *unnecessary* to this method of hearing from God. He might come across the word "move" in any number of places (a newspaper, comic book, or fortune cookie) and claim a personal message from God. A message received in this way has as much connection to the context in a newspaper as it does in the Bible. So, why do HVG teachers encourage looking for such messages in the Bible? Because Scripture provides a rich source of fodder for such abuses. Further, they can claim divine authority for their message if it is pulled out of the Word of God.

This is a superstitious view of Scripture, not an orthodox one. With no concern for the author's intended meaning in a text, they have adopted a post-modern "reader-response" approach to the

---

[26] Ibid., 77.

[27] The goal of reading and studying Scripture is to discern the original authors' intended meaning. An examination of context, genre, culture, history, and language are essential in determining that meaning. Scripture cannot have a "meaning" to us that it never had to its original audience.

Scriptures. Essentially, they ask, "What does this text mean *to me*?" and, "How does this passage speak *to my heart*?" This method doesn't seek to apply the meaning of the biblical text to the reader's circumstances. The meaning is irrelevant. He reads the Bible through the grid of personal circumstances to find some point of contact between the two, no matter how far-fetched. The Bible is the Magic 8-Ball of the HVG evangelical realm! Morris provides enough examples to tax even the most patient among us.

Morris claims that through a weird confluence of personal promptings, his daughter Elaine received direction from Revelation 4:1 to go to college in Tulsa, Oklahoma: "After these things I looked, and behold, a *door standing open* in heaven, and the first voice which I had heard, like the sound of a *trumpet* speaking with me, said, '*Come up* here, and I will show you what must take place after these things'" (Revelation 4:1).

She interpreted the words "open door" to refer to the "open door" to go to college, the "trumpet" was a reference to someone's challenge that struck her like a "trumpet call," and "come up" clearly pointed her to Tulsa since it was "due north" of their home. [28]

Morris claims he had a dream wherein God revealed he would build a church of 30,000 people that would reach 300,000 people in the Dallas-Fort Worth Metroplex.[29] The next day, Morris read 1 Samuel 11:8: "He numbered them in Bezek; and the sons of Israel were 300,000, and the men of Judah 30,000." He took this as "confirmation" of God's Word to him.

Morris claims God gave him the name "Gateway" for his church by an impression during a morning quiet time. A few days later, he saw the word "gateway" in the New Living Translation of Genesis 28:16-17. According to Morris, "That one phrase leapt out at me - *the very gateway to heaven*." Later, he felt this name confirmed to him while driving through an area of the potential church plant. There he saw a sign: "Coming soon! Gateway Shopping Plaza."[30]

This is a perfect example of how the words of Scripture are manipulated in the same fashion as the words on a sign announcing a shopping plaza. God spoke through both in the same way, with equal authority, and the same hermeneutic was applied to both. His claim that Scripture is unique rings hollow.

---

[28] Morris, *Frequency*, 57-58. Emphasis mine.

[29] Ibid., 81.

[30] Ibid., 84.

With a cognitive disconnect that staggers the mind, Morris offers his readers this warning: "Sometimes people open their Bibles at random, point to a verse, and claim it's from the Lord directly for their situation. And, yes, sometimes God may speak that way. . . . But more often than not, that's a method to take with a grain of salt."[31] In another place he warns, "I know people who use this method, and I never want to limit God from what He can do, but let me just say that this method has its risks."[32] Yet, this is primarily the method he employs for hearing God's voice.

I wish I could say this fortune cookie approach to Scripture is unique to Robert Morris. It isn't. Not even close. It is the stock in trade of HVG teachers. Scripture is treated as if it were a random collection of words which might "come alive" at any moment. If your personal message can't be found in one translation, look for it in another and just keep looking until you have your own personal word from God.

HOW TO GET YOUR OWN PERSONAL WORD

Morris offers a few suggestions on how we can receive God's specific Word tailor-made for us.[33] According to him, we need to develop the habit of hearing a "general word from God every day."[34] This is part of "the process of learning to value God's voice." It is only when the "general voice" comes alive that we are actually hearing God's "specific voice."

Morris offers four steps:
1. Set an appointment with God.
2. Be still and worship.
3. Pray and read.
4. Listen and write.[35]

"Listening" is essential to the HVG paradigm. Morris writes:

Listening to God is one of the hardest things for us to do. But if we learn to listen, then we will learn to hear God's

---

[31] Ibid., 16.

[32] Ibid., 48.

[33] Morris distinguishes between God's "general word" and "specific word." He refers to the Bible as God's "general voice" and the special impressions we receive when reading Scripture as God's "specific voice." He says, "Scripture is always the voice of God in the general sense that God inspired the words of Scripture (2 Timothy 3:16). God can also speak specifically to us through the Bible by drawing a particular passage to our attention, because the Word of God is living and active (Hebrews 4:12)." Morris, *Frequency*, 124. This distinction between "general" and "specific" is an artificial construct imposed on Scripture.

[34] Ibid., 88.

[35] Ibid., 88-95.

voice. I say listen and write because one of the best ways I've learned to hear the voice of God is to write down thoughts and prayers when I meet with Him.[36]

He then claims, "Listen and write. You will not be writing inspired words, as the writers of the Bible were doing, but you will be writing your personal application of inspired Scripture, following the pattern of action set by Bible writers."[37] That is complete nonsense. There is no biblical precedent for this. Nothing in Scripture instructs us to listen and write.

First, it is impossible for God's "specific word" to be less "inspired" than His "general word." This distinction in Morris's thinking is completely without biblical justification. He blurs the line by calling this "personal voice" of God "uninspired" and equating it with application. Meditating on God's Word and applying Scripture is not the same thing as receiving new revelation.

Second, the biblical writers did not set this "pattern of action." They were the instruments of divine revelation. The Holy Spirit superintended their writing to ensure that the result was the word of the human and divine authors. We have no examples of the biblical writers approaching Scripture in the way suggested by Morris. If this were their "pattern of action," we should expect to see it in Scripture. We don't. HVG teachers would have you believe that treating Scripture like a Magic 8-Ball is the apostolic pattern. It isn't.

SO, WHAT IS WRONG WITH THAT?!

Though this approach to Scripture is modeled in many pulpits and pursued by multitudes of Christians, it is fraught with problems.

First, the HVG approach demonstrates a low view of Scripture. HVG teachers don't believe the Bible is in itself the voice of God, but a vehicle or tool by which we might hear the voice of God. In practice, Scripture ends up being no more unique than a road sign, newspaper headline, or a fortune cookie. For them, the value of Scripture lies in its ability to help you recognize God's voice *outside* Scripture if it happens to come "wrapped" in Bible words.

Second, the HVG approach is not modeled in Scripture. There is *no record* of Paul, Daniel, Noah, Peter, or David handling Scripture this way. None of them ever conjured a personal message from Bible words in the manner taught in HVG circles.

---

[36] Ibid., 95.

[37] Ibid., 95.

The New Testament is full of quotations from the Old Testament, citing it nearly 350 times and alluding to it in hundreds of places. Yet in hundreds of allusions and quotations, you *will not find one example* of a New Testament author using Scripture in the way that HVG authors do. We never read of Paul "listening intently," waiting for a passage from the Psalms to jump off the page at him.

Third, the HVG approach is not taught in Scripture. Scripture does not distinguish between God's "general revelation" and His "special word" for our specific circumstance. HVG teachers claim that hearing personal messages is the heart and soul of Christian living and discipleship, but neither Jesus nor the apostles ever taught this.

Fourth, the HVG approach is a horrible abuse of the biblical text. In the quest to "hear God" the actual meaning of the biblical text is cast aside in favor of "personal words" and subjective impressions. No concern is paid to the intended meaning because no concern *needs* to be paid to the intended meaning. It is expected that a personal word is going to "come alive" *regardless* of the intended meaning. An ability to rightly handle the Word of Truth (2 Timothy 2:15) is unnecessary, and among HVG teachers, virtually nonexistent.

Fifth, this approach is inescapably subjective. Scripture is misused to confirm whatever message one might wish to see in any given text. Numbers, phrases, and individual words found in Scripture become nothing more than a Rorschach test for our own subjective and meandering thoughts. Rather than treating Scripture as the Word of God in an objective sense,[38] its value is determined by the ability of the reader to pick out their own "personal message." As evident from the examples given, there is no mishandling of Scripture that would be out of bounds in HVG theology. Though some more conservative HVG teachers might wince at these examples, their theology provides no limitations by which the subjective abuse of Scripture can be remedied.

Once Scripture becomes spiritual Play Doh molded to our own imaginings, no limiting factors *can* be put in place. No HVG teacher can say Robert Morris's twisting of Revelation 4:1 is worse than Henry Blackaby's misuse of John 11:4. Both treat Scripture the same way using the same approach. Though Morris's "personal

---

[38] By "objective," I mean its status and meaning as the Word of God is not dependent upon the response or actions of the reader (the subject). Whether or not the reader feels gripped, inspired, or impressed by the text, the Scripture remains the Word of God. Its meaning is not in any way determined by or dependent on the reader or their response.

word" is more fanciful than Blackaby's, it is no less egregious a mishandling of Scripture.

EXPLAIN THAT, MISTER!

"Well then, how do _you_ explain it?" you might be asking. "If a word or phrase 'coming alive' on the page of Scripture is _not_ the voice of God, then what is it?"

I did say at the beginning of this chapter that I have had this happen to me. It is not uncommon. In fact, it is not uncommon for even unbelievers to experience this phenomenon which is proof that it is not God's voice. Unbelievers aren't "listening" in the way taught by HVG advocates.

There is a very simple reason why words and phrases jump out at us, not only off the pages of Scripture, but also from road signs, newspapers, and the menu at the Chinese restaurant. It is the Baader-Meinhof Effect. This is sometimes called "frequency illusion" and refers to the way in which something recently encountered or learned suddenly seems to appear with improbable frequency.

Let me give you an example of this in action. My wife and I were in need of a new vehicle after the transmission in our minivan stopped working. At a nearby car dealership we found that price and features narrowed our options down to two Dodge Carvans – one red, one silver.

We would have preferred red as it is one of the colors of our favorite sports team, but the red van didn't have all the features the silver one had. So, we settled on the silver. We couldn't think of anyone who owned a silver van. In fact, I really couldn't have told you the last time I even _saw_ a silver van driving around our town. I thought we would be the only ones in town with a silver 2010 Dodge Grand Caravan.

You can guess what happened. We drove off the lot and saw 10 of them before we got home! They were everywhere! How did I not see those vans before? Where did they all come from? That is the Baader-Meinhof Effect. They were there all along, but I wasn't aware of them until I bought one.

Here is another example. You go to church and hear a missionary from Africa give an update on his church-planting ministry in Ethiopia. You resolve to pray for that missionary and the work he is doing on the continent of Africa every day of the following week. Then you hear _Africa_ by Toto on the 80s station at work on Monday, during lunch at the diner on Wednesday, and then in the mall on Friday. On Tuesday you see a cloud shaped like - you guessed it - Africa. On Saturday, you happen to read Acts 8 about the Ethiopian who trusts Christ. There it is again! Africa! Monday evening the news runs a story about elections in South Africa and on Thursday you see an online advertisement for an African Safari!

Why did you suddenly notice "Africa" everywhere you turned? Is this the voice of God trying to get your attention? No. It's the frequency illusion. Something happened in your life or came to your attention and you're now more aware of allusions or references to it.

Blackaby's daughter is sick and he remembers a verse that mentions sickness. Morris sees some numbers in Scripture that happen to be the same numbers he was contemplating earlier. If it isn't uncommon for me to see silver minivans everywhere I turn after buying one, why should I be surprised if I notice things in Scripture that are connected to recent thoughts I had or a decision I am faced with?

Noticing things in the pages of Scripture isn't the voice of God. It isn't God "trying" to get your attention. He isn't sending you personal messages. He isn't "whispering" to you. Let's stop claiming that everything that catches our attention is a message from Heaven. It's not. The Bible isn't a fortune cookie, a Magic 8-Ball, or a Rorschach test from which to wrench our own personal messages. This abuse of Scripture must stop!

Chapter 9

God Gave Me a Sign

9

When my children were younger, I was begrudgingly subjected to numerous episodes of "Blue's Clues." They would sit in rapt attention as a little, animated, blue, spotted dog followed clues to solve problems or find treasures. Blue's human companion, Steve, carried a notebook for writing down clues as they followed them to a solution.

Does this sound intriguing? Well, it's not. The target demographic for the program was either young children or adults with an IQ slightly lower than broccoli. I suspected watching the show was slowly turning my brain into mashed potatoes. It was enough to make watching CNN sound appealing.

For years I believed the Christian life was a more spiritual version of "Blue's Clues" for adults. Life is filled with mysteries: "Which house should I buy?" "Which job should I take?" "What should I name my child?" I was convinced God had a will for me concerning these things and, if I were going to be obedient to Him, I needed to listen for Him to reveal it. Without any direct, individual, and specific guidance in Scripture, I needed God to reveal His will to me. I believed He would do this through extra-biblical means: impressions, still small voices, and, of course, *signs*. I am not talking about a Mel Gibson movie, but hints, clues, confluences of events that, when properly interpreted, would point me in the right direction. God would lay out the breadcrumbs, I would follow them into His will.

What would this look like? It was a moving target. It might look different each and every day. A ringing phone might be a sign to call my mom. A Chinese word tattooed on the arm of the man next to me in the waiting room might be a sign I should have Chinese food for lunch. Hearing "Kokomo" by the Beach Boys in the elevator could be a divine directive to book a Caribbean Cruise.

Since the need for specific direction was constant, I needed to be alert, reading and heeding any sign that came my way. Anything and everything might be a sign.

HVG ON SIGNS

HVG advocates have an elaborate system for receiving and interpreting extra-biblical revelation. Central to their methodology is a reliance upon signs.[1]

Priscilla Shirer claims, "Our lives are an ever-changing catalog of intricately woven personal inquiries that we each need divine direction to navigate accurately."[2] With so many choices to make, supposedly, Scripture is not sufficient. As Shirer states:

> Sure, you do have the Bible to consult for guidance, but you know you can't just open it at random, taking verses out of context simply to affirm your own choices. *You genuinely want to hear from God.* You want to know whether the recent circumstances you've noticed around you are more than mere coincidence, or whether the comments you heard someone make to you might truly be a signal of God's will and direction.[3]

Allegedly, we must watch for the signs God drops in our path. Shirer speaks as if the only two options for receiving personal direction are "taking verses out of context"[4] or reading God's direction from circumstances and signs. According to her, the Bible has nothing to say about the important decisions. We must "*genuinely hear from God*" through the signs He is persistently sending! In *Discerning The Voice of God* she encourages us to ask, "What persistent, internal stirrings have I sensed? And how is He corroborating this message in other external ways?"[5]

---

[1] Not all HVG teachers make so much out of signs as a means of discerning God's voice. There are a couple of exceptions noted later in this chapter.

[2] Shirer, *Discerning the Voice of God*, 20.

[3] Ibid., 21.

[4] Shirer *habitually* takes verses out of context and misapplies them. She does this with John 10 ("My sheep hear my voice"), 1 Kings 19 ("still small voice"), and every instance where a word or phrase jumps off the page at her. She consistently quotes verses of Scripture that have *nothing* to do with the points she makes. She gives evidence by her use of Scripture that context is irrelevant to her. In fact, context can't be of any real importance in the HVG paradigm. What is significant in the HVG paradigm is not the intention of the original author but the impression on the reader.

[5] Ibid., 78.

These external signs are "confirmations" of internal stirrings, or what she calls "the still small voice." She says:

> When God speaks to you by the Holy Spirit within and also confirms it by other means from without, then be on the lookout for His directions. If you notice a consistent message confirmed through the leading of the Holy Spirit, the Scripture, your circumstances, and other people . . . pay close attention. God is repeating Himself to make sure you get the message.[6]

She describes this concurrence of signs as God's "persistence" or "His unrelenting attempts to speak to you and cause you to listen."[7] According to Shirer, the signs on the outside (circumstances and chance happenings) must line up with the persistent internal inklings that we sense: "Persistent, internal inklings matched by external confirmation is often the way God directs believers into His will."[8]

In HVG theology, words, phrases, or topics appearing with regular frequency is God persistently talking to us. A repeating thought that lines up with events in our life is God's attempt to get our attention. We are supposed to look for these themes. She cites an email received from Beth Moore that advised, "I know God is speaking to me about a certain matter when it seems like everything I hear or read for a while points toward the same issue. Anytime God gets 'thematic' with me, my ears start perking up."[9] Shirer finishes the chapter with this challenge: "Look for a theme or pattern in both your spirit and external circumstances when discerning God's leading."[10]

Mark Batterson agrees with Shirer saying:

> Can God speak audibly? Absolutely! But more often than not, He speaks in "sign language." I know this makes those who try to live by "the letter of the law" a little

---

[6] Ibid.

[7] Ibid., 79. God is "attempting" to speak to you? This view of God is unworthy of Him. What makes anyone think God "attempts" to do anything? The god of HVG theology is a god desperately trying to get our attention, communicate his will, and whisper in our ears. He is constantly frustrated in these attempts by our inability to hear. We don't "get good reception" (pg. 81), and so this god has to keep trying and trying, tenaciously at times, to get through to us. This is not the God of the Bible. The God of the Bible does not "attempt" to speak. He speaks.

[8] Ibid., 82.

[9] Ibid.

[10] Ibid., 89.

uncomfortable, and I understand why. Signs can be subjective. We'd rather rely on *sola Scriptura*. The problem with that limitation is that God speaks via sign language in Scripture.[11]

By "sign language" Batterson means not just an alignment of life's circumstances and repeated themes in our surroundings, but also "fleeces," "open and closed doors," internal peace, dreams, and visions.[12] He includes Moses' burning bush and Balaam's donkey as examples of "signs."[13]

Henry Blackaby is not opposed to all forms of being led by "signs." He teaches that God speaks to us through circumstances. He writes, "God does use circumstances to speak to us. But we will often be led astray if that is our *only* means of determining God's directions."[14] Blackaby's book is a manual on how to mine subtle signs for the voice and leading of God. He devotes a chapter to the subject: "God Speaks through Circumstances."[15]

Blackaby offers caution against seeking a "miraculous sign" for a confirmation of God's will, saying:

> Asking God for a sign, however, is often an indication of unbelief. . . . "Putting out a fleece" like Gideon is often a sign of your unbelief or an unwillingness on your part to trust God for an answer.
>
> When the scribes and Pharisees asked Jesus for a miraculous sign, Jesus condemned them as "an evil and adulterous generation" (Matt. 12:38-39). They were so self-centered and sinful, they could not even recognize that God was there in their midst. (See Luke 19:41-44.) Don't be like that wicked and adulterous generation by seeking for miraculous signs to validate a word from God.[16]

Yet, Blackaby's book encourages us to seek after a multitude of non-miraculous signs to validate a word from God. He encourages us to pursue signs in circumstances, interactions with others, our prayer life, verses of Scripture plucked from their

---

[11] Batterson, *Whisper*, 59.

[12] I will deal with some of these issues in future chapters.

[13] Ibid.

[14] Blackaby and King, *Experiencing God*, 89.

[15] Ibid., 117.

[16] Ibid., 88.

context, and things spoken to us by other believers, among others. All these "confirmations" are used to validate an alleged "word from God" on an issue. The only thing Blackaby cautions against is seeking a miraculous sign, which oddly enough, is the only thing that can give me 100% certainty on the validity of a message. In fact, it is the very thing Jesus cited to validate the divine origin of His words (John 5:36; 10:25, 37-38; 14:10).[17]

THE PROBLEM WITH SIGNS

Does God speak to us through signs dropped like breadcrumbs along life's path? Is it necessary that we learn to read circumstances and signs to discern the will of God? It is my contention that this approach to hearing from God and making decisions is completely unbiblical and in most cases, spiritually dangerous. There are at least three very serious problems with this approach.

First, this method is completely unbiblical, and I do mean *completely*. To establish this as a scriptural method for hearing the voice of God, HVG teachers need to demonstrate that it is both modeled and taught in Scripture. We find neither.

There is *no* example in Scripture of someone reading signs or interpreting circumstances in an effort to discern the voice of God. There are no examples of saints figuring out God's will by interpreting clues from their surroundings and circumstances. You don't read anything like this in Scripture:

> Paul woke up that morning thinking about Cyprus. In the marketplace he overheard two people talking about Cyprus. The next day he saw a ship leaving for Cyprus. Paul determined that God was getting "thematic" with him. He realized God was *trying* to get his attention and tell him something about Cyprus. Paul decided to go to Cyprus on his missionary journey. (Imaginations 15:12-14)

Moses didn't decide to go to Egypt and lead the Exodus because he kept seeing references to Egypt in his surroundings. He didn't interpret his circumstances and see a "theme" emerging.[18] Abraham didn't leave Ur of the Chaldeans because God dropped a series of ambiguous hints his way. God spoke to him - audibly. He

---

[17] Jesus' apostles cited the miraculous signs they performed as proof that they spoke from God (2 Corinthians 12:12; Acts 2:22; 14:3).

[18] Batterson's use of the burning bush as an example of a sign is absurd on its face. The burning bush was a visible and supernatural manifestation of the presence of God out of which God spoke clearly and unmistakably.

doesn't need to use breadcrumbs, subjective impressions, and vague clues to guide His people. God doesn't get "thematic" with us.[19]

Scripture tells the stories of hundreds of men and women who traveled, moved, married, worshipped, started families, named their children, built cities, waged war, engaged in commerce, started ministries, and made countless other decisions - *all without following a trail of divine breadcrumbs.* They lived their lives in obedience to the revealed Word of God, trusting that decisions made, and lives lived in obedience to God's revealed moral will would glorify Him and advance His purposes. There isn't one example of the modern HVG methodology being used. Not one.

We do read of men and women making decisions and following God's will when He spoke,[20] but that revelation was clear, audible, and unmistakable. It didn't come in nudgings, impressions, and vague signs.

Not only is there an absence of any examples, there is no clear biblical teaching of this method. If there were some clear teaching passages that described how this is done - what kinds of signs we should expect and how to interpret them - then we might have *some* justification for concluding that this method was used. If there were at least one passage that spelled this out in detail, then we would have some reason to believe the saints of old, the apostles, and the early church practiced it regularly. We might presume that even though it isn't modeled in great detail by way of example, it is clearly prescribed by means of instruction.

There is no such passage. We have passages with lengthy teachings on a multitude of issues central to Christian life and sanctification[21], but can you think of one, just one, that spells out for us how to discern God's voice in circumstances? Can HVG advocates cite one passage that commands us to seek guidance through hints and vague clues? Is there even one command to

---

[19] To counter, some may cite Gideon. I deal with Gideon and his fleece in a later chapter, but for now it's sufficient to say that the fleece wasn't a hint dropped into Gideon's path which God hoped he would notice. It was a supernatural test of God's prior revelation initiated by Gideon, not God. Therefore, it has nothing to do with what we are talking about here.

[20] Examples include Noah, Abraham, Isaac, Jacob, David, Solomon, Elijah, Elisha, Jeremiah, Daniel, Paul, Peter, John, etc.

[21] For instance, prayer (Psalms and Luke 11), giving (2 Corinthians 8,9), marriage (Ephesians 5 and 1 Corinthians 7), spiritual gifts (1 Corinthians 12-14; Ephesians 4; 1 Peter 4; Romans 12), relationship to authority (Romans 13 and 1 Peter 2), false teachers and false teaching (2 Peter and Jude), and dozens of other subjects.

"seek the voice of God in your circumstances and surroundings"? No.

If this were essential to Christian living, as HVG teachers claim, we should expect entire chapters, even entire books of the Bible to be devoted to its explanation. We should expect to find principles elucidated, questions answered, and difficulties resolved. Yet, there is no instruction, not a word. As this section adequately demonstrates, the passages usually cited have *nothing* at all to do with hearing the voice of God outside Scripture.

A SUBJECTIVE MUDDLE

Second, this method of reading signs provides nothing but a hopelessly subjective mix of feelings, impressions, and inklings. The danger of this method lies in its encouragement to look inwardly to thoughts and impressions rather than to Scripture. It encourages us to regard our thoughts and impressions as a divinely-given, authoritative source of revelation concerning the will of God.

It is common for HVG teachers to encourage their readers to write down their thoughts and impressions and spend time regularly praying over them.[22] Henry Blackaby suggests keeping a spiritual journal saying, "If you're not keeping a spiritual journal or diary, you need to. If the God of the universe tells you something, you should write it down. When God speaks to you in your quiet time, immediately write down what He said before you have time to forget."[23] Robert Morris says, "I encourage you to write down these impressions as well. Write down the thoughts that align with God's Word that are encouraging you,"[24] and, "I say listen and write because one of the best ways I've learned to hear the voice of God is to write down thoughts and prayers when I meet with Him."[25]

One never knows when that which might first appear to be a random thought ends up being a "word from the Spirit." By

---

[22] Sam Storms says you should "write down what you think may be the word of the Spirit." (Storms, *Practicing the Power*, 101.) Though Storms cautions against assuming "that every random thought that passes through your brain is from God," we are still left with the hopelessly subjective teaching that many of them may be.

[23] Blackaby and King, *Experiencing God*, 108. In the next paragraph, Blackaby describes writing down verses of Scripture that God uses to teach him about Himself. He does not limit this to *just* Scripture verses. Blackaby believes that God speaks through various means, including prayer. This quote comes from a chapter titled "God Speaks Through Prayer," and he claims that "what God says in prayer is far more important than what you say" (109).

[24] Morris, *Frequency*, 51.

[25] Ibid., 95. Completely abusing Habakkuk 2:2, Morris cites it as a model for us when we get "a word from the Lord."

comparing our recorded impressions with the confluence of circumstances and outward indicators, we are supposedly able to sense when God is being "thematic" with us. HVG theology doesn't direct people to the infallible and sufficient Word of God for wisdom and guidance. Instead, Christians are encouraged to take guidance from almost anything but Scripture. According to their view, Scripture gives "general principles" but is insufficient for guidance on the pressing, important, and daily issues we face.

If you need an example of where this theology logically and inevitably leads, I would remind you of the story Hybels tells in *The Power of a Whisper*. He describes one particularly tough time when he needed to "hear meaningful words from heaven."

> One day a few summers ago, I decided to spend an afternoon alone with God. I hopped on a boat, headed out on the lake and prepared to hear meaningful words from heaven. I sat there for an hour and heard nothing. I sat there for a second hour and heard precisely nothing. Partway through hour number three, I thought, "I love being on the water, but what's with the silence, God?"
>
> I was going through a tough time at Willow and desperately needed a little encouragement from above. But hour after hour I sat there, hearing nothing but the wind and the waves.
>
> Just as I was ready to haul up the anchor and motor back toward the harbor, I saw a Bud Light beer can float by. I stood there staring at the can, wondering, *"Is this a message from God? If so, what could it mean? Am I supposed to drink Bud Light? Am I supposed to tell my congregation not to drink Bud Light? Is there a message inside the can?"*
>
> After a few wasted minutes of silent inquisition, I figured God was probably just telling me to respect his [sic] creation, fish the can out of the water and toss it in the garbage.
>
> I got back to the house, and my family, all of whom knew I was investing an entire afternoon in some "meaningful dialogue" with God, said, "So, what did God say to you?"
>
> "Pick up the beer can - that's what he [sic] said."

We laughed, but there was little more to report. I had watched and waited and listened, but apparently God had nothing to say to me that day - or at least I couldn't hear it, despite my best efforts.[26]

Bill Hybels, pastor of one of the most influential churches in America over the last 40 years, was trying to exegete a message from God out of *a beer can*. If Hybels wanted to hear from God, why not open his Bible? If he needed truth to get him through a difficult time, why not read through the Psalms? He could turn to Paul's encouragement for downcast ministers in 2 Corinthians. Jeremiah's reflection on God's faithfulness in difficult times was written for our benefit (Lamentations). Instead, Hybels spent nearly three hours on a boat waiting for a word from God. We can only surmise that he believes more encouragement can be gleaned from a floating Bud Light can than from reading Scripture.

You may think I am cherry picking a ridiculous example to make a point. I am not. Once you believe messages from God come through thoughts, outward signs, and thematic circumstances, there is *nothing* that would keep you from trying to discern a message behind a floating beer can. If you think God is trying to speak through a song lyric,[27] a television broadcast, the shape of a cloud, or any other object which might catch your attention, then exegeting a floating beer can makes perfect sense. You wouldn't want to miss out on a desperately-needed whisper! This is the logical consequence of HVG methodology. We are abandoned to our feelings, hunches, and ever-shifting circumstances. We are told these are God's whispers to us.

This type of navel-gazing self-reliance is never commended in Scripture. Scripture warns against trusting in our own understanding (Proverbs 3:5-6), yet HVG teachers believe that in the bowels of the depraved human heart (Jeremiah 17:9), the most precious and reliable whispers from God are heard. Scripture never encourages us to write down our thoughts and examine them for divine messages. Scripture never suggests that God will speak to us through a confluence of events, circumstances, and outward happenings. No external sign can ever be reliably regarded as

---

[26] Hybels, *The Power of a Whisper*, 107-108. I cited a shorter selection from this passage in Chapter 2.

[27] Jack Deere says, "The other day I was running on a treadmill and listening through headphones to a portable CD player. . . . it was plain ol' country western. A love song came on, and the voice of God came through the words of the ballad" (Deere, *Surprised by the Voice of God*, 128).

divine revelation, no matter how "thematic" it is. Scripture *never* indicates that these things are the voice of God. HVG offers a hopelessly subjective muddle of confusion and uncertainty.

That leads us to the third problem: This subjective methodology requires an elaborate system of extra-biblical principles of interpretation. Since the method HVG teachers promote is neither taught nor modeled in Scripture, they need an elaborate system for interpreting God's voice. They admit their hopelessly subjective methodology inevitably opens them up to deception, mistakes, and even foolishness. Remember, there is a lot of "trial and error."

Most of the books cited here are "How To" manuals for hearing and interpreting God's voice. Though the authors repeatedly deny they are providing a "system" or "formula," that is, in fact, what they offer. They promote a complicated system for "tuning in" to God's frequency, getting into a receptive mood, and adopting spiritual disciplines that make us more likely to hear God's voice. We have to be quiet, undistracted, humble, teachable, willing to obey, spiritually hungry, holy, trusting, sacrificial, servant-hearted, receptive, seeking, and attentive.[28] These are biblical virtues, but Scripture nowhere suggests they are necessary to hear God.[29]

HVG teachers promote elaborate methods for reading signs. How can we know if a repeated thought is from God? Could it be a sign? It is *possible*! Shirer says God is "persistent" and gets "thematic" with us. But don't get too excited, because circumstances can be deceiving. We have to make sure that what is thematic is also challenging, personal, truthful, authoritative, and will bring us peace.[30] If a "word" is all those things, it *might* be from God. But maybe not! Satan may be trying to deceive us into disobeying God. We might be falling prey to our own deceptive hearts and desires, so it will all need to be "confirmed" by a complex system of checks and balances.

HVG teachers offer complicated systems of tests to ensure that fleshly, deceptive, or demonic impressions, circumstances, and signs are not mistaken for God's whispers. Impressions need to be confirmed, thoughts written down and prayed over, and signs

---

[28] All these qualities are recommended by Priscilla Shirer in her book *He Speaks to Me*. All the other HVG teachers follow suit. Shirer bases her book on the account of Samuel hearing God's prophetic call in 1 Samuel 3.

[29] I would offer Abraham, Moses, Saul of Tarsus, and Nebuchadnezzar as contrary examples.

[30] Shirer's book *Discerning the Voice of God* has an entire section detailing these qualities and providing examples.

examined. Circumstances must be interpreted. Beer cans must be exegeted. Inklings have to be deciphered. Random thoughts have to be scrutinized for any hint of a divine message.

All these "tests" are merely extra-biblical paradigms in search of proof texts. These are man-made systems of "divine guidance" foisted on Scripture. The passages normally cited as proof texts have nothing to do with the sophisticated and elaborate constructs promoted by HVG advocates. There is no passage of Scripture which provides these instructions for hearing and confirming the voice of God. Therefore, the methods and means for interpreting these "whispers" are just as subjective, fallible, and man-made as their theology of divine guidance itself. There is no escape from the subjective muddle they claim is the clear voice of God. The method is subjective. The message is subjective. The meaning is subjective.

A BETTER WAY

There is a better way: Scripture.

Contrary to the claims of HVG advocates, God has provided in Scripture "everything necessary for life and godliness through the true knowledge of God and of Jesus our Lord" (2 Peter 1:3). The Holy-Spirit-inspired Scripture is a "word made more sure" (2 Peter 1:19). It is "more sure" than experiences, signs, and subjective impressions.

The Scripture doesn't just *contain* the voice of God. It isn't just a *source* of the voice of God. The Scriptures *are* the voice of God. In them God has provided every truth, every principle, and every bit of wisdom necessary for all of life's decisions. Knowing God as He is revealed in Scripture is all that is necessary to live a life of obedience to Him and His divine will. Turn to the Book!

Chapter 10

God Opened a Door

10

But what about the infamous "open door"?

Commonly, Christians speak of "open and closed doors" in relation to the voice of God. It's a shorthand way of referring to God's direction in various decision-making contexts. According to HVG methodology, obediently following God's leading involves listening for His voice through "doors" - both open and closed. Similar to the "signs" critiqued in the last chapter, this source for God's voice requires us to examine circumstances to discern the will of God.

HVG TEACHING ON OPEN DOORS

Mark Batterson claims we need to learn to "speak the language of the Spirit. And one of His dialects is doors: open doors and closed doors."[1] He refers to these as a "sign language" of the Holy Spirit,[2] believing the leading of God through these signs is authoritative: "Ignoring signs is ignoring the God who speaks through them, and we do so to our own detriment."[3] According to Batterson, "open doors" and "closed doors" are indications of God's calling and leading: "In a sense, the closed door equates to 'released from' and the open door equals 'called to.'"[4]

He is aware of the inherently subjective nature of trying to discern the will of God through these kinds of signs: "I know that signs are subject to interpretation, and there is a very fine line

---

[1] Batterson, *Whisper*, 97.

[2] Ibid.

[3] Ibid.

[4] Ibid., 102.

between reading them and reading into them."[5] Batterson attempts to alleviate the concern about misreading signs by offering five tests to use when trying to discern God's voice through open and closed doors.[6]

First, does the direction suggested by signs give you "goose bumps"? He says that the "spirit-led life" is a "Wild Goose chase" (calling the Holy Spirit the "Wild Goose") and claims that the "will of God should make your heart skip a beat."

Second, do you have "a peace about it"? Misusing Colossians 3:15, Batterson claims the presence of peace regarding a course of action is an indication of God's leading.[7]

Third, does the "open door" align with wise counsel?

Fourth, is it crazy enough to qualify as a "God-sized dream"?

Fifth, make sure God has released you from previous obligations.[8]

These "tests" to prove the divine origin of a sign are intended to compensate for the *subjective* nature of conjuring guidance from circumstances. However, the tests themselves are a subjective quicksand of confusing and unbiblical principles. Nothing in Scripture teaches that God's providential leadings are crazy wild goose chases! How can my own subjective feelings be a reliable measure of divine authority? In other words, to avoid being led astray by my own thoughts and feelings, I should test them by my own thoughts and feelings. That's the HVG methodology in a nutshell.

HVG teachers cannot escape the subjectivity of being led by open and closed doors. Henry Blackaby, who does not hesitate to read the voice of God into circumstances, cautions against relying on this as a sole method for guidance. He writes:

> Some people try to hear God's voice and know His will only through circumstances. . . . The only problem is I don't see this as a pattern anywhere in Scripture. God does use circumstances to speak to us. But we will often be led

---

[5] Ibid., 97.

[6] We have yet another complex series of tests and checklists to avoid a false positive. None of these tests can be found in Scripture since Scripture does not give any method for testing the voice of God through "doors." The check against a hopelessly subjective source of guidance is nothing more than a hopelessly subjective list of manmade tests.

[7] I will address Colossians 3:15 and the "peace test" in Chapter 12.

[8] Ibid., 100–102.

astray if that is our *only* means of determining God's directions.[9]

Blackaby's sole caution is against relying *only* on circumstances for divine direction. He teaches that "open and closed doors" need to be confirmed by wise counsel, a passage of Scripture, something revealed in prayer, or the impression of an inner voice.

Dallas Willard includes the "open or closed doors of circumstances" as one of three "lights" which give us divine direction. He writes:

> Finally, the mere open or closed doors of circumstances cannot function independently of the other two lights or of *some* additional factor; for one does not know merely by looking at these doors who is opening or closing them - God, Satan or another human being. . . . Scripture and inner promptings must be brought into consideration to determine whether doors are open or closed.[10]

Like Blackaby, Willard teaches that "doors" are a reliable source for divine guidance, so long as they are confirmed or checked by some additional factors. He suggests "Scripture and inner promptings" as the proper guides for evaluating open and closed doors. As already noted, "inner promptings" are every bit as unreliable as circumstances and signs. If open and closed doors can be manipulated by Satan, why can't he manipulate my inner promptings as well? If both "lights" can be perverted and manipulated by Satan, how can one serve as a "check" for the other? Why should I trust either one?

DEFINING THE OPEN DOOR

According to HVG teaching, Christians must treat an "open door" as God's leading on a particular issue. "Open door" means an "unhindered opportunity." Faced with a decision, one choice might be fraught with obstacles while another appears free of opposition and resistance. The "open door" is assumed to be God's will for that circumstance. This constitutes the voice of God in a sign. According to HVG teachers, a path free of obstacles and adversaries is an "open door" God wants us to walk through. To ignore the sign is to ignore the God who is speaking through it. Conversely, a difficult

---

[9] Blackaby and King, *Experiencing God,* 89.

[10] Willard, *Hearing God,* 224.

path marked by obstacles should be taken as a sign God isn't leading in that direction.

In the HVG paradigm, the "open and closed door" test may be applied to nearly any area of decision-making. We receive guidance in important decisions through open and closed doors.

To summarize HVG teaching on "open and closed doors":

1. An "open door" is an option or course of action free of resistance, obstacles, or hindrances.

2. An "open door" is an almost certain indication of God's will. Not taking an open door is an act of disobedience to the revealed will of God.

3. The "open door" is not an infallible indicator and must be tested and confirmed by other expressions of "God's voice."

SCRIPTURE PASSAGES

Does Scripture teach that God leads us through "open and closed doors"? Are these signs treated in Scripture as the authoritative voice of God? Three passages are cited to show that "open and closed doors" are the voice of God.

1 Corinthians 16:8–9: "But I will remain in Ephesus until Pentecost; for a *wide door* for effective service has *opened* to me, and there are many adversaries."

2 Corinthians 2:12–13: "Now when I came to Troas for the gospel of Christ and when a *door was opened* for me in the Lord, I had no rest for my spirit, not finding Titus my brother; but taking my leave of them, I went on to Macedonia."

Colossians 4:3: "…praying at the same time for us as well, that God will *open up to us a door* for the word, so that we may speak forth the mystery of Christ, for which I have also been imprisoned."[11]

In all three verses, Paul was describing *opportunities for service in gospel ministry.* Paul had an opportunity in Ephesus for "effective service" and one in Troas for the "gospel of Christ." The prayer he requested of the Colossians was for an open door to

---

[11] Acts 14:27 also refers to an open door: "When they had arrived and gathered the church together, they began to report all the things God had done with them and how He had opened a door of faith to the Gentiles." This describes the gospel going to Gentile peoples through the ministry of Paul and Barnabas.

preach God's Word. This language is used *exclusively* of opportunities for gospel proclamation and ministry. "Open doors" aren't mentioned in connection with God's guidance for choosing a spouse, a house, a job, a church, or *any other sphere of decision-making* over which Christians often agonize.

The only place the "open door" is mentioned is in connection with opportunities for service to Christ in His gospel. Even if we were to assume this is a sure sign of God's clear leading, it's unwise at best, and presumptuous at worst, to apply this to *any other* area of decision-making. Though Paul speaks of an "open door" in connection with opportunities for gospel ministry, we aren't justified in assuming God will direct us this way in every sphere of life.

When we examine the passages and their historical context more closely, the problems for HVG theology on this issue only multiply.

THE OPEN DOOR IN EPHESUS

1 Corinthians 16:8–9: "But I will remain in Ephesus until Pentecost; for a *wide door* for effective service *has opened* to me, and there are many adversaries" (Emphasis mine).

The historical context provided by the book of Acts gives us some insight into Paul's meaning. Likely, the "wide door for effective service" was the unparalleled opportunity to teach at the school of Tyrannus for two years. Paul's time at that school resulted in the wide spread of the gospel. Luke notes that "all who lived in Asia heard the word of the Lord, both Jews and Greeks" (Acts 19:8-10). Thus, the Word of God spread throughout the entire region of Asia Minor.

Ephesus was filled with "many adversaries." The Jews in the Synagogue "were hardened and disobedient, speaking evil of the Way before the people" (Acts 19:8-9). Demetrius, a silversmith, stirred the city into a fevered rage that threatened Paul's traveling companions, Gaius and Aristarchus (Acts 19:23-29). The enraged worshipers of Artemis filled the city with their idolatrous chants and imperiled Paul as well as the other believers in the city (Acts 19:28-41). Many adversaries indeed! Though faced with life-threatening opposition, ardent adversaries, and entrenched resistance, Ephesus offered an unprecedented opportunity. Paul took advantage of the opportunity and remained in Ephesus for nearly three years (Acts 20:17, 31). His time in Ephesus is believed by many to be the most fruitful years of his life and ministry (Acts 19:20).

141

Paul mentions both an "open door" and "many adversaries." He did not view the presence of opposition, resistance, and adversaries as a "closed door." To the contrary, Paul saw an opportunity for effective service among hostile opposition as an "open door." In HVG theology, opposition or resistance is a clear sign that God "hasn't opened the door" or has "closed the door." This doesn't square with Scripture!

Have you ever heard a Christian say, "I have an opportunity to go serve the Lord. The adversaries are many, the challenges great, and the opposition is fierce. What an open door!"? If I lived a thousand years, I wouldn't hear an HVG teacher say such a thing. It's the path of least resistance that's considered an open door in HVG theology.

TITUS OR TROAS?

2 Corinthians 2:12–13: "Now when I came to Troas for the gospel of Christ and when a *door was opened* for me in the Lord, I had no rest for my spirit, not finding Titus my brother; but taking my leave of them, I went on to Macedonia" (Emphasis mine).

This second passage is no more friendly to HVG theology. The account of this journey is found in Acts 20. After the uproar in Ephesus (Acts 19) Paul exhorted the disciples and took leave of them "to go to Macedonia" (Acts 20:1). It appears Paul sent Titus to Corinth to deliver a letter (2 Corinthians 7:5-16).[12] Though the details of their arrangement aren't explicitly recorded in Scripture, we can surmise that Paul left Ephesus expecting to meet up with Titus in Troas.[13]

Paul spent 7 days in Troas, presumably waiting for Titus to arrive with news on the situation in Corinth. While there, on the first day of the week, Paul gathered together with the believers for a time of teaching. He taught until after midnight (Acts 20:6-12) to an eager and spiritually-hungry group who enthusiastically welcomed him. As in Ephesus, the needy church proved to be "a door opened in the Lord." Paul had a great opportunity for service in Troas. He could have stayed indefinitely. It was an open door!

---

[12] Titus was likely commissioned to deliver a letter Paul refers to as the sorrowful letter (2 Corinthians 2:4; 7:8). This letter coupled with Titus's faithful ministry to the Corinthians produced genuine repentance in the church (2 Corinthians 7:5-16).

[13] Paul mentions that he "came to Troas" but was unable to find rest for his spirit because he couldn't find Titus. It is believed that Paul had arranged to meet Titus there. When Titus never showed, Paul pressed on with his plans to travel to Macedonia, and eventually on to Jerusalem.

He left. Paul *left* the open door opportunity in Troas to find Titus. When presented with an open door for service in Ephesus, Paul stayed. When presented with an open door for service in the gospel of Christ in Troas, Paul left for Macedonia.

Wait! What?! How could he do that? If an open door is a clear voice from God, then how could Paul disobey it? According to Batterson, for Paul to ignore the open door is to ignore the God who gave him that sign! If what HVG advocates teach is true, Paul's departure for Macedonia constitutes a high-handed act of disobedience! He was disobeying God's clear direction revealed in the open door!

To counter, HVG teachers might argue that since Paul had "no rest in his spirit," he shouldn't have taken the open door. Willard, for example, would say this is an example of not being led by *only* an open door, but allowing an inner prompting to provide guidance. However, Paul's restless spirit wasn't an "inner prompting" or "still small voice." He was looking for Titus and awaiting a report on the Corinthian church. He didn't get a whisper telling him to leave Troas. He was moved by circumstantial concerns that pressed upon him a greater priority than ministry in Troas. Paul evaluated his options and made a wise decision in light of his circumstances and concerns.

Clearly he didn't regard an "open door" as a divine mandate. He didn't believe passing up an open door was passing up God's best, or ignoring the God who gave him a sign. In fact, Paul didn't regard the open door as a sign at all. For Paul, an "open door" was an opportunity for fruitful service and nothing more. He weighed the opportunity in light of pressing concerns and chose to pass it up. As Greg Koukl so aptly puts it, "Although God may have given him an opportunity, Paul did not consider the opportunity itself as a directive from God."[14]

All we can say about "open doors" in Scripture is that they are "gospel opportunities." They don't constitute divine guidance or direction. An open door is an opportunity that can be acted on or ignored, depending on other factors.

---

[14] *Decision Making and the Will of God* audio CD #1. This product is available from Stand to Reason (str.org) and is highly recommended for those seeking to understand the "Wisdom Model" of decision-making. Koukl offers a very helpful corrective to HVG theology and I have benefited richly from his work.

A COLOSSIAN PRAYER

Colossians 4:3: "...praying at the same time for us as well, that God will open up to us a door for the word, so that we may speak forth the mystery of Christ, for which I have also been imprisoned."

The mention of "open door" to the Colossians doesn't prove the HVG claims either. Paul was describing his desire for an opportunity to proclaim the gospel ("the mystery of Christ"), the very thing that led to his imprisonment in the cause of Christ. The reference to God opening a door had nothing to do with hearing the voice of God. It refers to Paul preaching God's Word, not hearing God's voice. He was praying for an effective opportunity for gospel ministry, not guidance in decision-making.

If you are curious what Scripture says about "closed doors," Garry Friesen perfectly summarizes it:

> The need for open doors certainly implies the existence of closed doors, though Scripture never uses the term. Paul did not have a "closed door" mentality. If he was sovereignly prevented from pursuing a sound plan, he simply waited and tried again later. He did not view a blocked endeavor as a "closed door" sign from God that his plan was faulty. He accepted the fact that he could not pursue that plan at that time. Yet he continued to desire, pray, and plan for the eventual accomplishment of the goal. This approach is clearly demonstrated in Paul's attempts to visit Rome. (Romans 1:10–13)[15]

PRACTICAL PROBLEMS

HVG teaching on "open doors" is fraught with problems.

First, the biblical teaching is opposite to what is taught by HVG teachers. They claim that a path free of obstacles constitutes an open door. Paul's open door was abounding with "many adversaries." HVG teachers claim an open door is an indicator of God's will. Paul walked away from an open door to pursue other concerns. HVG teachers must either say that Paul was disobedient to the voice of God or they must admit that their teaching on "open doors" is contrary to Scripture.

Second, Scripture neither teaches nor models this approach to decision-making. The Bible records the decisions and actions of hundreds of people making thousands of history-altering decisions.

---

[15] Friesen and Maxson, *Decision Making*, 212.

Not once did anyone look for "open doors" and make a decision on that basis.

If this means of hearing God's voice were as important as HVG teachers claim, it would be given prominent discussion in Scripture. These three references are all we find and none of them teach anything close to the HVG methodology. Yet, this doesn't keep HVG teachers from writing entire chapters on how to recognize, evaluate, test, and double-check "open doors" for the voice of God.

Third, treating "open doors" as the voice of God makes us susceptible to deception and/or dereliction of duty. How do we know if an "open door" is God's voice or a satanic deception? Maybe the devil is trying to lure us away from God's best through a temptation cleverly disguised as an "open door." Or what if the devil creates difficulty to disguise an open door as a closed one?

HVG teachers would say this is why "open doors" *by themselves* aren't adequate indicators of the will of God and must be confirmed with inner impressions and Scripture. However, impressions can be deceiving. How do I know the same devil making an "open door" isn't also whispering in my ear? If I am "checking" my open door by my "inner prompting" and checking my "inner prompting" by the "open door," where is the safeguard against deception? They can't claim Scripture is the safeguard since, according to them, Scripture is only a "general word" from God with nothing to say concerning my specific situation.

Fifth, this methodology does not provide the clarity and certainty that it promises. For instance, why should we assume obstacles are a sign of a closed door? Perhaps God wants you to push on closed doors. Might there be a reward for diligent perseverance toward a God-honoring goal in the face of difficulty?

If you push and the door opens, how do you know God opened it and not the devil? Perhaps in your flesh you opened a door God had closed. Maybe if you had waited, God would have opened the door or even opened a different one. But how do you know when you have waited long enough?

What if you push open a door God didn't want open? What if Satan opens one? Can Satan close open doors or open closed doors? What if you are not paying attention and don't see an open door? Are you in sin for not discerning God's voice in open doors?

I don't mean to sound petty with these questions, but if HVG advocates are going to claim we should make life- and ministry-altering decisions based on "open doors" and "inner impressions," these questions need to be answered. Scripture doesn't provide answers to these questions because Scripture doesn't teach this method of hearing from God. HVG teachers must admit their method is subjective and thus inherently uncertain and dangerous.

In order to bolster our confidence in their man-made methodology, they suggest that we add Scripture to the mix. "Always check it against Scripture!" they remind us. Of course, they presuppose that Scripture is silent on the issues in question, which is the very reason they claim we need to hear the voice of God through "inner impressions" and "open doors." What good is it to check the "open door" against Scripture if Scripture has nothing to say about it?

Willard promises that the "three lights" (Scripture, open doors, and inner promptings) will give us the clear voice of God. But only if Scripture is inadequate do I need the other two.[16] To compensate for what they perceive to be an inadequacy in Scripture, they offer a man-made system of subjective, confusing feelings and circumstances.

Sixth, trying to discern the voice of God in "open doors" leads to confusing and conflicting messages. When trying to decide whether to go back to Bible college for a second year, the "voice of God in my circumstances" provided no help at all. Scripture didn't give me personal direction on the issue, at least not the kind HVG teachers claim we need to make the right decision. There is no passage that specifically and directly addressed whether or not I should return the next school year.

Further, there seemed to be a big "closed door" in front of me prohibiting my return, namely, I didn't have any money for tuition. The only "open door" pointed home. I hadn't received any "inner impressions." I hadn't heard any whispers. When I turned inward to my own heart, I had no "peace" either way. I didn't feel peace about returning since I didn't have money for tuition. I didn't feel a peace about not returning because I really wanted to come back for more school.

Listening for the voice of God in places He has not promised to speak, inevitably creates this kind of subjective confusion.

---

[16] That is why they insist we *need* all these other sources of divine revelation (still small voice, doors, impressions, signs, fleeces, etc.). I willingly concede their point that Scripture does not provide detailed specific revelation on daily decisions. I contend that such specific direction is not necessary. If it were, we would be told so in Scripture. The principles provided in Scripture are *sufficient* information and guidance for the believer in *every* decision.

Chapter 11

I Put Out a Fleece

11

"'Put out a fleece?' What does he mean by that?" I wondered.

I was new to the Christian jargon. My friend, who had been instrumental in my salvation, spoke it fluently. "Putting out a fleece" was new to me, but judging from the way he talked, it was *the* way to discern God's will.

"What do you mean by that?" I inquired. If there was some secret to knowing God's will, I wanted in on it.

He recounted the story of Gideon in Judges 6-7. "Gideon needed to confirm God was telling him to fight the Midianites, so he put out a fleece - a piece of cloth. He asked God to cause the fleece to be wet and the ground dry by morning. God answered his prayer. To confirm God's will again, he asked for the opposite on the following night - a dry fleece and wet ground. God answered his request and confirmed His will to Gideon."

From the way other Christians talked, it sounded as if this was *the* method for confirming God's will. Which job should I take? Which college should I attend? Which car should I buy? Each and every one of these could be settled with a "fleece." Not a literal, actual fleece mind you, but something similar – a confirming test by which God would give direction through circumstantial happenings.

Allegedly, Gideon's approach to getting a "sign" from God was a model for us. When faced with two options, we can ask God for special guidance through a similar circumstantial confirmation. It sounded legit. After all, it was right there in the Bible!

THE PRACTICE DESCRIBED AND DEFENDED

Garry Friesen, in his excellent work *Decision Making and the Will of God*, describes the fleece this way:

Gideon's fleece has become the basis of a practice among some Christians which is called "putting out a fleece." In essence, when you put out a fleece you say to God, "If you really want me to carry out plan A, then please make the telephone ring at 9:10 p.m., then I will know that plan A is what you want." (You can make the "fleece" anything you wish, just so long as it can serve as a "sign" to you.)[1]

Robert Morris[2] unabashedly defends Gideon and the use of "fleeces" as a means of "confirming" personal revelations. In his book, *Frequency*, he writes:

I mentioned at the start of this book that the number one question I get asked as a pastor is "How can I hear the voice of God?" Well, I get asked an additional question about the number one question, and it's this: "How do I know if it is really God?" In other words, how do I know if God is truly speaking, and I'm not making up something in my mind? Is it okay to ask God to confirm His word?[3]

Morris assures the reader that "God always confirms His word. Let me repeat that: God *always* confirms His word."[4] He cites the story of Gideon saying, "The story of Gideon's fleece in Judges 6 is perhaps the best-known Bible story that relates to confirmation."[5] Likewise, Jack Deere cites fleeces as one of the "variety of ways" that "the people of the Bible heard God speak."[6]

---

[1] Friesen and Maxson, *Decision Making*, 213–14. Friesen is here quoting a definition he pulled from John White (John White, *The Fight* [Downers Grove, IL: Intervarsity Press, 1976], 165). Friesen notes that "White does not advocate putting out a fleece. In fact, his very next statement is, 'Forget about fleeces. If you've never used them, don't start. If you have, then quit.'" I highly recommend Friesen's book!

[2] There is some disagreement among HVG teachers on using "fleeces."

[3] Morris, *Frequency*, 104.

[4] Ibid.

[5] Ibid., 105.

[6] Deere, *Surprised by the Voice of God*, 19. Equating the "fleece" with the "voice of God" is a subtle rhetorical trick, and one that Deere heavily relies on in both his books. This is a category confusion in which anything and everything becomes the "voice of God." God did not speak through the fleece. The fleece was a sign, a miraculous and supernatural event confirming what God had already told Gideon on multiple, previous occasions. If there had been no prior revelation to Gideon, the odd happening of a dry fleece on wet ground, or a wet fleece on dry ground, would've been meaningless. It was only because of the clear Word of God to Gideon on the previous occasions that the "sign" of the fleece had any meaning at all. Technically, God did not "speak through the fleece." God performed a supernatural miracle to confirm something He had previously spoken. By calling the "fleece" the "voice of God," Deere ends up diluting the significance of genuine revelation. In the end, this is the result of all theologies which promote personalized extra-biblical revelation.

Dallas Willard suggests that we regularly ask God to speak to us through "friends, books, magazines, and circumstances."[7] Confident that if God "has something he really wants [you] to know or do," you will receive "an idea or thought with that peculiar quality, spirit and content that [we] have come to associate with God's voice." He suggests asking for further confirmation saying, "If you are uncertain if this is from you or from God, ask for further confirmation as Gideon did (Judges 6:11-40)."[8]

Mark Batterson promotes the use of signs for confirmation citing Gideon as "our biblical precedent."[9] Batterson claims, "Gideon did it in a spirit of humility, and God honored him with an answer both times. I think fleeces have God's stamp of approval, but let me offer a few warnings and instructions."[10] He offers three guidelines for using fleeces. "First, test your motives. . . . Second, delayed obedience is disobedience. . . . Third, set specific parameters in prayer."[11] He cautions, "If you don't define the fleece, it's easy to come up with false negatives or false positives. Notice the specificity of Gideon's fleece. And don't discount the fact that it required divine intervention."[12]

HOPELESS CONFUSION

We can't escape the confusion inherent in the HVG methodology. They claim that God speaks outside of Scripture today because we *need* clear direction. Since the Bible doesn't provide the clear and explicit direction we need, we must receive a clear and current word from God.

Is this what their methodology provides? Is there anything clear about the messages received through still small voices, impressions, and signs? If so, then why do we need confirmations? Willard candidly admits that a message received by "an idea or thought" is of uncertain origin. How do we know if the thought is from God, Satan, or self? Morris promises that "God always confirms His Word," but the confirmation is subject to deception and

---

[7] Willard, *Hearing God*, 260. In this context he is quoting James Dobson who claims to regularly receive divine revelation through these means. Regarding Dobson's example, Willard says, "This is exactly what we are to do."

[8] Ibid., 261.

[9] Batterson, *Whisper*, 108.

[10] Ibid.

[11] Ibid.

[12] Ibid., 108-109.

misinterpretation. Batterson warns that we might get "false negatives or false positives."

HVG methodology provides unclear and ambiguous parameters to confirm inconclusive and unreliable "voices" so we can test vague impressions of questionable origin. This they call a "clear and personal word from God." The man-made HVG system is a confusing, subjective, and hopelessly uncertain method, impotent to deliver what it promises, namely, the clear and unmistakable voice of God.

NOT ALL AGREE

Not all HVG teachers are as committed to the fleece as Batterson and Willard. Blackaby cites Gideon as an example of *unbelief* saying:

> Sometimes in Scripture God gave a miraculous sign to assure the person that the word was from Him. Gideon is one example (Judg. 6). Asking God for a sign, however, is often an indication of unbelief. In Gideon's case God had already sent fire from stones to consume a sacrifice and even the stones it was on. Yet, in his unbelief, Gideon asked for another sign. "Putting out a fleece" like Gideon is often a sign of your unbelief or an unwillingness on your part to trust God for an answer.[13]

Blackaby cites Gideon as an example of unbelief. Willard cites him as a model for confirming the Word of God. According to some HVG teachers, Gideon was questioning clear instructions. According to others, he was clarifying instructions because God had been unclear.[14] Blackaby teaches that Gideon's request was sinful

---

[13] Blackaby and King, *Experiencing God*, 88. On page 85, Blackaby notes that "Gideon lacked assurance" and so "God was very gracious to reveal Himself even more clearly." Blackaby rightly observes that Gideon was absolutely sure of God's Word (Judges 6:21-22) and yet he requested a sign anyway. This was a blatant act of unbelief.

[14] Robert Morris acknowledges that Gideon doubted God's voice, but lays the blame at God's feet saying:

> Why did Gideon doubt God's voice? If God had spoken to him in a big, booming voice, then why was Gideon so uncertain about the voice? I'm going to suggest that maybe God did not speak to Gideon in a big, booming voice as we often imagine. I think that God spoke to Gideon in a still small voice, the same kind of voice that He used to speak to Elijah in the cave at Horeb. I think God might have even impressed the message upon Gideon's heart, the same as He does for us today. (Morris, Frequency, 33-34.)

In other words, God's lack of clarity led to Gideon's doubt. As we will see, there was no lack of clarity in Gideon's mind regarding the will and command of God. Further, Morris horribly abuses the text of Scripture by misinterpreting the events of the passage to fit his

because he had a clear command from God, but Batterson claims that Gideon's actions have "God's stamp of approval" for confirming unclear commands from God.

I hope you see how confusing this is. Is Gideon an example of unbelief or faith? Is he a model of cowardice or confirmation? Was God's Word to Gideon clear or unclear? Is his example to be followed or avoided? Is Gideon an illustration of willing obedience or cowardly disobedience?

Ironically, we can get no certain answer from HVG teachers! We should expect, with something this important, to get clear teaching from those who claim to receive God's personal word. If God is truly speaking to these proponents of HVG theology, then maybe they could "confirm" whether Gideon's "confirmation" was an act of faith or fear. Blackaby and Batterson disagree on the purpose and function of fleeces. We need an HVG teacher to have an impression about fleeces. Of course, that won't be clear enough in and of itself, so we would need to have the impression confirmed. We need a confirmation of an impression about confirmations confirmed so we can know for sure that we can use fleeces to confirm impressions, even if they are impressions about fleeces. A confirmation of this kind is the only way we can know if an impression about confirmations is confirmed. Think of it as a fleece to confirm an impression about using fleeces to confirm impressions. While promising methods for receiving clear and sure words from God, HVG teachers sure seem confusing and unclear. They are unable to give us a clear message on how exactly we are supposed to get a clear message.

Examining the story of Gideon will go a long way toward clearing up the confusion that surrounds him. As we shall see, the example of Gideon is misused in the modern HVG movement.

GIDEON EXAMINED

Gideon lived during the time of the Judges - a series of military/political leaders God raised up to lead the nation of Israel. This period lasted from the death of Joshua (Judges 1:1) to the rise of Samuel (1 Samuel 7:15; 8:1-9). The ministry of Samuel transitioned the nation into the Jewish monarchy ruled by Saul, David, and then Solomon.

---

warped, man-made HVG paradigm. He assumes God spoke to Gideon in a "still small voice" and "impressed the message upon Gideon's heart," but there is nothing in the passage that suggests that. In fact, it's quite the opposite.

The book of Judges follows a predictable pattern. The nation would forget the goodness of God and turn to idols. God's wrath would burn against the nation bringing judgment through oppression by neighboring nations, or even people groups within their own borders. Israel, feeling the pain of temporal judgments, would cry out to God for deliverance. God would raise up a deliverer - a Judge "who delivered them from the hands of those who plundered them" (Judges 2:16). The deliverance was short-lived as the people would eventually turn from Yahweh, worship idols, and the whole process would repeat.[15] As Yogi Bera would say, "It's déjà vu all over again."[16]

Gideon came on the scene while the nation was oppressed by the Midianites for seven years (6:1). Judges 6:6 says, "So Israel was brought very low because of Midian, and the sons of Israel cried to the LORD." After the Lord sent a prophet to reprove the nation for their disobedience (vv. 7-10), we read, "Then the angel of the LORD[17] came and sat under the oak that was in Ophrah, which belonged to Joash the Abiezrite as his son Gideon was beating out wheat in the wine press in order to save it from the Midianites" (Judges 6:11). The conversation between the angel of the Lord and Gideon is recorded in Judges 6:12-18:

> The angel of the LORD appeared to him and said to him, "The LORD is with you, O valiant warrior." Then Gideon said to him, "O my lord, if the LORD is with us, why then has all this happened to us? And where are all His miracles which our fathers told us about, saying, 'Did not the LORD bring us up from Egypt?' But now the LORD has abandoned us and given us into the hand of Midian." The LORD looked at him and said, "Go in this your strength and deliver Israel from the hand of Midian. Have I not sent you?" He said to Him, "O Lord, how shall I deliver Israel? Behold, my family is the least in Manasseh, and I am the youngest in my father's house." But the LORD said to him, "Surely I will be with you, and you shall defeat Midian as one man." So Gideon said to Him, "If now I have found

---

[15] This sad history is summarized in Judges 2:11-23.

[16] https://en.wikipedia.org/wiki/Yogi_Berra#%22Yogi-isms%22.

[17] This angel was not an ordinary messenger from the angelic hosts. This was a pre-incarnate appearance of the second Person of the Trinity, the Divine Son. This same Person is identified later as "The LORD" Himself (Judges 6:14, 16, 23, 25, 27). This appearance is similar to other theophanies of Yahweh in the Old Testament (Genesis 16:7-14; 18:1; 32:24-30).

favor in Your sight, then show me a sign that it is You who speak with me. Please do not depart from here, until I come back to You, and bring out my offering and lay it before You." And He said, "I will remain until you return."

God's promise to Gideon was unambiguous: "The LORD is with you, O valiant warrior" (v. 12). Gideon questioned the promise, doubting whether the Lord was truly with them in light of their circumstances (v. 13). The command to Gideon was equally unmistakable: "Go in this your strength and deliver Israel from the hand of Midian. Have I not sent you?" (v. 14). Just as he had argued with the Lord concerning the promise, Gideon doubted the ability of God to deliver Israel through him (v. 15). The Lord repeated the promise, and the command (v. 16). Gideon responded by asking for a sign saying, "If now I have found favor in Your sight, then show me a sign that it is You who speak with me."

Though Gideon may have doubted the identity of the One Who spoke, there could be no doubt as to the meaning of what He said. Gideon was assured of two things: the Lord was with him, and he was to deliver Israel from the Midianites.

God granted Gideon's request for a sign. After he prepared a meal for the angel of the Lord, the Lord caused fire to consume it. Judges 6:20–21 says:

> The angel of God said to him, "Take the meat and the unleavened bread and lay them on this rock, and pour out the broth." And he did so. Then the angel of the LORD put out the end of the staff that was in his hand and touched the meat and the unleavened bread; and fire sprang up from the rock and consumed the meat and the unleavened bread. Then the angel of the LORD vanished from his sight.

Gideon realized with Whom he had been speaking. "When Gideon saw that he was the angel of the LORD, he said, 'Alas, O Lord GOD! For now I have seen the angel of the LORD face to face.' The LORD said to him, 'Peace to you, do not fear; you shall not die'" (Judges 6:22-23).

We haven't come to the test with the fleece yet, but already we can be certain of several things. First, *Gideon knew Who had given him instructions.* After the angel of the Lord vanished from his sight, Gideon "built an altar there to the LORD and named it The LORD is Peace" (6:24). He knew he had "seen the angel of the LORD face to face" (6:22).

Second, Gideon fully understood what God had promised and commanded. He commanded Gideon to deliver the people from Midianite oppression and promised His presence and power toward that endeavor. Gideon didn't receive an impression. He had a direct audible conversation with the angel of the Lord. God didn't whisper the command to his heart. He spoke it to Gideon's face. Gideon didn't sense a "feeling" or a "nudging." He didn't "feel led" by God through a recurring thought. Rather, the Lord manifested Himself to Gideon, face to face, and had an audible, intelligible conversation in which He told Gideon, in no uncertain terms, what he was to do.

Third, there was nothing to be confirmed. God hadn't been unclear. Though HVG teachers claim Gideon is a precedent for "confirming" God's revelation to us, there was nothing for Gideon to confirm. He knew exactly what God expected of him. Contrary to the unfounded claims of Robert Morris, God didn't whisper to Gideon's heart through a vague impression. Gideon had a full and clear conversation with the angel of the Lord.

He didn't ask for a sign out of humble faith but out of fear and doubt. Twice he argued with the Lord (6:13, 15) and three times he requested a sign (6:17, 37-40). After receiving a clear command to "pull down the altar of Baal" (6:25), Gideon obeyed and "did it by night" under the cover of darkness because "he was too afraid of his father's household and the men of the city to do it by day" (6:27). Even Gideon's act of obedience to a clear command was marked by cowardice. Gideon's problem was not clarity. It was cowardice.

HVG teachers tell us Gideon's request regarding the fleece was a desire to confirm an impression he had. There is nothing in the passage that even remotely hints at that. At no point is it even suggested that Gideon was unclear regarding what God had told him.

THE SIGN OF THE FLEECE
After Gideon tore down the alter of Baal, "all the men of the city arose" and tried to kill him for desecrating their idol (6:30). Joash, Gideon's father, refused to deliver his son over to them. The Midianites along with the Amalekites and the "sons of the east" assembled in the valley of Jezreel (6:33-35) to attack Israel.

This was Gideon's opportunity! The deliverance promised by the angel of the Lord was finally imminent. But, Gideon wanted *one more sign*. He asked for one more proof that God would keep His word and deliver Israel from their Midianite oppressors. Judges 6:33-40 says:

Then all the Midianites and the Amalekites and the sons of the east assembled themselves; and they crossed over and camped in the valley of Jezreel. So the Spirit of the LORD came upon Gideon; and he blew a trumpet, and the Abiezrites were called together to follow him. He sent messengers throughout Manasseh, and they also were called together to follow him; and he sent messengers to Asher, Zebulun, and Naphtali, and they came up to meet them. Then Gideon said to God, "If You will deliver Israel through me, as You have spoken, behold, I will put a fleece of wool on the threshing floor. If there is dew on the fleece only, and it is dry on all the ground, then I will know that You will deliver Israel through me, as You have spoken." And it was so. When he arose early the next morning and squeezed the fleece, he drained the dew from the fleece, a bowl full of water. Then Gideon said to God, "Do not let Your anger burn against me that I may speak once more; please let me make a test once more with the fleece, let it now be dry only on the fleece, and let there be dew on all the ground." God did so that night; for it was dry only on the fleece, and dew was on all the ground.

There we have it! That's the pattern promoted by HVG teachers as the God-given method for confirming personal divine revelation and guidance. Following HVG teachers, Christians pray for divine guidance by asking God to use similar fleeces to confirm what they suspect God might be whispering to them.

"Lord, if you want me to take the job in Atlanta, then let the Falcons win the football game this weekend. If you want me to take the job in Texas, then let the Cowboys win."[18]

"Lord, if you want us to buy this house, then when we arrive with the realtor, let there be blue carpet somewhere in the house. I will take blue carpet as a sign that buying this house is Your will."

"Lord, if Sue is the woman You want me to marry, then let her be wearing a dress at church this Sunday. If she is wearing pants, I'll take that as a sign she is not the one for me."

And so it goes. Life-altering decisions have been made on the basis of circumstantial happenings. God's will and whispers are

---

[18] I would object in the strongest possible way with anyone ever praying that the Dallas Cowboys might win a football game - any football game - unless the win would do harm in some way to the New England Patriots. Then, and only then, could such a prayer be allowable, and only if accompanied by great regret, contrition, and humiliation. I use this here for *illustrative* purposes only.

allegedly confirmed through signs and circumstances, treated as divinely authoritative confirmations from God.

Note three observations regarding Gideon's fleece from the narrative of Judges 6.

First, it deserves restating that Gideon was fully aware of what God had commanded and promised. We see that in the words Gideon used: "If You will deliver Israel through me, *as You have spoken*,..." (v. 36) and, "Then I will know that You will deliver Israel through me, *as You have spoken*" (v. 37).[19] Gideon didn't lack clarity regarding the revelation. He didn't need to confirm anything. The command had been so unmistakably clear that Gideon feared asking for a sign, since it might cause the anger of God to burn against him: "Do not let Your anger burn against me" (v. 39).

Gideon's request for a sign wasn't an act of confident faith but of cowardly fear. Doubt and disbelief inspired Gideon's request, not faith and humility. Even after God twice answered the request for signs, Gideon was still fearful. God directed him toward the Midianite camp so he would be strengthened by overhearing a conversation between two warriors (7:9-18).

Second, Gideon asked for two separate and distinct signs. He first asked that the fleece be wet and the ground dry. Then, on the subsequent night, Gideon requested the opposite. These were not one "confirmation" but two separate events.

Third, these were *miraculous* events, not natural happenings. A wet fleece and dry ground wasn't an ordinary happening, but a supernatural sign, a miraculous wonder that God wrought, contrary to the laws of nature, to satisfy Gideon's request.

Gideon, while doubting and fearful, clearly understood the command of God. He requested twice that God perform a miraculous sign to confirm what he already knew.

A MODEL FOR US?

Does this sound like a model for us? According to Morris, Willard, and others, Gideon is an example for the obedient, humble, and faithful Christian unclear about God's direction. Allegedly, this is another means by which we hear God's voice whispered to us. The examination of the narrative thus far is sufficient to demonstrate that the account of Gideon is stretched pretty thinly by HVG teachers. There are many problems with using Gideon as a model for modern day "confirmations."

---

[19] Emphasis mine.

First, though the actions of Gideon are *described in* Scripture, they aren't *prescribed by* Scripture. Not everything recorded in the Bible is intended to be a model for our own actions or experience. The Bible describes numerous events, actions, and experiences not intended to be patterns for us. Any sober-minded and discerning reader of Scripture *must* recognize this basic truth if they have any hope of making sense of what Scripture teaches.

The Bible describes Jesus walking on water, raising the dead, and multiplying bread and fishes. It describes Jesus' encounters with the demonic, His exorcisms, and His death on the cross, but we aren't commanded to duplicate any of them. Moses parted the Red Sea, struck a rock for water, and had a conversation with God in a burning bush, but these should never be interpreted as normative experiences for the believer. Elijah killed the prophets of Baal, and Paul struck a magician blind for his opposition to the gospel. Only the most extreme and undiscerning reader would think these are the normative experiences of believers. Why should we think Gideon's request for a divine sign is intended as a model for us? Why do HVG teachers think *this* is a model and not King Saul's consultation with a medium (1 Samuel 28)? They make a distinction between what is *described* and what is *prescribed* concerning King Saul, but their discretion vanishes with Gideon.

Second, there is *no* command in Scripture to follow this model. The apostles never cite Gideon as a model for decision-making or confirming God's will. Scripture doesn't promise God will "confirm" His Word[20] through circumstantial tests. In the New Testament, the apostles speak freely about knowing and doing the will of God,[21] but they never once suggest it can be discerned by Gideon-like fleeces.

Third, other than Gideon, there are no examples of such "fleeces" anywhere in Scripture. If this were intended as a model for believers, we would expect to see it numerous times in Scripture. We would expect to find it taught and modeled in the New Testament. We require instruction on fleeces: when to use a fleece, what kinds of fleeces to use, and how to avoid a "false positive." There is nothing in Scripture providing this necessary instruction.

---

[20] In this sense HVG advocates mean private revelations whispered in our minds or hearts.

[21] These are references to the moral will of God clearly revealed in the pages of Scripture and never to a hidden or secret will revealed through impressions and fleeces. See Chapters 3-7 in *Decision Making and the Will of God* by Garry Friesen.

Fourth, it's clear that modern HVG teachers *misuse* the example of Gideon. They claim Gideon's fleece test was motivated by faith and humility. It wasn't. They claim "putting out a fleece" will confirm an uncertain private revelation. Gideon was already certain of what God had said. They claim this is a method for modern decision-making. Gideon wasn't trying to make a decision.

HVG teachers don't get the details of Gideon's fleece right. They claim God will indicate which of two alternatives we are to choose by confirming one over the other through circumstantial signs. If that were true, Gideon's fleece would have looked something like this: "Lord, if it's Your will that I attack the Midianites, then let the ground be dry and the fleece wet. If it's not your will for me to attack the Midianite camp, then let the ground be wet and the fleece dry." That isn't what Gideon did.

He knew the obedient course because God had clearly revealed it to him. Gideon wanted another sign. After the sign was provided, he asked for yet another to confirm the exact same thing. Ironically, while touting Gideon as a model, HVG teachers don't follow his example.

Fifth, Gideon asked for a *supernatural* sign. On the first night he requested a wet fleece and dry ground. On the second night he asked that the ground be wet and the fleece dry. The answer to these requests involved supernatural intervention. Gideon requested a *miracle* not a common, ordinary happenstance.

This isn't what you typically hear Christians do today. If Gideon is the model, then those who use fleeces to determine God's will should follow it just as Gideon demonstrated. Most Christians will typically use lame fleeces - fleeces which are impotent, subjective, and require no miraculous intervention by God. These are coincidences or happenstance.

Asking God to provide direction through a normal life event (an available parking space, someone answering a phone, the color of carpet in a house, etc.) requires *no* miraculous intervention. That isn't following Gideon's model! It is time for HVG teachers to up their game. If we expect God to speak today, just like in Bible times, and if we are going to expect God to confirm His Word through signs, then let's go all in. Let's follow Gideon's example!

Here is what a fleece *should* look like. "Lord, if you want me to take that job, then when I wake up tomorrow morning, let my cherry tree be loaded with apples hanging from the branches." Now THAT would be a Gideon-like fleece! Or how about this: "Lord, if I am supposed to go on the missions trip, then make my car levitate off the ground." Or, "Lord, if it is your will for me to start this ministry at church, then show me a sign - make water come out of this rock." There's at least biblical precedent for that (Exodus 17:1-7). If we really want to make our "confirmations" follow the biblical models, we should ask for God to turn rods into snakes (Exodus 4:1-5), make the sun stand still (Joshua 10:13), or make a sundial move backwards (Isaiah 38:8). If you're going to commit to Gideon's model, then *commit* to Gideon's model. Stop with the half measures and wimpy fleeces! Ask for confirmations that leave no room for doubt.

That leads us to the sixth problem. Fleeces are liable to produce "false positives." Mark Batterson recognizes this danger when he cautions, "If you don't define the fleece, it's easy to come up with false negatives or false positives."[22]

What good does a "confirmation" do if it's prone to produce false results? The fleece is supposed to remove all doubt and confirm an impression, but it ends up producing no more certainty than all the other subjective means of "hearing from God." Since the terms of the fleece are chosen by the decision-maker, it's impossible to know with certainty that God has actually answered. How are we to *know* if we have put the proper parameters in place given that Scripture offers *no* instruction on this? Why should we assume that if we dictate the proper construct of circumstantial signs, God is obligated to arrange our reality accordingly? What's the proper construct of circumstantial signs?

The absurdity of this practice is illustrated in an episode of *The Simpson's*, where Homer is kneeling next to his bed praying:

> Dear Lord, the gods have been good to me and I am thankful. For the first time in my life everything is absolutely perfect the way it is. So here's the deal: You freeze everything as it is and I won't ask for anything more. If that is okay, please give me absolutely no sign. [pause] Okay, deal. In gratitude, I present to you this offering of cookies and milk. If you want me to eat them for you, please give me no sign. [pause] Thy will be done.[23]

Of course, Homer eats the cookies and milk.

---

[22] Batterson, *Whisper*, 108–9.

[23] This scene is available at https://www.youtube.com/watch?v=GxMJNmj5Iml (2:00 mark). Episode 2F10, "And Maggie Makes Three," original airdate January 22, 1995. I found this illustration in the notes of *Decision Making and the Will of God* audio series by Gregory Koukl of Stand to Reason (str.org).

Many Christians, thinking they are following Gideon's example, end up doing something very similar. They construct a fleece scenario that confirms what they want to hear God say to them. How can you ever be sure you haven't "loaded" the test in a manner that would produce an inaccurate outcome?[24] How can you be sure that Satan isn't keeping you from God's best by tricking you into a "false negative" or a "false positive"? There is only one way to know for sure - ask for a real Gideon-like sign. It has to be a miracle!

The entire HVG paradigm is fraught with subjective uncertainty and confusion. Why anyone would trust these methods for a "clear word from God" shall forever remain a mystery to me.

A LAST WORD ON GIDEON

There is one final issue regarding Gideon that we must address, namely, "How does everything I have written in this chapter fit the mention of Gideon in Hebrews?" The New Testament mentions Gideon and it seems contrary to what I have written of him here. Outside Judges 6-8, there is only one mention of Gideon in the rest of the Bible: "And what more shall I say? For time will fail me if I tell of Gideon, Barak, Samson, Jephthah, of David and Samuel and the prophets" (Hebrews 11:32).

Gideon is listed in the "Faith Hall of Fame," among other great examples of faith including, Able, Enoch, Noah, Abraham, Moses, Joshua, and Rahab. So, if Gideon is listed as a hero of faith (whom the author of Hebrews seems to suggest is worthy of emulating), how can I say he was fearful and *not* worthy of emulating? It does appear that my description of Gideon runs contrary to that in Hebrews 11:32.

I am not suggesting *nothing* in Gideon's life is worth emulating. I am saying that his fearful request for confirming signs is not worthy of emulating. Gideon is commended for an act of faith, namely, he finally believed God would deliver Midian into his hands (Judges 7:15-18) and attacked the Midianite camp with only 300 men, just as God had directed (Judges 7:1-8). Gideon's obedience, even after so many doubts, is a commendable act of faith. By it, he "conquered kingdoms" and "put foreign armies to flight" (Hebrews

------

[24] HVG believers might counter by suggesting that God will make sure to confirm His Word by providing confirmation according to whatever parameters we choose. However, Scripture hasn't promised this. Scripture doesn't suggest that God is obligated to confirm anything to our dictates at any time for any reason. We can make no demands on God to provide us signs according to whatever suits our fancy.

11:33-34). Gideon's request for a sign wasn't an act of faith and isn't commended by the author of Hebrews.

If one is going to argue that Gideon's act of faith in attacking Midian makes everything else he did a model worth following, then do you also commend his idolatry (8:22-26), polygamy (8:30), and adulterous fornication (8:31)? Gideon's obedience by which he defeated Midian was commendable. Doubting God's Word and asking for signs was not!

Gideon was a deeply flawed man, just like the other men listed alongside him in Hebrews 11: Barak, Samson, Jephthah, David, and Samuel. He serves as both a positive example (obey in faith) and a negative example (avoid idolatry and adultery). He is a vivid reminder of what God can do through mere men, even deeply flawed and doubting men. His act of obedient faith is praiseworthy. His fearful doubting of God's promise isn't. Gideon's fleece is an example of the latter.

Chapter 12

I Had a Peace About It!

12

I didn't have a peace about it! In fact, I was certain he would be the downfall of the Bible college.

During my second year at Millar, the school administrators were looking to hire a faculty member to oversee the new "Fourth Year Program." After considering several applicants, the academic committee decided to pursue a candidate working on his doctorate at Dallas Theological Seminary. His resume looked good. It looked *really* good.

They announced the decision to the student body during a chapel service. The applicant was coming to the school to interview for the position. His name was Phil. Phil would teach some classes, preach a couple of sermons, and mingle with the student body. Everyone on campus was excited to meet Phil. He arrived on campus and was introduced to the student body. He preached a morning chapel service, taught some classes, and preached the Sunday morning and evening services.

I started to sense something was wrong. After the Sunday evening service, I began to have serious doubts - an uneasy feeling deep in my heart. I sensed the man was dangerous. Poison. Bad news. I was sure of it. I may have used the phrase "wolf in sheep's clothing" to describe the danger I sensed. It was an impression I couldn't shake. Something was amiss, but I couldn't put my finger on it. I had a check in my spirit. I didn't have a peace about Phil. At first, I kept my concerns to myself, but eventually I shared my concerns with a couple of close friends. "You just wait," I said. "This man will turn out to be a false teacher - the ruination of this school!"

The "impression" about Phil was confirmed by a "check in the spirit," an absence of peace in my heart. The Bible warned about false teachers. The Scriptures, my impression, and my inner sense of peace all indicated the same thing: this man was bad news.

Whatever became of Phil? The college hired him. I gladly admit that I couldn't have been more wrong! Phil Powers was a fantastic addition to the Millar staff! Yes, this is the same Phil Powers mentioned in the acknowledgments of this book. An extraordinary teacher, a gifted expositor, and a superb theologian, Phil is one of the most gracious, humble, and generous men I have ever met. He and his wife, Neva, were a rich blessing to staff and students. He is one of the hardest working, most intelligent, mature, and godly men I have had the pleasure of knowing. In fact, he was my teacher when I came back for a fourth year at Millar. He taught me to preach. He was my counselor, mentor, and friend. Phil had a profound impact on my life and preaching ministry. His influence on my thinking resulted in this book as well as my book on spiritual warfare.[1]

MY EXPERIENCE PROVES NOTHING

Everything indicated that God was speaking to me. First, I felt a prompting (a still small voice) warning me of danger. Second, I lacked peace in my heart (sometimes referred to as "a check in the spirit"). Third, God's Word has something to say about false teachers and every time I read those passages, I sensed confirmation of my impression. All three agreed: the still small voice, the internal peace, and the Word of God. Each "voice" confirmed the others.

I could cite my own experience as proof the HVG methodology is false and unreliable, but my experience proves nothing. Someone else could easily produce an example of a time when a hunch turned out to be accurate, and so could I. HVG teachers load their books with these counterexamples. Bill Hybels' book, *The Power of a Whisper*, is bereft of biblical teaching and exegesis, but packed with stories of people hearing whispers and acting on them. In nearly every instance cited, things turned out well. Negative examples, if mentioned at all, illustrate failure to pay heed to some important element of the HVG method for hearing from God.

Experience *proves* nothing. Someone's positive experience doesn't prove God speaks through these means. My negative experience isn't proof that He doesn't. The fundamental question is:

---

[1] Jim Osman, *Truth or Territory: A Biblical Approach To Spiritual Warfare* (Kootenai: Kootenai Community Church Publishing, 2015).

"Does Scripture teach that God speaks to us through the absence or presence of an inner peace?"

THE INDISPENSABLE "PEACE"

According to HVG teachers, the "internal peace" is an indispensable component of hearing God speak. Nearly everyone who believes God speaks to us outside Scripture relies in some measure - great or small - on a feeling of internal peace. Most cite Colossians 3:15 as the key biblical text: "Let the peace of Christ rule in your hearts, to which indeed you were called in one body; and be thankful."

Charles Stanley writes:

When God speaks, one of the most prevalent signs is a sense of calmness in the spirit. It may not be tranquil at first. In fact, it may be full of conflict and strife, but the longer we listen, the quieter and more peaceful our spirits become. We begin to possess what the Apostle Paul called a peace "which surpasses all understanding" (Phil. 4:7). It is a peace that surrounds us like a fortress and keeps us from being overwhelmed with anxiety, worry, and frustration.[2]

Describing a time he felt peace in the midst of turmoil, Stanley says, "When that sort of peace comes to us, we *know* we've heard from God, and we are *confident* it is His Voice."[3] He cites Colossians 3:15.

Morris treats "peace" as God's confirmation of His Word: "This was the confirmation I was looking for. A peace that passes understanding came over me. The confirmation was felt deep in my heart."[4] Morris suggests we ask three questions to "confirm if we've heard a word from God."[5] The third question is, "Does peace reign in your heart?" Borrowing the language of Colossians 3:15, which he cites in that section, Morris writes, "You will have peace. This is one of the greatest confirmations of God's voice." Later he says, "If you have a feeling of unease in your heart and mind about a matter, then God probably does not want you to head down that road. But

---

[2] Stanley, *How to Listen to God*, 61.

[3] Ibid., 62. Emphasis mine.

[4] Morris, *Frequency*, 43.

[5] Ibid., 110–13. These three questions are: 1. Does it line up with the Bible? 2. Does godly counsel agree? 3. Does peace reign in your heart?

if God's peace is evident in a matter, then this is one of the main ways we can know if we've heard the voice of God."[6]

Priscilla Shirer makes much out of the "internal peace." In her book, *Discerning the Voice of God*, in a chapter titled "He Brings Peace" she claims, "As you grow in your relationship with Him, learning how to hear His voice and respond in obedience, *peace becomes one of your determining factors in knowing* when He is leading and speaking to you."[7] She likens peace to "getting a 'green light.'"[8] She writes, "It's the same way in hearing from God. As you sense His leading, ask yourself, 'Am I sensing a "green light" in my spirit? Am I confident and at peace about moving forward, *even if* I don't like what I'm being compelled to do?'"[9]

Citing Colossians 3:15 she claims that common decisions like which job to take, which employee to hire, which contractor to use on a remodel, and even whether to take a ministry position, can all be determined by paying "close attention to what you're hearing and sensing."[10] According to Shirer, this is how "peace reigns in a matter," namely, when "God's voice is accompanied by deep assurance and permission."[11]

For Shirer, the sense of inner peace is indispensable, "When it comes to discerning His voice, always remember. . . Peace rules."[12] Shirer quotes Kay Arthur saying, "A reigning sense of God's peace confirms His voice to me. There may have been turmoil getting to that peace, but when I have settled in on His desire for me, I am assured of that by the peace that accompanies it."[13] Mark Batterson assures us that "one of the best ways to gauge the will of God is to discern whether or not the peace of Christ is ruling in your heart."[14]

Joyce Meyer claims, "inner peace" is the single greatest evidence God is speaking outside Scripture saying, "You might ask, 'Joyce, how do you know for sure God was talking to you, that your mind was not just making it up?' The answer is that I had peace

---

[6] Ibid., 113.

[7] Shirer, *Discerning the Voice of God*, 108. Emphasis mine.

[8] Ibid.,

[9] Ibid., 109.

[10] Ibid., 110.

[11] Ibid.

[12] Ibid., 111.

[13] Ibid.

[14] Batterson, *Whisper*, 40.

about what I was receiving. It felt right inside me. My spirit confirmed it as being truly from the Lord."[15]

For Meyer, the internal sense of peace determines *everything*. She says, "I run my life by finding peace."[16] Taking nearly any verse that mentions "peace" out of context and misapplying it, Meyer tries to make the case that "When God speaks, He gives us a deep sense of internal peace to confirm that the message is truly from Him,"[17] and, "Peace is true confirmation that you are hearing from God."[18]

Appealing to Colossians 3:15 as a proof text, she says, "We should never act without peace. One might say that peace is an 'internal confirmation' that action being taken is approved of by God."[19] She claims the "inner peace" is essential for decision-making and counsels, "Don't make serious decisions and commitments without doing an 'inner check' to see if true peace abides within you."[20]

We could summarize HVG teaching on "the peace" with the following three statements:

First, God speaks through "peace in the heart." This peace "surpasses all understanding" (Philippians 4:7). It is an inner feeling, a calmness and tranquility of heart, even in the midst of chaos. The "peace" is the voice of God in your heart signaling His will in a decision, His approval of an action, or His confirmation of an impression.

Second, it is an essential, certain, and reliable means of confirming the voice of God. Peace is an unfailing confirmation of the voice of God. It is the means by which we *know* God has spoken. His voice will *always* be accompanied by a peaceful disposition of the heart.

Third, Colossians 3:15 teaches this. Colossians 3:15 is the primary text that instructs us to govern our lives, make our decisions, and confirm God's voice by an internal peace.

Colossians 3:15 is the *only passage* pressed into service to teach that a peace in the heart is the voice of God. It's the only passage where HVG teachers make an attempt at exegesis to

---

[15] Meyer, *How to Hear from God*, 23.

[16] Ibid., 82.

[17] Ibid., 81.

[18] Ibid., 82.

[19] Ibid.

[20] Ibid., 84.

prove this claim. Consequently, the assessment of this teaching is very straightforward. We simply have to determine if Colossians 3:15 teaches that "inner peace" is the voice of God for decision-making and guidance.

THE HVG CASE FOR COLOSSIANS 3:15

Colossians 3:15: "Let the peace of Christ rule in your hearts, to which indeed you were called in one body; and be thankful."

The entire HVG case for hearing the voice of God through an inner peace rests on Colossians 3:15, and I do mean the *entire case*. If you have never been exposed to HVG theology and the accompanying method of decision-making, then you are likely wondering what the verse has to do with hearing the voice of God. Here is how HVG teachers make their case.

Robert Morris claims Colossians 3:15 "is a foundational verse."[21] Attempting to explain the significance of the verse through weak exegesis, he writes, "The word *rule* used here (*brabeuo* in Greek) means so much more than simply to let peace be present in your hearts. This verse is not simply a call to chill out. The word *rule* in the Greek means 'to be an umpire.' It means 'to reign' or 'to arbitrate, judge, decide, or control.'"[22]

Shirer makes the same case:

> The Greek word for "rule" is significant. It means to act as a judge or umpire. So Paul was telling the church that in the same way a modern day baseball umpire manages a game according to the rules, the Holy Spirit was to serve as the "umpire of their hearts," and the Colossians were to make decisions in accordance with His calls. Christ wanted the Colossians to be committed to and ruled by the assurance given or not given by His Spirit as they sought to discern God's will. In other words, His peace wasn't supposed to be merely a part of their lives; it was to rule them, direct them, and govern everything they did.[23]

Shirer applies this principle to decisions about jobs, ministries, contractors, and career changes. Allegedly, just as a baseball umpire calls balls and strikes, the "peace in our hearts" gives us a green light or red light in confirming the voice of God for decision-

---

[21] Morris, *Frequency*, 113.

[22] Ibid. In the very next paragraph, he cites Philippians 4:7: "And the peace of God, which surpasses all comprehension, will guard your hearts and your minds in Christ Jesus."

[23] Shirer, *Discerning the Voice of God*, 109–10.

making. Or as Joyce Meyer summarizes it, "The Bible says that peace is like an umpire that decides what is 'safe' or what is 'out.' No peace? It's 'out'! We are to *let* the inner harmony in our minds and souls rule and act as an umpire continually in our hearts, deciding and settling with finality all questions that arise in our minds."[24]

Is that what Paul meant?

THE TEACHING OF COLOSSIANS 3:15

Colossians 3:15 has a context and it isn't friendly to HVG claims regarding this verse. It's obvious from HVG teaching on Colossians 3:15 that they give no thought, and even less exegesis to the larger context. I suspect that few, if any, would be able to explain the context and how their interpretation of the verse fits with it.

Colossians 3 begins with a grand statement of our identification with Jesus Christ.[25] Since we have "died with Christ" (2:20) and "been raised up with Christ" (3:1), we have been freed from sin (3:5). The implications of our union with Christ are explained in 3:5-11. We are to "consider the members of [our] earthly body as dead to" all sins mentioned in those verses. Believers have put those sins aside (v. 8-9) and have "put on the new self" (v. 10) fashioned after the image of Christ. United in Jesus Christ and brought together in one body (the Church), believers enjoy a fellowship "in which there is no distinction between the Greek and Jew, circumcised and uncircumcised, barbarian, Scythian, slave and freeman, but Christ is all, and in all" (3:11).

Addressing a church filled with individual believers of various ethnicities and nationalities, Paul instructed them to live in harmony with one another (3:12-13). He described a perfect unity, a spiritual communion in the church where racial, ethnic, national, tribal, and social distinctions mean nothing. In contrast to the sins listed in the previous paragraph (vv. 5-11), Paul commends the virtues that mark "those who have been chosen of God, holy and beloved." Though addressing the corporate body, the individual instructions to God's elect, when obeyed, will have a salutary impact on the unity and love in the body of Christ.

---

[24] Meyer, *How to Hear from God*, 82.

[25] I would strongly encourage the reader to read the entire passage for themselves. Don't take my word for it. Read the context! For the sake of space, I will cite the verse numbers here without quoting the passage at length.

That brings us to the paragraph that includes v.15:

So, as those who have been chosen of God, holy and beloved, put on a heart of compassion, kindness, humility, gentleness and patience; bearing with one another, and forgiving each other, whoever has a complaint against anyone; just as the Lord forgave you, so also should you. Beyond all these things put on love, which is the perfect bond of unity. *Let the peace of Christ rule in your hearts, to which indeed you were called in one body; and be thankful.* Let the word of Christ richly dwell within you, with all wisdom teaching and admonishing one another with psalms and hymns and spiritual songs, singing with thankfulness in your hearts to God. Whatever you do in word or deed, do all in the name of the Lord Jesus, giving thanks through Him to God the Father. (Colossians 3:12–17, emphasis mine)

Ignore for a moment the italicized words (v. 15) in question. Judging from the first part of the paragraph, what would you say Paul is addressing? What is the subject matter?

Notice the repetition of the words "one another" and "each other" in verses 13 and 16. Compassion, kindness, humility, gentleness, patience, forbearing, forgiving, and loving, all commanded in verses 12-14, must characterize our treatment of *one another*. These describe the manner in which believers, in the body of Christ, relate to each other. Selfless, others-centered love in the body of Christ produces a perfect bond of unity (v. 14). Those graces, flowing from new life in Christ, promote *harmony and peace* among brethren in the congregation.

Skipping over verse 15 for the moment, we can see how the rest of the paragraph also describes our relationships within the body of Christ. Being filled with the Word of God; we are to be "teaching and admonishing *one another* with psalms and hymns and spiritual songs, singing with thankfulness in your hearts to God" (3:16). This describes the selfless, others-centered living that must characterize a congregation of blood-bought saints.

This passage instructs believers on harmonious living in the body of Christ. That Paul was dealing with interpersonal relationships is made abundantly clear in the next few paragraphs as he focused on specific relationships within the church. Verses 18-19 touch on the husband/wife relationship. Verses 20-21 deal with the parent/child relationship. Verses 3:22-4:1 address the relationship between masters and slaves. Clearly, Paul was concerned with how believers, in the context of various social and family relationships, treat one another.

This passage has *nothing* to do with decision-making or confirming divine revelation. Paul wasn't giving guidelines for confirming impressions and making decisions. He was reminding them of the Christlike virtues that characterize a Spirit-filled believer. HVG teachers claim Paul wants us to look inward to a personal feeling of peace. Actually, he told them to look outward to the interests of others. Verse 15 isn't about how we feel, but about how we treat others. HVG teaching on this passage completely misses the point.

Read the paragraph again, and this time, let's insert the HVG meaning of verse 15 into the paragraph and see if it makes sense:

> So, as those who have been chosen of God, holy and beloved, put on a heart of compassion, kindness, humility, gentleness and patience; bearing with one another, and forgiving each other, whoever has a complaint against anyone; just as the Lord forgave you, so also should you. Beyond all these things put on love, which is the perfect bond of unity. [*Let the feeling of inner peace in your heart act as an umpire in your daily, individual decision-making. It is God's confirmation of His whispers. Always be led by the inner feeling of peace.*] Let the word of Christ richly dwell within you, with all wisdom teaching and admonishing one another with psalms and hymns and spiritual songs, singing with thankfulness in your hearts to God. Whatever you do in word or deed, do all in the name of the Lord Jesus, giving thanks through Him to God the Father. (Colossians 3:12–17, with my insertion)

Does that fit the context?

"PEACE" AND "THE UMPIRE"

If verse 15 is not about an "internal peace" acting as a judge to confirm God's voice, then what is Paul talking about?

The key to understanding this verse is not the word "rule" but the word "peace." HVG teachers *assume* this is an inner feeling of tranquility in the heart. They never stop to consider whether or not that definition of "peace" even fits the context.

The word translated "peace" can have two different meanings First, it can refer to an inner harmony or emotional tranquility. Th

173

is how it is used in Philippians 4:7.[26] Second, it can refer to a "lack of conflict between two parties" who were formerly at enmity with each other as in Ephesians 2:14-15.[27] Paul uses it that way in Romans 5:1: "Therefore, having been justified by faith, we have *peace with God* through our Lord Jesus Christ."[28] The result of our justification is peace with God.[29] Hostilities have ceased. We aren't under God's wrath. Once His enemies, we have been reconciled through the work of Jesus Christ. Which definition of "peace" do you think best fits the context, "an inner feeling of tranquility" or "a lack of conflict between two parties formerly at enmity"?

Remember the context. In the preceding paragraph, Paul described the church as a body in which there is "no distinction between Greek and Jew, circumcised and uncircumcised, barbarian, Scythian, slave and freeman." Outside the church, all of those ethnic, national, and social distinctions created conflict. Jews hated Gentiles and Gentiles hated Jews. Slaves hated their masters, and masters hated their slaves. In the world, every social structure, societal category, and ethnic tribe, is in a constant state of opposition, war, and hostility against various other factions. Hostility, war, and enmity are the norm *outside the church.*

When believers obey the commands of Colossians 3:12-14 and "put on a heart of compassion, kindness, humility, gentleness and patience," "bear with one another," "forgive one another," and "put on love" for one another, the result is peace. A body of Christians characterized by these qualities will dwell together in peace, regardless of their former worldly distinctions. Hostility, strife, and enmity between husbands and wives (3:18-19), children and parents (3:20-21), and slaves and Masters (3:22-4:1) will dissolve.

---

[26] Philippians 4:7: "And the peace of God, which surpasses all comprehension, will guard your hearts and your minds in Christ Jesus." As in Colossians 3:15, Paul is not talking about decision-making or hearing the voice of God. Philippians 4:7 describes a state of spiritual tranquility (the opposite of anxiety mentioned in v.6) resulting from prayer offered in a spirit of thanksgiving. Our continual trust in the Lord, which manifests itself in a comprehensive prayer life, brings a settled peace in our spirit and freedom from anxiety.

[27] Ephesians 2:14–15: "For He Himself is our peace, who made both groups into one and broke down the barrier of the dividing wall, by abolishing in His flesh the enmity, which is the Law of commandments contained in ordinances, so that in Himself He might make the two into one new man, thus establishing peace."

[28] Emphasis mine.

[29] Justification is the judicial act of God whereby He declares "righteous" the believing sinner based on the merits of the work of Christ alone through faith alone by grace alone.

Again, judging from the context, which definition of "peace" fits the passage? Paul was describing a "lack of conflict between two parties" formerly at enmity. This peace was to so characterize the Colossian believers that it would "rule and control" the life of the congregation as they lived in harmony in the body of Christ.

The word translated "rule" is the word *brabeuo* (βραβεύω). According to the Theological Dictionary of the New Testament:

> Common from the time of Euripides, this word refers originally to the activity of the umpire (βραβεύς, βραβευτής) whose office at the games is to direct, arbitrate and decide the contest. In the wider sense it then comes to mean "to order," "rule," or "control." The translators were correct to translate this word "rule" rather than "act as an umpire." [30]

Paul was not saying "peace" should act as a "red light" or "green light" for decision-making and confirming God's voice. He was teaching that peace among those formerly at enmity must control the hearts of the Colossian believers as evidence of their love for one another.

That is quite different from the interpretation offered by HVG teachers! In fairness, we should read the entire paragraph and see if the interpretation I have offered makes sense in the context. Does it fit the flow of Paul's instruction? In place of Paul's words in verse 15, I have inserted the interpretation I have offered:

> So, as those who have been chosen of God, holy and beloved, put on a heart of compassion, kindness, humility, gentleness and patience; bearing with one another, and forgiving each other, whoever has a complaint against anyone; just as the Lord forgave you, so also should you. Beyond all these things put on love, which is the perfect bond of unity. [*Let peace between people once at enmity, the peace that results from our reconciliation in Christ, rule in your hearts and govern your treatment of one another, since you were called one body, and do this with thankfulness.*] Let the word of Christ richly dwell within you, with all wisdom teaching and admonishing one another with psalms and hymns and spiritual songs, singing with thankfulness in your hearts to God. Whatever you do in

---

[30] E. Stauffer (1964–). βραβεύω, βραβεῖον. G. Kittel, G. W. Bromiley, & G. Friedrich (Eds.), Theological Dictionary of the New Testament (electronic ed., Vol. 1, pp. 637–638). Grand Rapids, MI: Eerdmans.

word or deed, do all in the name of the Lord Jesus, giving thanks through Him to God the Father. (Colossians 3:12–17, with my insertion.)

It fits quite well. That understanding of "peace" and "rule" fits the previous context and makes sense with the rest of verse 15. HVG teachers typically ignore the rest of verse 15, quoting only the first half of the verse: "Let the peace of Christ reign in your hearts." They don't bother to cite the rest of the verse: "... to which indeed you were called in one body; and be thankful." Nor do they attempt to explain how their interpretation fits it. Paul wasn't talking about an internal peace that confirms God's voice. He was describing our relationships within the body of Christ! That is why Paul mentions being "called in one body." HVG teachers don't just ignore the preceding context, they ignore *the rest of the sentence.* They take a passage describing relationships in the congregation and turn it into a passage describing their feelings about a decision. That is an egregious abuse of a biblical text!

This passage has *nothing* to do with decision-making or hearing the voice of God. That topic was nowhere near the mind of Paul as he wrote those words. To teach otherwise is to completely miss the point of the whole passage.

THE PROBLEMS WITH THE "PEACE"
HVG teachers take Colossians 3:15 out of context. They abuse the text to prop up their specious modern doctrine of hearing God's voice. Only strong tradition coupled with entrenched Christian lingo could cause one to think this passage is a reference to "inner peace" that confirms God's voice. That isn't the only problem with the HVG view of inner peace. Here are a few more.

First, as with the other alleged sources of God's voice, this is inherently subjective. Rather than pointing us to an objective source of divine truth (the Word of God), HVG teaching tells us to look for the will of God in our feelings and ever-fluctuating emotions. This approach to decision-making has great potential for disaster and ruin. Scripture *never* directs believers to determine God's will by their feelings. Never!

Second, often doing the right thing, the biblical thing, can be very unsettling. Do you think Moses had a peace about going to Egypt to deliver Israel (Exodus 3:11, 13; 4:1, 10, 13)? Did Gideon have a peace about attacking the Midianites (Judges 6:17, 27, 36-40; 7:9-14)? Did Joshua have a peace about taking over for Moses (Joshua 1:1-9)? What if you waited until you were at peace in your heart before you shared the gospel with someone? Would you ever do it? Would anyone ever do it?

Third, there is an opposite danger, namely, doing something foolish or unbiblical because you "had a peace in your heart." It's possible to have a peace about things that are clearly wrong. I've heard people justify the most unbiblical and immoral choices claiming, "I prayed about it and I have a peace about it." I know a woman who had an affair, divorced her husband, and continued to live in unrepentant adultery, all while claiming she had a peace about her decisions. Try talking to someone about the wisdom or morality of a decision they believe was confirmed through an "inner peace," and you will find out how utterly disastrous this teaching can be.

HVG teachers will counter by claiming that the "inner peace" and the "Word of God" must agree. If a peace in the heart is contrary to Scripture, then it should not be followed. According to them, this serves as a check on the abuse of this method. But if the Word of God has something to say on an issue, then of what value is peace in the heart? If Scripture already provides guidance, why would anyone need an inner peace to confirm it? If Scripture doesn't speak on the issue, then it can't serve as a check to protect against abusing the inner peace.

HVG theology treats peace in the heart as a source of divine revelation, the means by which we *know* we are hearing from God. Thus, it's authoritative and binding. Given a choice between the Word of God (written to a different people at a different time half a world away) and the inner word of God (spoken directly to the heart in the here and now), which will the HVG believer choose? Will they obey the "fresh word of God" or the ancient Scriptures? Will they follow today's feelings or a command given to someone else 2,000 years ago? Ninety-nine times out of one hundred they will choose a "whisper from God" over the Word of God. They will choose the personal, authoritative whisper over an impersonal authoritative Word nearly every time. What else should we expect when people are taught to be guided and ruled by their feelings?

In theory, HVG teachers believe the Word of God acts as a check against an illegitimate or unbiblical peace. In practice, they fail to appreciate the depth of corruption and self-deception that resides in the human heart. To quote a sage of our age, "The heart

177

wants what it wants."[31] When you tell the heart that a feeling of peace constitutes the voice of God and provides authoritative divine direction, you have a recipe for a moral disaster. This is why Scripture *never* tells us to make decisions based on a feeling of peace. This is why the Word of God is our only source of divine revelation.

Why would we rely on the feelings of the human heart, notoriously fickle, wicked, and unreliable as they are? We're easily deceived by our feelings. We don't need our feelings *to confirm* the truth of Scripture. We need our feelings to be *conformed by* the truth of Scripture.

Our feelings are just feelings. They are no sure guide of truth.

---

[31] According to online sources, those words were written by Emily Dickinson and used by Woody Allen and Selena Gomez.

Chapter 13

I Felt Led

13

"I felt led . . ."

"The Lord led me . . . "

"The Lord is leading me to . . . "

It's difficult to determine what someone means when they say, "The Lord led me to. . ."

They may be speaking of a random thought they believe is the leading of the Lord: "The Lord led me to pray for you. This morning I was out for a walk and you came to mind."

It may describe a feeling they had: "The Lord led me to write the letter. I felt so strongly that I should, and I just couldn't shake it."

They may be describing a series of events that led them to take action: "I got a $1,000 bonus check this week. At church, a visiting missionary said their African mission is raising $1,000 for a new well. Then, in the restaurant after church, we heard the song *Africa* by Toto. These are signs God is leading me to give my bonus check to the African missionary."

The language is used to describe a message received through an elaborate system employed for hearing and confirming the "voice of God": "The Lord led me to volunteer for the children's ministry. I felt an impression that I should volunteer for it. The Lord opened that door and while praying about it, I sensed the Spirit whisper in my ear, 'You lead.' I asked the Lord to confirm His will through a fleece. I decided that if the position wasn't filled by next Sunday, I would take that as the Lord's confirmation that I should volunteer. I prayed about it again and heard the still small voice nudging me to volunteer. On Saturday, while reading through 2 Kings 19 I saw these words in verse 3: 'For *children* have come to birth and there is no *strength* to deliver.' The words 'children' and 'strength' jumped off the page at me. I felt the Holy Spirit speak to my heart through that verse and promise me *strength* to serve in the *children's* ministry. I sensed a peace fill my heart. On Sunday, the Lord confirmed the fleece when I heard the position was still open. I volunteered."[1]

THE COMMON TEACHING

The Bible describes Christians as those "led by the Spirit." Two specific passages use this language:

Romans 8:14: "For all who are being *led by the Spirit* of God, these are sons of God."

Galatians 5:18: "But if you are *led by the Spirit*, you are not under the Law."

This terminology is so commonly and widely used in evangelical circles that I was surprised to find that, among the many HVG teachers I have read, only two cited Romans 8 and none referenced Galatians 5. Wayne Grudem's work on this subject is a notable exception to the pattern. Grudem is a reformed theologian responsible for excellent exegetical and theological contributions in a number of areas. He is also a continuationist[2] who has given substantial attention to Romans 8 and Galatians 5 in attempts to defend his belief in private revelations.[3]

Though references to these passages are rare among HVG teachers, the use of the language is not. They commonly use "I felt led" verbiage to speak of receiving personal divine direction for

---

[1] That scenario incorporates nearly every aspect of this methodology I have critiqued thus far.

[2] "Continuationism" is the belief that miraculous sign gifts of the New Testament continue in operation within the church today. All New Apostolic Reformation, Word of Faith, Charismatic, and Pentecostal theological streams are continuationist in theology. There is a growing movement within conservative, reformed, Calvinistic evangelicalism that promotes an "open but cautious" approach to the revelatory gifts. They are open to the gifts of tongues, word of knowledge, and prophecy, and some believe they should be cultivated in the church today. Wayne Grudem is the most notable theologian in a reformed continuationist camp that includes John Piper, D.A. Carson, Sam Storms, Matt Chandler, and C.J. Mahaney of Sovereign Grace Ministries. I will address Grudem's arguments later in the chapter.

[3] Grudem deals with these texts as part of a response to Garry Friesen's book *Decision Making and the Will of God* in his own book *Christian Ethics* (Grudem, *Christian Ethics: An Introduction to Biblical Moral Reasoning*, pgs. 174-177), and in his systematic theology (Grudem, *Systematic Theology*, 642–644). His most comprehensive treatment is found in a paper representing his address to the Evangelical Theological Society (ETS) titled "What Does It Mean to Be 'Led by the Spirit' (Rom. 8:14; Ga. 5:18)?" available on his website: http://www.waynegrudem.com. His book titled *The Gift of Prophecy in the New Testament and Today* contains no reference to either of these passages. Given his influence on this subject, his work is deserving of a more thorough critique, though that is outside the scope of this book.

decision-making and guidance. I've had numerous interactions with people who use "I was led" language and cite these verses as proof that God leads through subjective impressions and promptings. For that reason, I have included a study of these verses here.

Before we look at the passages, it'll be helpful to see how they are used in HVG teaching. In my reading, I didn't note any references of the Galatians passage, but Dallas Willard and Priscilla Shirer make use of Romans 8:14. Willard writes:

> It is just such a conversational manner of presence that is suited to the personal relationship with God so often spoken of in the Christian community. This turns Paul's statement that "all who are led by the Spirit of God are children of God" (Rom 8:14) into a *framework for personal development.* Being "led by the Spirit of God" is neither blind, robot-style obedience nor feeling stuck interpreting vague impressions and signs.[4]

That comes immediately after Willard claims that "God is also with us in a conversational relationship: he [sic] speaks with us individually as it is appropriate - which is only to be expected between persons who know one another, care about each other and are engaged in common enterprises."[5]

He claims our understanding of God's "conversational relationship" with us *turns* Romans 8:14 "into a framework for personal development." In other words, Romans 8:14 becomes the paradigm for "personal divine guidance." Giving no consideration to the context of Romans 8:14 he *turns the passage* into something that fits his theology of divine guidance. This is twisting the meaning of Scripture to match a theology.

Priscilla Shirer describes a sensational way in which God allegedly spoke to her and then counsels:

> He has not promised to lead us in a way that appeals to one of our five senses but rather to our spirits - by the leading of the Holy Spirit within us. "For all who are being led by the Spirit of God are children of God" (Romans 8:14 NLT).
>
> As His Spirit speaks, personalizing His message in a vast variety of ways, we hear His voice. Inside us. Compelling. Encouraging. Convicting. Challenging.

---

[4] Willard, *Hearing God,* 68.

[5] Ibid., 67-68.

Teaching. And guiding us right smack-dab into His will for our lives.[6]

Shirer and Willard quote the verse without any explanation of context or meaning. They *assume* that if the Bible uses the words "led by the Spirit," it *must* be describing private, individual guidance by the voice of God.

Are they justified in using this passage in that way? What does Paul mean by the phrase "led by the Spirit"? Does it describe the Spirit leading us through impressions, nudges, whispers, and other means of hearing God's voice?

Let's look at each verse in their individual contexts.

BEING LED - ROMANS 8:14

Romans 8:14: "For all who are being *led by the Spirit* of God, these are sons of God."

Without looking at the context we can know two things for sure. First, the Spirit of God *leads* the sons of God. Second, all those so led are children of God. There is one thing we *cannot* know with any certainty from the verse by itself, namely, "What is the nature of the *leading*?" There is nothing in the verse that indicates what Paul has in mind by the phrase "led by the Spirit of God." For that, we must look to the context.

It is not an overstatement to claim that HVG teachers *assume* this refers to receiving divine guidance by the voice of God. The only way we can know what Paul meant by the phrase "led by the Spirit of God" is to follow his argument and teaching throughout the context. As Garry Friesen rightly says, "The context, however, deals a deathblow to such an [HVG] understanding of this passage."[7] Death blow indeed. Paul's intended meaning is not difficult to discern.[8]

In Romans 7, Paul described his ongoing war against the sin that remained in his "body of this death." We are familiar with the struggle of doing "the very thing I do not want to do" (Romans 7:14-20). He fought indwelling sin that remained even after conversion. Putting sin to death and living as a slave of righteousness (6:12-23) requires constant battle against the flesh and its desires.

---

[6] Shirer, *Discerning the Voice of God*, 72.

[7] Friesen and Maxson, *Decision Making*, 99.

[8] For the sake of space, I won't quote the entire passage here. I would encourage the reader to follow along in the passage as verses are cited.

In Chapter 8, Paul taught that even though the struggle against sin is a reality for the believer, condemnation for it isn't. For those in Christ Jesus, "there is no condemnation" (8:1). That law which once demanded justice is now fulfilled in those "who do not walk according to the flesh but according to the Spirit" (8:4).

Verses 5-13 note a number of contrasts between those who set their mind on the flesh and those who set their mind on the Spirit (8:6). Slavery to righteousness (6:17-18), putting to death the deeds of the body (8:13), and final deliverance from indwelling sin (7:24-25) are impossible for those "in the flesh" since "those who are in the flesh cannot please God" (8:8). They don't walk according to the Spirit and so they fulfill the desires of the flesh. This passage contrasts *those who walk according to the Spirit in holiness of life and those who walk according to the flesh in fulfilling their sinful desires.*

Here are the verses immediately preceding the reference to being "led by the Spirit of God" in verse 14. Two groups are mentioned: those who live in the flesh and those who live in the Spirit.

> However, you are not in the flesh but in the Spirit, if indeed the Spirit of God dwells in you. But if anyone does not have the Spirit of Christ, he does not belong to Him. If Christ is in you, though the body is dead because of sin, yet the spirit is alive because of righteousness. But if the Spirit of Him who raised Jesus from the dead dwells in you, He who raised Christ Jesus from the dead will also give life to your mortal bodies through His Spirit who dwells in you. So then, brethren, we are under obligation, not to the flesh, to live according to the flesh - for if you are living according to the flesh, you must die; but if by the Spirit you are putting to death the deeds of the body, you will live. *For all who are being led by the Spirit of God, these are sons of God.* (Romans 8:9–13)

In verses 9-10, Paul teaches that *all the sons of God* have the Holy Spirit. Those who don't have the Holy Spirit do "not belong to Him." As those who have the Holy Spirit, we are under obligation to live according to the Spirit. The one living according to the Spirit is "putting to death the deeds of the body" (v. 13).

Verse 13 is the *immediate context* of the statement in verse 14 about being "led by the Spirit of God." In that immediate context, what is Paul talking about? Is he describing decision-making or the voice of God? Is he teaching us about the nature of a "conversational relationship" where the Spirit whispers instructions about which job to take, which contractor to choose, or what restaurant to visit for lunch? Is there *anything* in the context that speaks of promptings, whispers, still-small voices, fleeces, or reading signs? No. Romans 8 is describing Spirit-led holy living. If Paul had any "decision-making leading" in mind at all, it's only the decision to put to death sinful deeds and live righteously in the power of the Spirit.

I would never suggest that the Spirit of God *does not lead us.* Of course He does! But this leading is not whispers and voices. He leads the sons of God to mortify sin and live in holiness. He does this for all believers, since all believers have the Holy Spirit. In Romans 8, "living according to the Spirit" and "being led by the Spirit" are synonymous. The one "led by the Spirit" is "living according to the Spirit" and thus "putting to death the deeds of the body" (v. 13). The one living a fleshly lifestyle isn't "led by the Spirit" because he doesn't have the Holy Spirit in him. This is the obvious and straightforward meaning of the passage.

To demonstrate how badly HVG teachers misuse the verse, let's take their understanding of "led by the Spirit" and insert it into the paragraph. Here is Romans 8:12-14 in HVG theology:

> So then, brethren, we are under obligation, not to the flesh,
> to live according to the flesh - for if you are living according
> to the flesh, you must die; but if by the Spirit you are putting
> to death the deeds of the body, you will live. [*For all who
> are hearing whispers, voices, and nudgings from the Spirit
> for daily guidance are sons of God.*]

To suggest Romans 8:14 is teaching *anything* concerning hearing God's voice, is an abuse of the passage. Being led by the Spirit of God has *nothing* to do with hearing whispers from Heaven, and everything to do with holy living.

But how about Galatians 5:18?

BEING LED - GALATIANS 5:18

Galatians 5:18: "But if you are led by the Spirit, you are not under the Law."

Regarding this verse, Garry Friesen correctly notes: "This verse, which is very similar to Romans 8:14, is often cited with it in support of the traditional view of guidance [HVG theology]. But the context of Galatians 5 makes an even stronger case for ruling out such an interpretation."[9]

As with Romans 8:14, we can't determine the meaning of the phrase "led by the Spirit" from the verse in isolation. In order to understand what Paul means by "led by the Spirit," we must look at the context and the argument Paul is making to the Galatians.

The context of Galatians 5 is very similar to Romans 8. In Galatians, Paul is addressing the relationship of a believer to the Old Testament law. The Galatians had embraced the Judaizer's message that Gentiles saved by faith in Christ needed to submit to the forms and signs of the Old Covenant, particularly, circumcision. Galatians is an extended refutation of that legalistic perversion of the gospel. Paul explained that Gentile believers are not under the law (3:10-14). Having been justified by faith alone (3:23-29) they had no obligation to keep the civil and ceremonial demands of the law. Those seeking to be justified by law were estranged from Christ (5:2-6). They were to reject the false gospel and stand firm in their justifying faith and freedom in Christ (5:1).

Like in Romans 8, Paul was discussing the law and the believer's relationship to it. He taught that the righteous requirements of the law are fulfilled in those who walk according to the Spirit. This is what it means to be "led by the Spirit." We should not be surprised to discover that the same author, addressing a similar subject, using the same phrase would mean *the same thing* in Galatians 5 and Romans 8. There was a contrast in Romans 8 between the "flesh" and the "Spirit." We find the very same contrast in Galatians 5.

Here is the immediate context of verse 18:

> For you were called to freedom, brethren; only do not turn your freedom into an opportunity for the flesh, but through love serve one another. For the whole Law is fulfilled in one word, in the statement, "YOU SHALL LOVE YOUR NEIGHBOR AS YOURSELF." But if you bite and devour one another, take care that you are not consumed by one another. But I say, walk by the Spirit, and you will not carry out the desire of the flesh. For the flesh sets its desire against the Spirit, and the Spirit against the flesh; for these are in opposition to one another, so that you may not do the things that you please. But if you are led by the Spirit, you are not under the Law. (Galatians 5:13–18)

---

[9] Friesen and Maxson, *Decision Making*, 102.

Notice the repeated contrast between "Spirit" and "flesh." Two different orientations toward sin are in view: living in sin or warring against it. The teaching is identical to Romans 8. We see from the preceding verses (vv. 13-17) what Paul means by "led by the Spirit." Those "led by the Spirit" don't serve the flesh, but instead, serve others in love (v. 13). They fulfill the law of God by loving their neighbors (v. 14). They don't bite and devour one another (v. 15). They "walk by the Spirit" and do not "carry out the desire of the flesh" (v. 16).

The verses directly below verse 18 are equally telling. Those in the flesh do the "deeds of the flesh" listed in verses 19-21: immorality, impurity, sensuality, etc. Those who practice the deeds of the flesh "will not inherit the kingdom of God" (v. 21). By contrast, those "led by the Spirit" put to death the deeds of the flesh and produce the fruit of the Spirit (Galatians 5:22-24). Paul made the same point in Romans 8. Those who walk in the flesh are not believers (Romans 8:6-9; Galatians 5:21). The sons of God "put to death the deeds of the body" (Romans 8:13; Galatians 5:16) because they have the Spirit of God and are led by Him. Paul's meaning is the same in both passages. The ones "led by the Spirit of God" are believers who produce the fruit of the Spirit and do not live according to the sinful desires of the flesh.

Nothing in the context of Galatians 5 has anything to do with hearing the voice of God, receiving divine revelation, or listening to the Spirit's whispers. Paul was describing Spirit-empowered holy living not listening for God's whispers.

To demonstrate how foreign the HVG understanding of the text is to Paul's meaning, I'll insert the HVG interpretation of the verse into the paragraph. Here is how Galatians 5:13-18 reads in HVG theology:

> For you were called to freedom, brethren; only do not turn your freedom into an opportunity for the flesh, but through love serve one another. For the whole Law is fulfilled in one word, in the statement, "YOU SHALL LOVE YOUR NEIGHBOR AS YOURSELF." But if you bite and devour one another, take care that you are not consumed by one another. But I say, walk by the Spirit, and you will not carry out the desire of the flesh. For the flesh sets its desire against the Spirit, and the Spirit against the flesh; for these are in opposition to one another, so that you may not do the things that you please. But if you are [*hearing God's*

voice, following impressions and promptings,] you are not under the Law. (Galatians 5:13–18)

Does the HVG interpretation fit that context? Clearly, no. HVG teachers lift the phrase "led by the Spirit" from its context and assign it a meaning completely unrelated to that intended by the apostle. According to HVG teachers, being "led by the Spirit" is "hearing God's whispers as He gives guidance" about which turkey to buy for Thanksgiving or which contractor to hire for the remodel. If they are going to hold to that interpretation of Romans 8 and Galatians 5, then they need to be consistent and say that "living according to the flesh" describes believers not hearing whispers. If being "led by the Spirit" means "listening to divine whispers," then "living according to the flesh" must mean "not hearing divine whispers."

The context clearly describes holy living and not heavenly whispers.

WHAT ABOUT GRUDEM?

This brings us back to Wayne Grudem's arguments pertaining to these two passages.[10] In an earlier footnote (#3) I mentioned the various works Grudem has published on these passages attempting to show that they support a theology of personal revelations and divine guidance.

His most thorough treatment is in a paper titled "What Does It Mean to Be 'Led by the Spirit' (Rom. 8:14; Gal. 5:18)?" which accompanied an address he gave at the Evangelical Theological Society on November 13, 2018 in Denver Colorado.[11] His book, *Christian Ethics*, provides the second-most thorough treatment of the subject. In *Christian Ethics*, Grudem offers a method to guide Christians in ethical decision-making. He claims the Holy Spirit gives personal, specific, and individual guidance to every believer for daily decision-making. Listing "Guidance from the Holy Spirit" as one of "Nine Sources of Information and Guidance" available to the Christian for ethical decision-making, he cites Romans 8:14 and

---

[10] I have tremendous love and respect for Wayne Grudem. Though we have never met, he has had a salutary impact on my life. I appreciate his works on ethics, theology, and economics. I do not doubt Dr. Grudem's sincerity or love and devotion to his Lord. His affection for Christ is evident in his teachings and writings. My respect for Dr. Grudem notwithstanding, I believe his perspective in this area is entirely unbiblical. I believe Dr. Grudem commits logical and exegetical fallacies that he would never countenance if made by others in other important areas of theology and Christian living.

[11] This paper is available at his website: http://www.waynegrudem.com/. I was unable to find any accompanying audio of that presentation.

Galatians 5:18.[12] In the same chapter, Grudem offers a response to Garry Friesen's book *Decision Making and the Will of God*,[13] a book I wholeheartedly recommend.

LEADING FOR ALL CHRISTIANS?

Grudem believes special leading by the Holy Spirit is available to all Christians, and "direct guidance from the Holy Spirit is the normal component of the life of Christians generally."[14]

Noting the universal nature of the Spirit's leading, Grudem says, "Paul wrote to Christians in Rome, whom he had not yet met, about an experience of being led by the Holy Spirit that he seems to have thought of as a characteristic of the lives of Christians in general: For *all who are led by the Spirit of God* are sons of God (Rom. 8:14)."[15] Using Galatians 5:18 he claims, "Paul is speaking of personal guidance from the Holy Spirit to individuals, and he indicates that this experience is characteristic of the lives of all Christians."[16]

As I have already demonstrated, the passage Grudem cites is *not* "speaking of personal guidance from the Holy Spirit to individuals," at least not in the sense that Grudem means when he speaks of "personal guidance." This is assumed by Grudem and the assumption is not warranted from the text.

I believe that true believers are "led by the Spirit." I also concur that such leading is for ALL believers and not just the apostles.[17] Thus, the kind of "leading" Paul describes in Romans 8 and Galatians 5 is for *all Christians.* However, Grudem defines this "leading" in a way not supported by the contexts. This is apparent when he writes, "All of these passages speak about an expectation that Christians in general will experience a measure of leading or

---

[12] Wayne Grudem, *Christian Ethics: An Introduction to Biblical Moral Reasoning*, (Wheaton: Crossway, 2018),152–60.

[13] Ibid., 171–84. This response to Friesen's work is helpful as it demonstrates the stark difference between two models for decision-making. For further study, I would recommend Friesen's book and a reading of Grudem's response in *Christian Ethics*. I will not address all Grudem says in response to Friesen. In this chapter, I will only deal with Grudem's handling of these two passages in question: Romans 8:14 and Galatians 5:18.

[14] Ibid., 159.

[15] Ibid.

[16] Ibid., 160.

[17] Earlier in the same section Grudem asks, "But is direct guidance from the Holy Spirit part of the life of all Christians, or was it unique to Paul and the other apostles in the book of Acts?" (Ibid., 159.) By "leading" Grudem means personal decision-making and private revelation.

guiding by the Holy Spirit, who [sic] will influence their evaluation of various choices and courses of action in a subjectively perceived way."[18]

Grudem sneaks into the discussion his assumption about what kind of "leading" Paul intends. The context indicates Paul was not describing decision-making or private revelations. These passages have *nothing* to do with an "evaluation of various choices and courses of action in a subjectively perceived way."[19] They have everything to do with the work of the Holy Spirit in divinely enabling the child of God to mortify sin (put to death the deeds of the flesh) and live holy lives. Grudem uses two verses that describe the Spirit leading all Christians in mortifying sin and uses them to prove that the Spirit will lead all Christians in decision-making.

Grudem attempts to define the term "led" used in these passages, but in so doing he commits another exegetical fallacy.

WHAT IS THE NATURE OF "LEADING"?

Grudem addresses the meaning of the verb translated "led." After citing Friesen's claim that the "leading of the Holy Spirit" in these passages has to do with God's moral will and holy living, Grudem responds:

> However, this interpretation does not sufficiently account for the actual word that Paul uses for "led," which is the Greek verb *agō*, "to lead." This verb is common in the New Testament (it is used 69 times), and it gives a picture of someone specifically leading a person (or even an animal) from one location to another.[20]

He cites eight places where "*agō*" is used in the New Testament.[21] Based on those uses, he claims that first-century readers would have understood Paul to "speak of one person leading or guiding another person from one place to another."[22] In the paper that accompanied his address to the ETS in 2018 he

---

[18] Ibid., 160.

[19] By this, Grudem means any of a large number of inner, personal, and private impressions, feelings, thoughts, nudgings, burdens, or hunches.

[20] Ibid., 177.

[21] Grudem cites Matthew 21:2; Mark 13:11; Luke 4:1, 9; 10:34; John 1:41-42; 18:28; and 2 Timothy 4:11.

[22] Ibid., 178.

offers a far more comprehensive attempt at establishing the meaning of "*agō*."[23]

It's true that the Greek term "*agō*" often describes a personal agent leading someone or something else in a specific situation. It's also true that it almost always refers to physical leading, like an animal or a prisoner. However, it is entirely wrong to conclude that this same word refers to vague, fallible impressions, voices, and signs in Romans 8 and Galatians 5. It is flawed exegesis to take the meaning of this term in *another* context and insert it into these passages.

Context determines the meaning of "*agō*" in these passages, and the context is obvious. Paul wasn't talking about receiving impressions and nudges for daily decision-making. He was describing the indwelling work of the Holy Spirit who *leads* us in holiness as we put to death the deeds of the flesh. The Holy Spirit (a personal agent) leads every child of God in a progressive pursuit of holiness. He leads us (like one might lead an animal from one place to another) from sin to righteousness.

Grudem begs the question when he writes:

> When first-century readers (who frequently used the verb *agō* to speak of one person leading or guiding another person from one place to another) saw that Paul used this verb to speak of being "led" by the Holy Spirit, they would have understood it to mean detailed, specific guidance in the various choices and decisions of everyday life.[24]

No, they would not. When they read Matthew 21:2[25] - "Go into the village opposite you, and immediately you will find a donkey tied there and a colt with her; untie them and bring [*agō*] them to Me" - would they have thought the disciples were giving "detailed, specific guidance in the various choices and decisions of everyday life" to the donkey? Of course not! The meaning of "led" is determined by the context in which the word is used. In Galatians 5 and Romans 8, the first-century readers would have understood that Paul was

---

[23] Citing both New Testament and Old Testament (LXX) usages, Grudem says it refers to "situation-specific, directional guidance that leads to a particular location or decision," "of human agents leading a person or animals to a specific place," "God guiding Israel through the wilderness," "guidance by a personal agent," and "guidance from the Holy Spirit." (Grudem, W. [2018] "What Does It Mean to Be 'Led by the Spirit' [Rom. 8:14; Gal. 5:18]?") available at http://www.waynegrudem.com.

[24] Ibid., 178.

[25] This is a verse cited by Grudem as an example of how *agō* is used in the New Testament.

speaking about holy living, not hearing the voice of God, since that is what the context is clearly describing. Unwittingly, Grudem allows the use of this word in an unrelated context to color his understanding of this word in the verses in question.

EXPANDED CONTEXT

I believe there is a third error Grudem makes in these passages. He expands his understanding of the context of Romans 8 and Galatians 5 to make room for a theology of personal divine guidance. Grudem is not *ignorant* of the context of these passages. He just does not believe that they speak *only* of righteous living in the revealed, moral will of God. He writes:

> I agree with Friesen that the context in both verses shows that those who are led by the Holy Spirit will not live in a pattern of sin against God's moral laws. However, that idea fits well in a context of specific guidance from the Holy Spirit, because Paul is saying that if you are led by the Holy Spirit, you will be following the desires of the Holy Spirit, and those desires will guide you to fulfill God's moral law: "Walk by the Spirit, *and you will not gratify the desires of the flesh*" (Gal. 5:16).
>
> This does not mean that the leading of the Holy Spirit is *confined* to teaching us to follow God's moral law in Scripture, but it means that the leading of the Holy Spirit, in whatever detailed path of conduct he [sic] chooses, will always be *consistent* with the character of the Holy Spirit, and so will necessarily conform to God's moral law. But the leading of the Holy Spirit is a broader reality than just giving us a desire to follow those moral laws - it is an actual *leading* through the path of life.[26]

The idea of living in the moral will of God may "fit well in a context of specific guidance from the Holy Spirit," but these verses aren't in the "context of specific guidance from the Holy Spirit." They are in the context of "putting to death the deeds of the flesh" and living in the power of the Spirit. Since, in Grudem's mind, these concepts "fit well" together, he inserts the notion of divine guidance into a context where it isn't present - not even remotely. He then claims that "the leading of the Holy Spirit is *a broader reality* than just giving us a desire to follow those moral laws." It might be, but

---

[26] Grudem, *Christian Ethics*, 178.

Paul isn't speaking of any "broader reality." He has one specific, narrow subject in mind.

Of course, I don't think the *only* thing the Holy Spirit does is help us obey God's moral will. That doesn't mean we are free to read any and every aspect of this "broader reality" into a passage that is describing something specific. The leading of the Spirit also involves gifting for service, sealing us until the day of redemption, empowering our acts of service, giving us a love for the brethren, calling us unto the Savior, regenerating us, and glorifying Christ. Those things are all part of the "broader reality," but Paul isn't addressing any of those issues in Galatians 5 and Romans 8. Neither is he speaking of personal divine guidance for decision-making.

Grudem is essentially arguing that because Topic A (personal divine guidance) is not *inconsistent* with Topic B (holy living), we can *assume* that Topic A is intended by the author even though he is only discussing Topic B, and doesn't mention or allude to Topic A at all. Then the passage is quoted and applied as if it were actually discussing Topics A *and* B.

If anyone tried this trick with any other passage, Grudem would rightly cry "foul." To illustrate, imagine we are discussing Romans 5:1: "Therefore, having been justified by faith, we have peace with God through our Lord Jesus Christ," and I say:

> I agree with Grudem that the passage in the context shows we are justified by faith. *However, that idea fits well in a context* of good works. Certainly, those justified by faith will engage in good works as these two things are not *inconsistent.* Salvation isn't *confined* to just faith. It is *a broader reality than just* faith alone. So, when Paul says "we are justified by faith," it is a *broader reality* in view. Therefore, we are justified by works also.[27]

That is the same exegetical method Grudem employs in his treatment of Romans 8 and Galatians 5 and it is fundamentally flawed. I don't believe he would make that mistake if he didn't have a theology of divine guidance he was trying to force into the text. Grudem would never countenance that exegetical reasoning if employed in any other context.

Do Romans 8 and Galatians 5 teach that all Christians will receive personal divine guidance from the Holy Spirit for daily

---

[27] I have intentionally used the language and arguments of Grudem and put his words in italics.

decision-making? No. These passages teach no such thing. The context is clear. These passages teach that all who belong to God are led by the Holy Spirit into a sanctified, sin-mortifying life of holiness.

Chapter 14

I Had a Dream

14

Claims of revelatory dreams and visions in charismatic circles are common. Dreams are the "coin of the realm" among the leadership as charismatic preachers attempt to outdo one another with increasingly spectacular accounts.

Even in non-charismatic circles, many believe God still speaks through dreams and visions. This is indispensable in HVG theology! If God is speaking through floating beer cans, billboards, and random thoughts, why not dreams and visions?

DREAMS IN HVG METHODOLOGY

Nearly all HVG teachers believe God speaks today through dreams and visions.[1] Dallas Willard lists dreams and visions among the ways God speaks to us saying, "God addresses us in various ways: in dreams, visions and voices; through the Bible and extraordinary events; and so forth. Once again, this is obvious in humanity's experience of God in general. It is also clearly marked out within the biblical accounts."[2] For Willard, nearly anything can serve as a vehicle for God's voice. Willard claims there are "six ways God addresses people within the biblical record: a phenomenon plus a voice, a supernatural messenger or an angel, *dreams and visions*, an audible voice, the human voice, the human spirit or the 'still, small voice.'"[3]

---

[1] Some HVG teachers are hesitant to promote dreams without reservation. Others are cautious about offering guidelines for interpreting dreams.

[2] Willard, *Hearing God*, 115.

[3] Ibid., 120-121. Emphasis mine.

He suggests visions and dreams play a lesser role today than in early biblical history, though he doesn't deny that they "continue to play some part."[4] According to Willard, dreams and visions indicate "*a less-developed spiritual life both in the individual and in the church group.*"[5] Consequently, we should be seeking to move beyond dreams into "a life in which one hears from God amid frequent times of conversational prayer."[6] In other words, an impression, nudging, or still small voice is preferable to dreams and visions.

Robert Morris abuses Scripture to confirm his dreams claiming:

In a dream one night in 1993, God gave me a vision for ministry. It was a larger vision than I could have ever come up with on my own, and it was one of the most specific words from the Lord I'd ever received. God was speaking to me in the dream. This was His word to me: *I want you to build a church of thirty thousand people that reaches three hundred thousand in the Dallas-Fort Worth Metroplex. I also want this church to reach three million people in Texas, thirty million people in America, and three hundred million people around the world.*

Wow! I could hardly imagine a ministry with those kinds of numbers. . . . I wondered if maybe I had misunderstood the Lord.

But the very next morning I read 1 Samuel 11:8: "When he numbered them . . . the children of Israel were 300,000, and the men of Judah 30,000." Immediately when I read those numbers, the Lord confirmed in my heart that the dream I'd had the night before had been from Him.[7]

With complete disregard for the intended meaning, Morris uses 1 Samuel 11:8 as confirmation of his dream. The mere presence of similar numbers in a biblical text served as proof he had received a word from God. 1 Samuel 11 has nothing to do with planting a church in Dallas Texas, but that didn't stop him from using it as God's confirmation of a personal revelation.

Jack Deere says Paul's vision in Acts 18:1-18 is proof he "had come to rely on the voice of the Lord, not only in the Bible, but in

---

[4] Ibid., 146.

[5] Ibid.

[6] Ibid., 147.

[7] Morris, *Frequency*, 81.

dreams and visions, in his human spirit, and in other ways."[8] That Paul had a vision of Jesus is not evidence that he "had come to *rely*" on them. There is no evidence of that. There is ample evidence in Paul's writings and preaching that he *relied* on Scripture. As he drew near to death (2 Timothy 4:6-8), he didn't encourage Timothy to rely upon dreams and visions, private revelation, or a continuing prophetic office. He pointed Timothy to Scripture (2 Timothy 3:16-4:5).

Deere admits, "I frequently use examples like this one to encourage people to believe that hearing God in dreams, visions, impressions, and in other ways is simply normal New Testament Christianity."[9] He claims that "with the New Testament coming of the Holy Spirit, dreams, visions, and other prophetic experiences *become the normal experience* for the whole church (Acts 2:17-18). . . . they are common ways for God to speak to his [sic] children."[10]

Mark Batterson claims, "The language of dreams is the fourth love language, and it's God's lingua franca. There is no dialect that God speaks more fluently or frequently in Scripture. Whether it's dreams by night or dreams by day, God is the Dream Giver."[11] Batterson defines "dreams" so broadly as to be almost meaningless. He includes nocturnal sleeping dreams, hopes, desires, and ambitions in this category.

THE SUBJECTIVE SWAMP OF DREAM INTERPRETATION
My family will tell you I don't enjoy hearing about people's dreams. I would rather listen to fingernails grind down a chalkboard than someone's dream. "Hey, want to hear about the dream I had last night?" No. I do not. Not ever. I have no interest in hearing a completely imagined story filled with absurd details ending suddenly without plot or point.

HVG teachers would beg to differ. Jack Deere writes, "If we are ever going to hear all that God wants to say to us, we must adjust to his [sic] ways of speaking. And one of his [sic] favorite ways of speaking is through dreams."[12] In HVG theology, dreams are an

---

[8] Deere, *Surprised by the Voice of God*, 50.

[9] Ibid.

[10] Ibid., 145.

[11] Batterson, *Whisper*, 117. The term "lingua franca" refers to a common or commercial language used among people of different languages. For instance, when traveling in Israel I found that among those who speak Hebrew, Arabic, Romanian, Italian, and Russian, English was the lingua franca (common language) everyone spoke.

[12] Deere, *Surprised by the Voice of God*, 219.

indispensable means of hearing God's voice. Though notoriously confusing, mystifyingly irrational, and often downright silly, dreams are, according to HVG teachers, one of God's favorite ways of speaking to His people.

To counter, they would argue that the confusing nature of dreams requires they be interpreted and confirmed by other "voices." In *Surprised by the Voice of God*, Jack Deere includes what he expects to be a helpful section on interpreting dreams.[13] Though intended to bring clarity, the guides for the interpretation of dreams are a dog's breakfast of confusion and subjectivity.

Since "you can't interpret dreams if you don't remember them," Deere encourages his readers to regularly write them down.[14] He even suggests you "keep a tablet or a recorder near your bed. If you dream every night, you obviously can't record all of your dreams. You will have to be selective and record the ones you think are most meaningful."[15] This counsel doesn't seem at all wise in light of the HVG theology of dreams. Deere says that tuning into dreams is necessary if "we are ever going to hear all that God wants to say to us," and then suggests that some of these divine communications are not worth writing down! How do we determine this? What are the guidelines? Where does Scripture teach this? How can we possibly know which are "most meaningful"? What if dreams I deem to be least meaningful are actually very significant? What if God is desperately trying to tell me something in a dream but I don't deem it worth recording?

Deere recounts a time he had an important dream that woke him up in the middle of the night. Since he did not write it down and review the dream before it left his memory, he was unable to recall it in the morning, "All I could remember in the morning was that I had an important dream during the night. I couldn't recall a single detail."[16] He offers this as a cautionary tale of missing God's voice. This shows the impotency of the god of HVG theology. He has an important message for us, he is *trying* to get our attention, *trying* to

---

[13] Ibid., 224–28.

[14] Ibid., 224. As precedent for this, He cites Daniel 7:1: "In the first year of Belshazzar king of Babylon Daniel saw a dream and visions in his mind as he lay on his bed; then he wrote the dream down and related the following summary of it." It is true that Daniel wrote down that particular dream. It is also true that Daniel had already been confirmed as a divinely called, divinely gifted prophet of God. Daniel, as a prophet, had every reason to believe that the vision/dream of Chapter 7 (a close parallel to a vision recorded in Chapter 2) was divine revelation. This is markedly dissimilar to our modern situation and modern dreams.

[15] Ibid.

[16] Ibid., 225.

communicate, but alas, his efforts are thwarted because we don't record our dreams!

According to Deere, dreams need to be interpreted. Since they can be difficult to interpret, he counsels:

> Don't let the symbolism of your dreams intimidate you. Symbolism often makes a dream difficult to interpret, just as the symbolic visions of the prophets were and are difficult to interpret. Frequently, however, the most symbolic dreams are also the most meaningful dreams. One benefit of symbolism in our dreams is that it causes us to depend on God for the illumination of the dream. Symbols also let us know that we didn't make up the dream. Dreaming in symbols we don't normally use and can't understand is a sign that the dreams are not coming out of some conscious opinion that we hold.[17]

Or it might be a sign that you ate too much pizza before going to bed! According to Deere, the presence of "symbols we don't normally use and can't understand" is proof the dream is "meaningful" and comes from God. By this measure, the more disconnected from reality - the more irrational, unusual, and bizarre a dream is - the more likely it comes from God and carries significant meaning. That is disastrous theology!

This swamp of subjectivity only gets murkier! Deere claims:

> I find it common for God to give a "dream vocabulary" to those who dream regularly. For example, a baby might appear in your dreams as a recurring symbol of some ministry the Lord has given you. To someone else the baby might function as a symbol of immaturity.[18]

Not only do you get your own private revelations, but now you have your own "dream vocabulary" as well. Only *you* can interpret the symbols of your dreams because they are as unique to the dreamer as the dreams themselves. Deere claims "all of the rules for the interpretation of symbols in the Bible are also valid for interpreting symbols in dreams."[19]

You'll search Scripture in vain for any mention of "dream vocabulary" or the teaching that symbols in dreams have radically different meanings to different people according to their "dream

---

[17] Ibid.

[18] Ibid.

[19] Ibid.

vocabulary." How did Joseph know Pharaoh's "dream vocabulary" (Genesis 40-41)? What if seven skinny cows in Pharaoh's "dream vocabulary" means seven gallons of skim milk and not seven years of famine? What if seven fat cows was symbolizing drinking only whole milk for seven years? How did Daniel know Nebuchadnezzar's personal "dream vocabulary" (Daniel 4)? What if Daniel and Joseph were interpreting the symbols according to *their own* "dream vocabulary" instead of the "dream vocabulary" of those who had the dream? Wouldn't they get the meaning wrong?

Though some might have a personal "dream vocabulary," Deere says "there are some things that seem to function as universal symbols."[20] He says:

> After listening to people's dreams for a number of years, I have found that clean, moving water often symbolized the power of the Holy Spirit. Cars sometimes symbolize a particular ministry. Trains may symbolize movements or denominations. And I have already noted that a faceless man may represent the Holy Spirit.[21]

How is this determined? Experience. Are these biblical guidelines? No, they're invented out of whole cloth in the mind of Jack Deere based on his experience. Those who follow this advice will end up interpreting their dreams in light of their current circumstances, thoughts, and desires. How can they avoid making their dreams mean whatever they want them to mean? How do we know for certain if a symbol is a "universal symbol" or one from a personal "dream vocabulary?" Attempting to interpret the fickle, unstable, and dubious imaginations of their sleeping consciousness, HVG practitioners inevitably arrive at an interpretation that confirms their current desires or fears. Convinced the dream and interpretation are "from the Lord," they stamp their midnight musings with the imprimatur, "The Lord told me."

It is mystifying that anyone would think the incoherent imaginations of their slumbering subconsciousness are messages from God. The Word of God is "more sure" (2 Peter 1:19) than any personal dream, vision, or experience. It contains all God needs to say to you.

---

[20] Ibid.

[21] Ibid.

THE LACK OF BIBLICAL INSTRUCTION

Given the emphasis HVG teachers place on dreams and visions, we should expect to find an abundance of scriptural teaching on this means of hearing from God. Allegedly, this is "normal New Testament Christianity."[22] These prophetic experiences have "become the normal experience for the whole church," the "common ways for God to speak, to his children."[23] If that is true, there should be ample teaching on this subject in Scripture.

We should find passages that promise God will speak to us in dreams. We should find chapters devoted to describing the value, benefits, and glories of prophetic dreams, just like we find in Psalm 119 for the Word of God. We could reasonably expect Jesus to cite "dreams and visions" in the same manner He cites the Old Testament in the Gospels.[24] We could expect the apostles, following His example, to repeatedly direct their readers to dreams and visions as a means of hearing from God just as they did the written Word of God.[25] Scripture doesn't emphasize dreams and visions. It points us to the written Word of God.

Since Satan is a deceiver appearing as an "angel of light" (2 Corinthians 11:13-15), we need clear teaching from Scripture on how to discern whether a dream is from God, the devil, or the fitful and fevered imaginations of our own unconscious minds. Which dreams are important, and which are unimportant? Are ALL dreams the "voice of God" or only some, and how do we know which ones? Where are the guidelines from Scripture on how to determine this?

---

[22] Ibid., 50.

[23] Ibid., 145.

[24] Jesus frequently cited the Old Testament as authoritative divine revelation to answer questions, settle disputes, and reprove His challengers. He appealed to the Word of God by asking, "Have you not read what is written?" (Matthew 12:3, 5; 19:4; 22:31; Mark 12:10, 26; Luke 6:3) or by declaring, "It is written," prior to citing the Old Testament Scriptures (Matthew 4:4, 7, 10; 11:10; 21:13; 26:24, 31; Mark 7:6; 9:12, 13; 11:17; 14:21, 27; Luke 4:4, 8; 7:27; 10:26; 18:31; 19:46; 20:17; 21:22; 22:37; 24:44, 46; John 6:45; 8:17; 10:34; 15:25).

[25] Though the apostles occasionally received dreams and visions for divine direction, they never commended this to other believers. They quoted the Old Testament frequently in their writings (Romans 1:2; 4:3; 9:17; 10:11; 11:2; 15:4; 16:26; 1 Corinthians 15:3-4; Galatians 3:8, 22; 4:30; 1 Timothy 4:5-6, 13; 5:18; 2 Timothy 2:9, 15; 3:14-4:5; Titus 1:3, 9; 2:5; James 2:8, 23; 4:5; 1 Peter 2:6; 2 Peter 1:20; 3:16), yet never taught that God will speak through dreams and visions as a part of a "normal experience for the whole church" (Deere, *Surprised by the Voice of God*, 145). Even a brief survey of the book of Acts shows how dependent the apostles were on the written Word of God for their preaching, teaching, and decision-making (Acts 2:16-21; 3:17-26; 4:11, 23-26; 7:2-7, 18, 27-50; 8:32-33; 13:16-41, 47; 14:15; 15:16-18; 23:5; 28:26-27).

Further, if dreams are as essential as HVG teachers claim, Scripture would give instructions for interpreting them.[26] We find none. Though Scripture records dreams and interpretations (Daniel, Joseph, Paul, etc.) we are never told what hermeneutical parameters guide the interpretations. Scripture says nothing of "dream vocabularies." We have to read Jack Deere to find out that "cars sometimes symbolize a particular ministry" and that "[trains] may symbolize movements or denominations."[27]

In Scripture, dreams either provided direct, unmistakable guidance or they required interpretation. The interpretation was itself a form of divine revelation. The dream given to Joseph is an example of unmistakable guidance: "Now when they had gone, behold, an angel of the Lord appeared to Joseph in a dream and said, 'Get up! Take the Child and His mother and flee to Egypt, and remain there until I tell you; for Herod is going to search for the Child to destroy Him'" (Matthew 2:13). No interpretation was necessary. The "child," the "mother," and "Egypt" were not symbols from his personal "dream vocabulary."[28] He didn't conclude that "Egypt" was symbolic of a local restaurant and that he should take the family out for dinner.

Other dreams appeared to have no obvious connection to the divinely-revealed interpretation. Who would think that Nebuchadnezzar's dream of a single statue with a gold head and feet of clay was a revelation of world history through four pagan kingdoms followed by a Messianic Kingdom (Daniel 2:31-35)? Nobody could know that apart from the divinely-revealed interpretation (Daniel 2:36-45). In this case, both the dream and the interpretation were revealed to Daniel (Daniel 2:1-24). Are there any "dream interpretation" specialists like Jack Deere, who can recount the dreams of others and the interpretation? This isn't asking too

---

[26] HVG teachers may counter by saying, "God speaks in Scripture and yet we don't find instructions in Scripture for interpreting Scripture; therefore we should not expect to find instructions in Scripture for interpreting dreams." It is true that we don't find instructions in Scripture for interpreting Scripture. However, the medium of Scripture, the written Word, presupposes a particular hermeneutical methodology. When we hear human speech or read words on a page, our mind automatically interprets the words to discern the author's intended meaning. We apply the normal rules of grammar, syntax, and language (considering genre and context), to interpret words on a page. In other words, the medium of the written word assumes its own principles and standards of interpretation. This is not true and cannot be true for dreams. Jack Deere's invention of a "dream vocabulary" is a tacit admission of this fact.

[27] Deere, *Surprised by the Voice of God*, 225.

[28] Joseph also received this kind of divine direction indicating it was safe to return to Israel (Matthew 2:19-20) and to settle in Galilee (Matthew 2:22).

much. They claim the dreams of Scripture and the methods of interpretation are the model for modern-day dreams. They claim God speaks today *just like He did* in the Bible.

A cursory look at the "dreams" and "interpretations" of HVG advocates will show that what passes as "dreams from the Lord" in those circles is nothing close in kind to the dreams detailed in Scripture. The personal "dream vocabulary" and "universal symbols" described by Jack Deere are completely absent from the scriptural accounts of dreams.

Scripture gives no instruction on when to expect dreams, what kinds of dreams to expect, how to interpret dreams, who should interpret dreams, how to confirm the interpretation of dreams to avoid confirmation bias, or how to discern revelatory dreams from ordinary dreams. This total lack of biblical instruction indicates one of two things. Either the Holy Spirit has failed to provide the information necessary for us to avoid deception and rightly hear all that God has to say to us, or HVG teaching on dreams is unbiblical and dangerous.

Scripture gives examples of God speaking through dreams in the past, but there is *no* indication this is a feature of "normal Christian experience."

BIBLICAL CITATIONS: THE HVG CASE

HVG teachers typically offer two lines of "biblical evidence" for hearing God's voice through dreams.

First, like Charles Stanley, they point out that "God spoke through dreams"[29] in Scripture and assume He must be doing the same today. This ignores the distinction at the heart of Hebrews 1:1-2, where the modes of revelation belonging to previous eras are replaced by the full revelation in the Son: "God, after He spoke long ago to the fathers in the prophets in many portions and in many ways, in these last days has spoken to us in His Son, whom He appointed heir of all things, through whom also He made the world."[30] Ignoring that distinction they cite examples of God speaking through dreams (Pharaoh, Jacob, Nebuchadnezzar, Joseph, etc.) and claim they are a pattern for today.

Second, they cite passages that they claim are promises God will speak to us through dreams. The two passages most frequently cited by HVG teachers are Joel 2:28 and Job 33:14-16.

---

[29] Stanley, *How to Listen to God*, 10.

[30] I provide a longer treatment of this passage in the next chapter.

Job 33:14–16: "Indeed God speaks once, Or twice, yet no one notices it. In a dream, a vision of the night, When sound sleep falls on men, While they slumber in their beds, Then He opens the ears of men, And seals their instruction."

This is Elihu's response to Job's lament (Job 27-31). Elihu falsely accused Job of two things: first, claiming God had invented a pretext against him in order to treat him as an enemy (a slander against the justice of God), second, claiming God had not sufficiently warned him of his sin. Job had not actually charged God with either of those two wrongs. Elihu was misrepresenting Job's lament (33:8-13).

It is the second slanderous misrepresentation that pertains to the text in question. Elihu claimed Job had complained against God for not sufficiently revealing His righteous standards: "Why do you complain against Him That He does not give an account of all His doings?" (33:13). To answer the alleged complaint, Elihu claimed that God does speak and reveal truth to men in dreams while they sleep. These are the words often cited by HVG proponents:

> Indeed God speaks once, Or twice, yet no one notices it. In a dream, a vision of the night, When sound sleep falls on men, While they slumber in their beds, Then He opens the ears of men, And seals their instruction, That He may turn man aside from his conduct, And keep man from pride; He keeps back his soul from the pit, And his life from passing over into Sheol. (Job 33:14–18, Emphasis mine)

According to Elihu, God reveals His dealings in dreams to warn men of coming judgment for their sin. He claimed in verses 19-22 that God afflicts men with suffering for the same purpose, to turn them from sin lest they face His judgment.

Elihu's slander didn't stop there. In the next chapter He charged Job with heinous sins against God:

> What man is like Job, Who drinks up derision like water, Who goes in company with the workers of iniquity, And walks with wicked men? For he has said, "It profits a man nothing When he is pleased with God." Therefore, listen to me, you men of understanding. Far be it from God to do wickedness, And from the Almighty to do wrong. For He pays a man according to his work, And makes him find it

according to his way. Surely, God will not act wickedly, And the Almighty will not pervert justice. (Job 34:10–12) [31]

Elihu's argument is straight forward: God is just and doesn't afflict men with suffering unless they deserve it. Job suffered, therefore, Job deserved it.

What does any of this have to do with God speaking in dreams (33:14-16)? The context is important. In the passage cited by HVG teachers, Elihu levels a subtle but unmistakable slander at Job: "Indeed God speaks once, Or twice, yet no one notices it" (Job 33:14). Elihu alleged that God was speaking to Job in dreams to turn him from his sin, but Job didn't perceive it. He didn't listen to God. The result: Job's current suffering.

We could paraphrase Elihu's claim this way: "God tried to speak to you in a dream to warn you, but you didn't pay attention (33:13-18). He's speaking to you through your suffering and you *still* don't get it (33:19-22). You continue to assert your own innocence while you charge God with wrongdoing (33:8-12)."[32]

HOW JOB GETS ABUSED

Elihu's speech is one long defamatory slander of Job's life and character. Just as he was slanderously abused by his "comforters," the book that bears his name is abused by HVG teachers who take Elihu's slanderous charge and turn it into a promise of revelatory dreams! Elihu was not promising that God's voice would come in dreams. He was falsely claiming that God had warned Job in a dream. God had done no such thing. It is clear from Job 1:22 and 42:7 that Job had *not sinned* against God so as to deserve the suffering he experienced. If Job had *not sinned*, then God had *not warned him* in a dream of the suffering to come. Therefore, Elihu's claim that God warns men in dreams before judging them for sin, was *false*. It was a lie, a slander against a good and righteous man. HVG teachers take a falsehood spoken by a lying slanderer (Elihu) impugning God's righteous servant (Job) and use it to "prove" that God speaks to us today through dreams and visions. Elihu's statement wasn't true then and it isn't true now.

---

[31] Read the entirety of Elihu's speech in Chapters 33-37 of Job and note the many unjustified accusations against Job and pious-sounding defenses of God's justice.

[32] Though this was the accusation from all of Job's "friends," it was not true. Job 1:22 says, "Through all this Job did not sin nor did he blame God." In the end, Job was vindicated by God when He reproved Eliphaz saying, "My wrath is kindled against you and against your two friends, because you have not spoken of Me what is right as my servant Job has" (42:7).

Further, the passage they cite doesn't promise the kind of direction HVG teachers claim to receive from dreams. Elihu said God spoke through dreams to turn men from iniquity lest they be judged. HVG teachers claim God speaks in dreams to provide timely instructions. I have yet to read *one* HVG proponent who limits revelatory dreams to the purpose actually specified in the text they cite. Even if we ignore the context and assume this does teach that God will speak to us through dreams, the *most we could say* is that God will do so to turn people away from their sin. HVG teachers would be hard-pressed to explain why many millions of wicked people are never warned in dreams to turn from their sin, as Elihu allegedly promises.

The HVG handling of this text is an inexcusable abuse of Elihu's words! Does Joel 2:28 fare any better at their hands?

BUT WHAT ABOUT JOEL?

Joel 2:28: "It will come about after this That I will pour out My Spirit on all mankind; And your sons and daughters will prophesy, Your old men will dream dreams, Your young men will see visions."

The passage from Joel was cited by Peter in his Pentecost sermon recorded in Acts 2. At Pentecost, the Holy Spirit filled believers and gave to some the ability to speak in languages they hadn't previously learned. Hearing this, some were amazed and some began to mock, suggesting the phenomena was the result of drunkenness (2:12-13). Peter corrected them saying:

> For these men are not drunk, as you suppose, for it is only the third hour of the day; but this is what was spoken of through the prophet Joel: "AND IT SHALL BE IN THE LAST DAYS," God says, "THAT I WILL POUR FORTH OF MY SPIRIT ON ALL MANKIND; AND YOUR SONS AND YOUR DAUGHTERS SHALL PROPHESY, AND YOUR YOUNG MEN SHALL SEE VISIONS, AND YOUR OLD MEN SHALL DREAM DREAMS; EVEN ON MY BONDSLAVES, BOTH MEN AND WOMEN, I WILL IN THOSE DAYS POUR FORTH OF MY SPIRIT And they shall prophesy. AND I WILL GRANT WONDERS IN THE SKY ABOVE AND SIGNS ON THE EARTH BELOW, BLOOD, AND FIRE, AND VAPOR OF SMOKE. 'THE SUN WILL BE TURNED INTO DARKNESS AND THE MOON INTO BLOOD, BEFORE THE GREAT AND GLORIOUS DAY OF THE LORD SHALL COME. AND IT SHALL BE THAT EVERYONE

WHO CALLS ON THE NAME OF THE LORD WILL BE SAVED."
(Acts 2:15–21)[33]

Acts 2 is significant in HVG theology since Joel mentions dreams, visions, and prophecy in connection with the Holy Spirit: "And your sons and your daughters shall prophesy" (Joel 2:28; Acts 2:17). Those who believe the revelatory gifts (prophecy, tongues, word of knowledge, etc.) continue today, appeal to this passage to prove that the Holy Spirit intends these gifts for the entirety of the church age. The argument of HVG teachers is straightforward: The Holy Spirit was given on the day of Pentecost to fulfill Joel's promise. Joel promised a day when the Spirit would give revelatory dreams and visions. Peter's quotation of the promise at Pentecost indicates that that day has arrived. Therefore, God speaks today through dreams and visions.[34]

UNDERSTANDING JOEL AND DREAMS

Joel predicts events that accompany the "Day of the Lord." The phrase "Day of the Lord" is used a number of times in the Old Testament to "refer to any time God acts in judgment."[35] The ultimate and final "Day of the Lord" is the return of Christ in judgment upon the nations and the unbelieving wicked who dwell therein.[36] Joel mentions the "Day of the Lord" 5 times (1:15; 2:1, 11, 31; 3:14) giving graphic descriptions of the judgments that will accompany it.[37] For instance, Joel 3:1-3 describes judgment of the nations in the valley of Jehoshaphat "in those days." That is a reference to the "Day of the Lord" described in the very passage that Peter quotes in Acts 2.

Though Peter quoted part of the description of the "Day of the Lord" from Joel, he did not intend to suggest that *every* element of Joel's prophecy was fulfilled on the day of Pentecost. There were

---

[33] The quotation comes from Joel 2:28-32a. The last half of v. 32 is not included in Peter's citation. Peter had an evangelistic intention for not quoting the rest of the verse. After quoting Joel's promise that "everyone who calls on the name of the Lord will be saved," Peter preached about Jesus (Acts 2:22) indicting his hearers for their rejection and crucifixion of the Messiah, Whom God had raised from the dead.

[34] They would argue that if these gifts accompanied the ministry of the Holy Spirit at Pentecost, and if we have the Holy Spirit today, then these signs must also accompany the ministry of the Holy Spirit at this present time.

[35] John MacArthur, *The MacArthur New Testament Commentary: Acts 1-12*, (Chicago: Moody Press, 1994), 54. See Isaiah 13:6, 9; Ezekiel 30:2-3; Amos 5:18-20; Obadiah 15; Zephaniah 1:14-18.

[36] 1 Thessalonians 5:2; 2 Thessalonians 2:2; 2 Peter 3:10.

[37] See Joel 1:15-2:17.

no "wonders in the sky above" or "signs on the earth below" that included "blood, fire, and vapor of smoke" (Acts 2:19). The sun did not "turn to darkness," nor "the moon to blood" (Acts 2:20) as Peter described. Judah and Jerusalem were not restored to glory and prosperity (Joel 3:1) nor were the nations judged in the Valley of Jehoshaphat (Joel 3:2). Clearly, not all that Peter cited was fulfilled on the Day of Pentecost. We could say the same thing about dreaming dreams, seeing visions, and prophesying (Joel 2:28-29). There is no record that any of those phenomena made an appearance at Pentecost.

In the larger context of the passage quoted by Peter, Joel described the phenomena that will accompany the establishment of the Messianic Kingdom, including blood, fire, and smoke.[38] In Matthew 24:29-30, Jesus described changes in the sun, moon, and stars that will attend His return. There is no indication dreams, visions, or prophecy happened on the day of Pentecost, so it is best to understand that these will take place in connection with the second coming of Christ. As John MacArthur says, "It is only in those days (the millennial kingdom) that such extensive prophesying will take place. The nature of the prophesying, dreams, and visions that will take place remains a mystery."[39]

So what *was* fulfilled on the Day of Pentecost? The Holy Spirit was poured out! This was something for "all mankind" (Joel 2:28) as the Church includes Jews and Gentiles. The giving of the Spirit was accompanied by a miraculous event (fluently speaking in an unlearned human language)[40] which was itself a sign of coming judgment upon the nation for their unbelief. Tongues were a sign of judgment (1 Corinthians 14:21-22). That made Peter's citation of Joel appropriate.

The miraculous events of Pentecost foreshadowed something to come. The gift of the Holy Spirit in this age is a taste of the blessings, power, and supernatural phenomena that will attend the

---

[38] These elements are mentioned in Joel 2:30. Cross reference with "blood" mentioned in Revelation 6:8; 8:7-8; 9:15; 14:20; 16:3, "fire" mentioned in Revelation 8:5, 7-8, 10, and "smoke" mentioned in Revelation 9:2-3, 17-18; 18:9; 18:18.

[39] MacArthur, *Acts 1-12*, 53–54.

[40] Luke connects this miraculous sign to the coming of the Holy Spirit on at least two other occasions: the salvation of Cornelius (Acts 10:1-11:18) and the salvation of some disciples of John the Baptist (Acts 19:1-7). It is possible that tongues attended the Samaritan believers' receiving of the Spirit (Acts 8:4-24), but it is not mentioned by Luke, therefore, we should not assume they were present. For an excellent discussion on the purpose and nature of these events in Acts, see John MacArthur's book *Charismatic Chaos*, particularly Chapter 8 titled, "What Was Happening in the Early Church."

establishment of the Kingdom of Christ.[41] There is more to come! The Messianic age will be accompanied by even greater manifestations of the works of the Holy Spirit.

Does Peter's citation of Joel prove God has promised revelatory dreams and visions? Yes! But those things, along with signs in the heavens and earth, and the judgment of all nations in the valley of Jehoshaphat, will accompany the establishment of the Messianic Kingdom. The giving of the Holy Spirit at Pentecost was God's down payment on the promise.

HVG teachers take a passage describing the events associated with the future second coming of Christ and use it to support their doctrine of listening for the voice of God in dreams. This is another inexcusable abuse of a biblical text by a movement that claims to love Scripture.

When the Lord Jesus returns, and all the signs of Joel 2 are fulfilled, we won't need Jack Deere's guidelines for writing down and interpreting dreams. The ministry and power of the Holy Spirit will be so evident we won't be guessing the meaning of vague visions and dubious dreams.

DIFFERENT BUT THE SAME

HVG teachers insist that the voice of God in dreams today is the same as in Bible times. According to HVG advocates, God speaks through dreams *just like in Scripture*. God uses symbols *just like in Scripture*. Dreams can be difficult to interpret *just like in Scripture*. Interpreting dreams requires the illumination of the Holy Spirit, *just like in Scripture*.

A closer examination reveals that their insistence that modern dreams are "*just like those in Bible times*" is a thin veneer intended to mask the glaring differences. They claim God's most common method of speaking is dreams. In Scripture, revelatory dreams were rare and treated as unique by all involved. Those in Scripture didn't write down their dreams so as not to miss the voice of God. The Bible doesn't teach that dreams need to be "confirmed," that we can expect God to speak through dreams, that we can learn how to interpret dreams, or that we each have a "dream vocabulary." All

---

[41] We must reject the teaching in Charismatic and New Apostolic Reformation circles that we must exercise dominion over this world through supernatural manifestations in order to usher in the coming Kingdom. The Kingdom of Christ will not be established through human methods and means. Isaiah 9:7 promises that the "zeal of the Lord of hosts will accomplish this." He will not accomplish it through teachers and movements fraught with disastrous fruit and heretical teaching.

these things are taught by those who insist that God speaks through dreams *just like He did in Bible times.*

They caution against the danger of misunderstanding the meaning of a dream. Scripture never cautions against this because God always ensured that the meaning of the dream was clearly and perfectly understood by the recipient, either because it was interpreted via divine revelation or because the dream didn't need an interpretation. They claim the voice of God in a dream isn't as infallible, inspired, or authoritative as Scripture, but no such distinction exists in Scripture. Scripture nowhere suggests that God's voice in a dream isn't as authoritative and inspired as written Scripture.

While claiming that the voice of God in modern dreams is the same as when God spoke through dreams in Scripture, the teaching and guidelines of HVG advocates betray them. Nearly everything they teach regarding dreams is completely foreign to Scripture.

I Had a Dream

Chapter 15

I Saw a Man in White

15

According to reports, Muslims are converting to Christianity in unprecedented numbers.[1] Reports like these bring joy to the hearts of Christians. We rejoice at the news that God is calling His sheep out of the false religion of Islam to Christ. However, not every testimony that comes back from Muslim lands is cause for unmitigated joy.

For instance, a Gospel Coalition article cautions against believing every report of Muslim conversions. It tells the story of a U.S. short-term missions team that went to a park in Athens and held up Greek signs that read: "We will interpret your dreams."[2] After a busy day of "evangelistic ministry" they reported to a local pastor that they had led fourteen people to Christ that afternoon. The short-term missionaries left with a great success story while the fourteen "converts" were never seen in a local church.

It's common to hear reports of Muslims being converted to Christianity through spiritual dreams in which converts see bright lights and a man dressed in white. The man in white is understood to be either an angel or Jesus. In some instances, they receive instructions directing them to someone - a missionary or pastor - who shares the gospel with them.[3] Some accounts are accompanied by claims of miracles and angelic messengers.

---

[1] That is the headline of an online article at Open Doors, a ministry dedicated to supporting persecuted believers in more than 60 countries (https://www.opendoorsusa.org /christian-persecution/stories/muslims-turn-to-christ-in-unprecedented-numbers-pt-1/).

[2] https://www.thegospelcoalition.org/article/muslims-dream-jesus/.

[3] A good sampling of these accounts can be found in the Gospel Coalition article referenced in the previous footnote.

These accounts have been enthusiastically received in many evangelical circles, even where claims of continuing revelation might otherwise be rejected. For instance, in June 2018, during their annual gathering, David Platt gave a missions report to the International Mission Board of the Southern Baptist Convention. He claimed Muslims are having visions and dreams that result in salvation. Platt told the story of a Southern Baptist missionary who loaned a large white t-shirt to a fellow believer, a man named Amad, who donned it for a motorcycle ride. When it started raining, Amad pulled over under an awning where he was invited inside by the occupants of a nearby house. Amad shared the gospel with them and was taken aback at their quick and positive response to the message. According to Platt:

> The man said, "You don't understand. I've had several dreams over the last three nights. And in each dream a man wearing white has told me he had the way to salvation for my family and me…Last night, a man, that man, appeared to me again, and told me a man dressed in white would come to my home the next day telling me the way of salvation. When we saw you standing outside we knew we needed to invite you in and hear whatever you had to say to us."[4]

Platt concluded, "This formerly Muslim couple is now a follower of Isa the Messiah." He received loud applause and a standing ovation at a convention of churches that supposedly reject modern revelations, visions, and dreams.

We might expect these claims from charismatic sources, and indeed, they are not difficult to find.[5] But these testimonies are not relegated to the fringe sectors of Christianity where discernment is in short supply. They are mainstream in circles that, until a few years ago, would have greeted reports of modern revelations with warranted skepticism.

What are we to make of these accounts? Should reports of evangelistic dreams and visions be uncritically embraced as evidence God is doing a work among Muslim peoples in closed countries? Is skepticism regarding these claims warranted? If so,

---

[4] A transcript of Platt's address to the IMB can be found here: https://www.facebook.com/notes/the-end-time/david-platt-report-to-imb/1889399824455873/.

[5] https://www.charismanews.com/opinion/63635-dreams-and-visions-of-jesus-are-fueling-the-explosive-growth-of-christianity-in-muslim-nations-worldwide.

what biblical considerations should guide our evaluation of these reports?

I will argue in this chapter that claims of Muslim conversions through dreams and visions should be rejected based on four lines of New Testament teaching. First, these accounts don't conform to the revealed God-ordained means of evangelism. Second, the finality of God's revelation in Christ make these dreams unnecessary. Third, the apostles gave no indication that they believed Jesus would appear to people after His ascension. Fourth, the apostles warned against believing in visions. Let's take each of these in turn.

THE GOD-ORDAINED MEANS OF EVANGELISM

First, God has revealed His evangelism strategy and it does not include dreams and visions. He hasn't ordained visions, dreams, or prophetic revelations as His chosen tools to reach the lost. He has ordained the preaching of the Word of God - the proclamation of gospel truth, through human instruments.[6] This is foolishness to some and the very reason God has chosen this method - to confound the "wise" (falsely so-called).

Paul explained this in 1 Corinthians 1:18-2:5.[7] In spite of their hostility to the truth, their pagan background, and open opposition to his message (Acts 18:6), the Lord converted some Corinthians through Paul's preaching. Paul's commission was clear: "For Christ did not send me to baptize, but to preach the gospel, not in cleverness of speech, so that the cross of Christ would not be made void" (1 Cor. 1:17). The means of Corinthian conversion was the faithful, accurate, Spirit-empowered gospel proclamation of the apostle. To those who rejected the message, Paul's preaching was foolishness: "For the word of the cross is foolishness to those who are perishing, but to us who are being saved it is the power of God" (1 Corinthians 1:18).[8]

God's elect are saved through the gospel message, faithfully, boldly, and accurately preached by human messengers, not through dreams and visions of shining lights. Paul explains:

---

[6] I am indebted to Fred Butler for this observation. See his article at https://biblethumpingwingnut.com/2018/11/05/the-man-in-white-appearing-in-muslim-dreams/.

[7] For the sake of space, I do not quote the entire passage here. I encourage the reader to follow along as I cite selected verses.

[8] Paul makes the same point in Romans 1:16 when he said the gospel is "the power of God for salvation to everyone who believes, to the Jew first and also to the Greek."

> For since in the wisdom of God the world through its wisdom did not come to know God, God was well-pleased *through the foolishness of the message preached* to save those who believe. For indeed Jews ask for signs and Greeks search for wisdom; but *we preach Christ crucified*, to Jews a stumbling block and to Gentiles foolishness, but *to those who are the called*, both Jews and Greeks, Christ *the power of God and the wisdom of God.* (1 Corinthians 1:21–24 Emphasis mine)

Though Jews asked for signs, Paul gave them preaching. God didn't convert them through miraculous dreams and visions, but through the preaching of Christ crucified. The effectiveness of Paul's message wasn't in his eloquence or oratory abilities:

> And when I came to you, brethren, I did not come with superiority of speech or of wisdom, proclaiming to you the testimony of God. For I determined to know nothing among you except Jesus Christ, and Him crucified. I was with you in weakness and in fear and in much trembling, and *my message and my preaching* were not in persuasive words of wisdom, but in demonstration of the *Spirit and of power*, so that your faith would not rest on the wisdom of men, but on the *power of God.*" (1 Corinthians 2:1–5 Emphasis mine)

The gospel message preached through a human instrument is powerful not because of a human preacher, but because it's God's message, accompanied by God's Spirit (1 Thessalonians 1:5), delivered by the God-ordained means, namely, preaching. Paul didn't expect God's elect would be converted through dreams apart from gospel preaching. He argues in Romans 10:14-15:

> How then will they call on Him in whom they have not believed? How will they believe in Him whom they have not heard? And how will they hear without a preacher? How will they preach unless they are sent? Just as it is written, "HOW BEAUTIFUL ARE THE FEET OF THOSE WHO BRING GOOD NEWS OF GOOD THINGS!"

In Paul's thinking, there is no alternative means for evangelizing lost peoples. He cited Isaiah 52:7 in answer to his own question: "How lovely on the mountains Are the feet of him who brings good news, Who announces peace And brings good news of happiness, Who announces salvation, And says to Zion, 'Your

God reigns!'" His citation of an Old Testament text is telling.[9] The evangelization of the lost by the preaching of the gospel was anticipated in the Old Testament and fulfilled in the New Testament. Paul stood in a long line of men who proclaimed the good news of a God who loves and saves sinners. By this means - the faithful preaching of the gospel - God brings the good news to a lost and dying world. This includes those in the Muslim world today.

Many would say there are a number of possible answers to Paul's question: "How shall they hear without a preacher?" Paul would answer, "They can't, so we must go!" Many today would answer, "It could be by a preacher, a vision, a dream, or private revelation."

Scripture doesn't entertain the possibility that God will convert lost peoples through visions, dreams, or private revelations. He has ordained the preaching of the gospel through human messengers. This is the impetus for gospel ministry, gospel proclamation, and obedience to the great commission: "Go therefore and make disciples of all the nations, baptizing them in the name of the Father and the Son and the Holy Spirit, teaching them to observe all that I commanded you; and lo, I am with you always, even to the end of the age" (Matthew 28:19–20).

The lost are saved through God-ordained, Spirit-empowered, Christ-exalting preaching of the gospel. Paul's command to Timothy to "preach the word . . . in season and out of season" is not far removed from his encouragement to "do the work of an evangelist" and "fulfill [his] ministry" (2 Timothy 4:1–5). Why? Because evangelistic gospel ministry is not "dream-centered" but "Word-centered." Evangelism isn't helping Muslims interpret their dreams. Evangelism is sharing the truth of Scripture with them.

This God-ordained means of evangelism was lived out in the ministries of the apostles. The church was born when Peter preached an exposition of Old Testament texts on the day of Pentecost. That Scripture-centered ministry of the Word was the power behind the explosive growth of the early church in Jerusalem (Acts 6:7) even in spite of staunch opposition and persecution (Acts 6:8-15; 7:54-60). Paul followed the Word-centered preaching approach that characterized the ministries of Peter and John. Luke summarized Paul's entire ministry in his description of his time in

---

[9] It is noteworthy that this passage from Isaiah 52:7 is only seven verses removed from the section of Isaiah that describes the life, death, burial, and resurrection of Jesus Christ (Isaiah 52:13 - 53:12). This "Suffering Servant" section of Isaiah's prophecy describes the substitutionary death of the Lord Jesus Christ – "the good news of good things."

Rome. He "was welcoming all who came to him, preaching the kingdom of God and teaching concerning the Lord Jesus Christ with all openness unhindered" (Acts 28:30-31).

We have clear and repeated teaching in Scripture that the God-ordained, Spirit-empowered means of bringing the lost to Christ is gospel preaching through human instruments. This is the teaching of the New Testament and it is modeled in the lives and ministries of the apostles.

HEBREWS 1

Second, the fullness and finality of the revelation of God in Christ make dreams and visions unnecessary. Hebrews 1:1-2: "God, after He spoke long ago to the fathers in the prophets in many portions and in many ways, in these last days has spoken to us in His Son, whom He appointed heir of all things, through whom also He made the world."

A notable feature of the first two verses in Hebrews is the cluster of prepositional phrases: "after He spoke long ago," "to the fathers," "in the prophets," "in many portions," "in many ways," and, "in these last days." The prepositional phrases provide a number of contrasts intended to show the superiority of the Son over previous modes of revelation.[10] If we ignore the prepositional phrases for a moment, we are left with a simple subject and verb: "God...has spoken." The rest of the phrases fill in the details answering key questions,[11] namely, "When did God speak?" "To whom did God speak?" "How did God speak?" and, "Does He continue to speak?"

When did God speak? The author notes and contrasts two periods of God's revelation: "long ago" and "last days." The "last days" refers to the time period in God's redemptive plan marked by the arrival and revelation of the Messiah. We live in the period of human history between two advents of the Christ known as "the last days."

To whom did God speak? God's previous revelation "to the fathers" is contrasted with what He has spoken "to us." We have received revelation that the fathers who lived in Old Testament

---

[10] Hebrews is a long argument demonstrating the superiority of Jesus over all the forms and functions of the Old Covenant. Jesus is superior to the angels (Ch. 1-2), Moses and Joshua (Ch. 3-4), the Old Testament Sabbath and the Promised Land (Ch. 4), Melchizedek (Ch. 7), Aaron and the Levites (Ch. 5-7), the Levitical priesthood (Ch. 7), the sacrifices, temple, and ministry of the Old Covenant (Ch. 8-10), etc.

[11] To hear a sermon I preached on this passage providing much more detail, please visit our church website, kootenaichurch.org, where you will find an entire series of messages on the book of Hebrews.

times never had. God spoke to "the fathers" then and "to us" now. His revelation to us, is found in Jesus Christ. According to Hebrews 2:3-4, both the author and the recipients had received the truth second-hand.[12] They were only thirty years removed from the coming of Christ, but like those to whom Peter wrote, they had not seen Christ themselves (1 Peter 1:8-9).

God has spoken to us in the Son. We may be further removed from the moment of God's revelation in Christ, but we are no further removed from its meaning, significance, or sufficiency. We are in the same situation as most of those to whom the New Testament books were written. We haven't seen Jesus personally, yet we are still those to whom "God has spoken."

How did God speak? The prior revelation came "in the prophets in many portions and in many ways." The revelation to us has come in the Son.[13] The Old Testament came through prophets who spoke and wrote the Word of God. The full and final revelation is in the Son. He wasn't merely a "messenger of God," but "the radiance of His [God's] glory and the exact representation of His nature" (Hebrews 1:3).[14] Revelation in Christ is qualitatively greater than that which came by the prophets.

Revelation to the prophets came "in many ways," describing the variety that characterized that revelation. Old Testament revelation came through audible voices, dreams, visions, divine words, angelic messengers, theophanies, prophetic events, types, shadows, symbols, handwriting on the wall, and even a donkey.

Revelation came to the prophets "in many portions," meaning "in many parts." This describes the fragmentary nature of Old Testament revelation. No one prophet received all the fullness of information about the Messiah. Old Testament revelation consisted of puzzle pieces given at various times, in various ways, over thousands of years. There was a progressive nature to that revelation as information was added over time.

---

[12] The author does not place himself in the group of people who had firsthand knowledge of Christ. He says in Hebrews 2:3–4: "How will we escape if we neglect so great a salvation? After it was at the first spoken through the Lord, it was *confirmed to us* by *those who heard*, God also testifying *with them*, both by signs and wonders and by various miracles and by gifts of the Holy Spirit according to His own will" (Emphasis mine).

[13] According to Homer A. Kent, Jr., "The absence of the Greek article (thus not 'the Son' nor 'his Son') throws the emphasis upon the nature or quality of the noun itself. It is the 'son-ness' that is being stressed. In contrast to the Old Testament prophets, great as they were, God has now spoken in one who is a Son." (Homer A. Kent, Jr., *The Epistle to the Hebrews: A Commentary*. [Winona Lake: BMH Books, 1972], 36.)

[14] See also John 1:1, 14, 18; Colossians 1:15-20; 2:9.

That is radically different than the revelation of Christ. He is the full, complete, and perfect revelation of God in human flesh. In Christ, all the "portions" of Old Testament revelation come together into one full, glorious, all-sufficient revelation of God's nature and saving work.

Does God continue to speak? The passage from Hebrews provides the answer to that question. All we need to do is follow the argument of the text.

Hebrews contrasts two separate eras of revelation: "long ago" and "last days." These two eras were marked by different kinds of revelation: partial and complete. Further, the two eras had different means of revelation: "many ways" and "in the Son." To us, in these last days, God has spoken (past tense) in His Son. Visions and dreams characterized the former era of incomplete and enigmatic revelation. These are clearly *inferior* to what we have revealed in Christ.

To say God is speaking today in the same ways He spoke throughout Bible history is to ignore the distinction made by the author of Hebrews. Visions, dreams, and signs belong to a previous era of revelation characterized by enigmatic and partial modes. God speaking in the Son is clearly superior to dreams, visions, and voices. Having spoken with unimpeachable clarity in the highest and greatest revelation, why would God return to the inferior means of the Old Covenant?

Throughout the book of Hebrews, Jesus is compared with the people, features, and forms associated with the Old Covenant. He is superior to them all. In every case where the superiority of Christ is shown, God has abandoned what is eclipsed by Christ. For example, the "rest" provided in Jesus is superior to the Sabbath rest mandated under the Old Covenant. Christ is the substance that has eclipsed the shadow (Hebrews 4:1-11). The Melchizedekian priesthood of Jesus is superior to the Levitical Priesthood (7:1-10). Since Christ has been appointed to serve as our High Priest, the Levitical priesthood, with all it's accoutrements, has been abolished (7:12, 18; 8:7,13). If God has abandoned the inferior covenant (priesthood, law, sacrifices, offerings, temple), why would He return to the inferior modes of revelation that characterized that inferior covenant?

In every instance in Hebrews where Jesus is presented as superior to a previous system, that system is rendered obsolete and inoperable. Proponents of continuing revelation must argue for one lone exception - God speaking. In this one case they must assert that God has continued doing what He has always done, in spite of the fact that God speaking in the Son has rendered the previous modes unnecessary.[15] Why would this be the exception to the pattern of Hebrews?

The perfection of Christ's sacrifice renders animal sacrifices obsolete (Hebrews 9:11-14). The perfection of His priesthood and intercession renders the Levitical priesthood obsolete (Hebrews 7:11-25). The perfection of the New Covenant initiated by Christ renders the old obsolete (Hebrews 8:7, 13). The perfect rest in Christ fulfills the Sabbath on our behalf (Hebrews 4:1-11). Likewise, the perfection of the revelation in Christ renders all the former means unnecessary and obsolete.[16] There is nothing about Christ that is inadequate or unclear, therefore, there is no need for further messages from Heaven. How could God improve upon what He has said in His Son?

WHAT THE APOSTLES EXPECTED

A third evidence from the New Testament teaching is the implicit expectation of the apostles. The apostles gave no indication that they believed Jesus would appear to people after His ascension. Should we expect God to improve upon His revealed ordained means of evangelizing the lost? Is Scripture open to the possibility that Jesus will appear in evangelistic dreams? The writings of the apostles show that they didn't expect Jesus to appear after His ascension to Heaven (Acts 1:1-11). We will briefly look at

---

[15] Some would cite Hebrews 13:8 - "Jesus Christ is the same yesterday and today and forever"- in an attempt to prove that since God doesn't change, we should expect Him to speak to us today in the same way He did to Moses, Noah, Abraham, etc. They will say this while ignoring the fact that Hebrews is full of examples of God changing the ways in which He deals with people and administers His redemptive plan. For instance, God no longer works through the Levitical priesthood, the Old Covenant, the animal sacrifices, the Aaronic priesthood, the festivals, the feasts, the Sabbath, or any of the physical laws that regulated the old priesthood (Hebrews 7:12, 18; 8:7,13).

[16] Some could argue that there was further revelation after the coming of Christ, which revelation constituted the New Testament. Cornelius, Peter (Acts 10), and Paul (Acts 18:9-10) all had visions. Decades after Christ ascended, John had his vision on the island of Patmos. They would contend that revelation clearly did not cease with the birth of Christ. In answer, that is technically true. However, the revelation that came in the years after the birth, life, death, and resurrection of Christ, was all centered around Him. The Gospels record biographically God speaking through the Son. The epistles explain the implications of God speaking through the Son. Revelation describes the coming return of the Son. Therefore, the writings of the apostles in the New Testament are not, in fact, revelation given in addition to God's speaking in His Son, but instead they are the revelation of God speaking in His Son. We come full circle to the question at the heart of this issue: "Why is further revelation necessary?"

five passages that should preclude us from expecting modern evangelistic dreams and visions, even in the Muslim community.[17]

THE APOSTLE JOHN

In the introduction to his first epistle, John describes his personal knowledge of Jesus as something he, but not his audience, knew by visual and sensory experience:

> What was from the beginning, what *we* have heard, what *we* have seen with our eyes, what *we* have looked at and touched with *our* hands, concerning the Word of Life - and the life was manifested, and we have seen and testify and proclaim to *you* the eternal life, which was with the Father and was manifested to *us* - what *we* have seen and heard *we* proclaim to *you* also, so that *you* too may have fellowship with *us*; and indeed our fellowship is with the Father, and with His Son Jesus Christ. These things we write, so that our joy may be made complete. (1 John 1:1–4, emphasis mine)

The pronouns in that passage are instructive. John distinguished between *his* knowledge of Christ in the incarnation (heard, seen, touched) and the knowledge of his readers who had only heard what had been proclaimed to them. He was among those (we, us, our) who had personally seen Christ. His audience wasn't. If John believed that Jesus would appear in dreams and visions and such appearances should be expected, the distinction would be meaningless. John wasn't writing in case Jesus hadn't appeared to *some* of them. He was writing because he assumed that Jesus had appeared to *none* of them. Their understanding of eternal life and their enjoyment of fellowship with the Father rested on the apostolic witness, not dreams and visions. John assumed no one in his audience had firsthand knowledge of Christ. He could never assume that if he expected Jesus to appear in dreams and visions.

Consider what he says in 1 John 4:5–6:

> They are from the world; therefore they speak as from the world, and the world listens to them. We are from God; *he who knows God listens to us; he who is not from God does*

---

not listen to us (emphasis mine). By this we know the spirit of truth and the spirit of error.

The dividing line between those who belong to God and those who do not, is one's response to apostolic testimony. Christ's sheep hear and obey His message through the apostles. Such is the nature of the apostolic witness. It is essential and indispensable. If salvation can come by listening to a man in white appearing in dreams, then apostolic testimony may be helpful, but it wouldn't be essential. Personal visions render apostolic witness unnecessary and apostolic witness makes personal visions and dreams unnecessary.

THE APOSTLE PETER

The Apostle Peter presumed that the believers to whom he was writing had *not* seen Christ: "And though *you have not seen Him*, you love Him, and though *you do not see Him now*, but believe in Him, you greatly rejoice with joy inexpressible and full of glory" (1 Peter 1:8-9). These believers had joy inexpressible in their salvation. Their faith had endured the fiery trial of persecution (1 Peter 1:6-7) and was evidenced in their love for the Savior. It was a remarkable faith because they had believed in Christ and loved Him even though *they had not seen Him*. Twice Peter makes this point. They "had not seen Christ" (past tense) and "do not see Him now" (present tense). As my friend and fellow pastor Dave Rich pointed out in a sermon on this text, "Love and faith in a Person that had been communicating with them either directly through physical visits or spiritual visions, would not be marvelous or commendable. It would be reasonable, normal, human faith."[18]

Does it sound like Peter thought dreams and visions were common among first century Christians? Did Peter expect that any of his readers would have seen Christ in a vision or dream? The self-evident answer is "no."

In his second epistle, Peter made the same distinction as John when he spoke of himself as an eyewitness of Christ in contrast to those to whom he was writing:

> For we did not follow cleverly devised tales when *we* made known to *you* the power and coming of our Lord Jesus Christ, but *we* were eyewitnesses of His majesty. For when

---

[18] Dave preached this sermon in a Sunday worship service. It is archived at the church website: kootenaichurch.org. I borrowed this wording from the sermon manuscript he provided.

He received honor and glory from God the Father, such an utterance as this was made to Him by the Majestic Glory, "This is My beloved Son with whom I am well-pleased" - and *we* ourselves heard this utterance made from heaven when *we* were with Him on the holy mountain. (2 Peter 1:16–18, emphasis mine)

Peter owned a unique privilege not enjoyed by others. He was an eyewitness of the glory of Christ. If he believed Jesus would appear in dreams and visions after His ascension, then Peter could not make that distinction at all. In fact, Peter's audience would have no need for him to remind them of any truth (1:12-15) if they were to receive it through personal visions and dreams. Peter didn't believe Jesus would be appearing to people.

THE APOSTLE PAUL

Paul regarded Christ's appearance to him on the Damascus Road as the "last" post-resurrection appearance saying, "And last of all, as to one untimely born, He appeared to me also" (1 Corinthians 15:7–8, emphasis mine). Paul lists himself as the last person to see Jesus after His resurrection. Paul would never list himself as "last of all" if he expected Jesus to appear regularly in dreams and visions.[19]

One might argue that Paul was *not* the last one to receive a vision since decades later John received a vision of Jesus while exiled on the Island of Patmos (Revelation 1:9-20). While this is true, John's vision was markedly different in kind than what is allegedly resulting in Muslim conversion accounts.

First, John was already a believer. Therefore, his vision on Patmos was not an evangelistic encounter leading him to faith in Christ. It cannot be considered instructive for our purposes here nor is it a model for what we might expect in the Muslim community.

Second, John was one who had already seen Christ. He spent three years with Jesus during his earthly ministry and was an

---

[19] Jesus also appeared to Stephen (Acts 7:55-56) when he was martyred. Though Paul heard Stephen say that he saw "the heavens opened up and the Son of Man standing at the right hand of God" (Acts 7:56-58), Paul did not list Stephen in 1 Corinthians 15. It seems the vision that Stephen received was markedly different than Paul's in a number of ways. First, the appearance to Paul did not happen while he was a believer. It resulted in his conversion to Christianity (Acts 9:1-19). Stephen was a believer when he was allowed to see into Heaven prior to his death. Second, in Stephen's vision he saw Jesus standing and nothing was said to him. Paul's vision of Christ included a brief conversation. Modern claims to evangelistic visions would have to cite Paul and not Stephen as their model, and yet, in describing it, Paul says he was "last of all."

eyewitness of His transfiguration and resurrection (Matthew 17:1; John 20:1-31). John's vision on Patmos did not add him to the list of those who had seen Christ. He was already on that list and had been since Resurrection Sunday.

Third, John was an apostle, chosen by Christ as a vehicle of inspired revelation. It is special pleading to ignore this detail and claim that the apocalyptic revelation given to an apostle (resulting in inspired Scripture) is proof that Jesus is appearing today dressed in white to evangelize Muslims.

OTHER CAUTIONS

A fourth reason we should reject claims of evangelistic dreams and visions is the apostolic warnings regarding the dangers of these kinds of experiences.

For instance, Paul warned the Colossians about false teachers who "keep defrauding you of your prize by delighting in self-abasement and the worship of the angels, taking his stand on visions he has seen, inflated without cause by his fleshly mind" (Colossians 2:18–19). He didn't commend them for seeking visions. He cautioned them of the danger of listening to those who claim to receive them.

The Apostle Paul, who had his share of revelatory visions, was slow to speak of them (2 Corinthians 12:1-6). He only did so reluctantly when forced by the Corinthian church's rejection of his apostolic authority.[20] Paul didn't teach that visions should be expected by anyone else. His unqualified warning to the Colossians is evidence that he regarded claims of supernatural visions as worthless at best and spiritually dangerous at worst.

Further, Paul's warning to the Corinthians regarding Satan's deceptions should weigh heavily in our evaluation of these claims:

> For such men are false apostles, deceitful workers, disguising themselves as apostles of Christ. No wonder, for even Satan disguises himself as an angel of light. Therefore it is not surprising if his servants also disguise themselves as servants of righteousness, whose end will be according to their deeds. (2 Corinthians 11:13–15)

Satan counterfeits the genuine work of Christ. To deceive the undiscerning, He disguises himself as a messenger of light. I don't

---

[20] Paul spends the bulk of 2 Corinthians defending his apostolic credentials and ministry to a church that had rejected him in favor of spiritually abusive teachers who slandered him at every turn.

believe it is coincidental that light is such a pronounced feature of the Islamic visions. Many Christians uncritically embrace the stories of these visions, even though we are warned that Satan's deceptions will appear as if their source is the kingdom of light.

The apostles never provide instructions on interpreting visions or dreams. If this were part of God's evangelistic methodology, we could expect some instruction on it. How can we tell if a vision is a heavenly vision or a demonic deception? Who might receive these visions and under what circumstances? Concerning the church's embrace of visions, the only apostolic instruction we have is a warning against the dangers and deception inherent in them.

SOME POSSIBLE OBJECTIONS

I am certain my skepticism and dismissal of Muslim conversions through dreams and visions will be met with some objections. Here are a couple I would expect.

1. "Saul of Tarsus was converted through a vision of Jesus (Acts 9:1-19), why shouldn't we expect the same today?"

Answer: Saul of Tarsus was called to be an apostle, so why *should* we expect the same today? Given that Paul's vision of Jesus was connected with his apostolic calling and authority (1 Corinthians 9:1; Galatians 1:11-12), we cannot appeal to him as an example of what might be normative for others. Paul never suggested he was an example of how others might be converted. However, he did teach that God's ordained means of bringing the lost to faith in Christ was through preaching.

2. "Since revelatory dreams are such a big part of the Islamic worldview, God is accommodating His method to reach them."

Answer: Since when does God accommodate pagan worldviews and theologies instead of calling people to abandon them? Why would God lend credibility to a satanic religious system by adopting its teachings to reach Muslims? God doesn't need to adopt their methods to reach people in Islamic cultures. The preaching of the gospel is the power of God unto salvation (Romans 1:16). The Holy Spirit is perfectly able to bring the lost to saving faith and regenerate human hearts through the ordained means of gospel proclamation without Jesus appearing in a vision (John 16:5-15; 1 Corinthians 1:21-25). I see no reason in Scripture why the Islamic community should warrant an exception. They are no more lost or hostile than other unbelievers have been for the last 2,000 years.

Though missionaries have found the Muslim world largely unreceptive to the Christian gospel and evangelistic results have been less than optimal, it doesn't necessitate that God use a methodology (dreams and visions) specially crafted to reach Muslims. God chooses His elect, brings them the gospel, grants them faith and repentance, regenerates their heart, and causes them to be born again to a living hope.[21] The fact that some are within the Muslim community doesn't hinder God's work or God's will concerning the lost He intends to save. One would only argue that dreams are necessary to accomplish the task if they first assume the Spirit-empowered proclamation of the gospel is insufficiently powerful.

FINAL CONSIDERATIONS

Stories can be powerful and personal experiences persuasive, but they can't ever be allowed to dictate our theology. Christians aren't obliged to set aside the teaching of Scripture to accommodate anecdotes from the mission field. Nor are we obligated to exegete anyone's experience. Often we are expected to interpret Scripture in a way that aligns with another's personal experience. Nobody is obliged to do so. Our personal experiences must be explained in conformity with the truth revealed in Scripture. So it is with the accounts of Muslims having dreams and visions.

Just because one claims he was directed by a "messenger of light" does not mean we should assume it was Jesus or a holy angel. Nor should we assume every Muslim who was told in a dream to "believe in Jesus" actually believed savingly on the Jesus revealed in Scripture. Did they repent of their sin and believe the Christian message or did they syncretistically embrace a watered-down Christian "gospel" devoid of hard truths and exclusive claims? Did they embrace the "Jesus" of Islam or the God-man of Scripture? Most of the anecdotes coming out of Islamic regions do not adequately answer these questions.

I acknowledge that even if the dreams and visions phenomena among Muslims is primarily a demonic deception, God may be saving some Muslims in spite of it, using what Satan intends for evil to accomplish His purposes. God can draw a straight line with a

---

[21] Ephesians 1:4; John 6:35-45, 65; Acts 3:26; 11:18; 16:14; Ephesians 2:8-9; Philippians 1:29; 2 Timothy 2:25; James 1:18; 1 Peter 1:3.

crooked stick. That doesn't mean we are justified in either believing the dreams are of divine origin or promoting the anecdotes as evidence that God is at work in Muslim cultures. The acceptance of these stories could discourage people from going to the mission field to spread the gospel among Muslims by the God-ordained means. Why would anyone give up the comforts and safety of life in the West to go and preach the gospel if Jesus is converting Muslims through dreams?

Finally, we cannot ignore the fact that many of the alleged conversion accounts are fraught with problems.[22] Some of the accounts lack documentation. Like stories of "healings" and "resurrections" among charismatic hucksters, many of the accounts lack any documentable details. In the repeated retelling, they come to sound like this: "My aunt's church supports a missionary in Pakistan who heard about a pastor who knows a Muslim Christian whose cousin in another church knows a guy who was converted from a dream."

We can't ignore the likelihood that Muslims would "convert" to Christianity in order to receive financial aid from Christian ministries in Muslim lands. Others could make up stories to "fit in" among certain environments or to satisfy an ever-increasing hunger for sensationalized conversion stories. In a culture where maturity and spirituality are measured by the number and clarity of their revelatory dreams, they would have ample motive to "spice up" their testimony. We know that this happens in America among those who want to enjoy a little time in the spotlight. That same financial motivation exists among those needing to raise money for ministry purposes in those areas. The more sensational and supernatural the story, the more likely it is to gain the financial support of Christians in America who want to know they are contributing to a genuine "work of God."

CONCLUDING CLARIFICATIONS

By critiquing the claims of evangelistic dreams among Muslims, I am not claiming that God *cannot* convert Muslims through dreams. My position has nothing to do with God's *omnipotence* and everything to do with His *ordinance*. I am not talking about what is *possible* for God, but rather what God has revealed about His ordained means. God *can* speak to me through a leprechaun in my

---

[22] For more on this, see the article at https://www.thegospelcoalition.org/article/muslims-dream-jesus/.

refrigerator. However, I have no good reason to believe He will and a lot of good reasons to believe that He won't. Just because God *can* do a certain thing does not give us latitude to claim that He *is* doing or *will do* that certain thing.

Am I claiming every account can be explained in this way? Am I trying to impugn the motives and credibility of any and all who have embraced accounts of Muslim dream conversions? No. But neither should we uncritically embrace these accounts as if none of these concerns are valid. Scripture isn't silent on this issue, and I believe that we are more than justified in a skepticism that seeks to honor the teaching of the Word of God over sensationalistic stories.

Part 4

Tying Up Loose Ends

Chapter 16

How the Apostles Made Decisions

16

If HVG theology is biblical, we would see it taught and modeled in the book of Acts. Acts is the inspired record of the early Church under the direction and oversight of the apostles. Commonly associated with miraculous events like tongues, miracles, prophecy, and visions, HVG proponents believe Acts teaches "that hearing God in dreams, visions, impressions, and in other ways is simply normal New Testament Christianity."[1] Jack Deere surveys "the book of Acts to determine just how common supernatural revelation was in the early church," claiming that Acts "gives us realistic portrayals of how the first century Christians *actually* lived."[2] He says "that *normal* Christian experience is depicted in the book of Acts."[3] In light of the assumptions made by HVG teachers, Deere isn't overstating his case. If we could reasonably expect to see HVG methodology employed *anywhere*, it would be the book of Acts.

HVG teachers claim God speaks today just like He did in Bible times. The lives and experiences recorded in Scripture are regarded as normative for every believer. If that is the case, we should expect to see the following things in the narrative of Acts:

1. Receiving revelation was the common experience of all Christians. There can't be anything special about apostles and

---

[1] Jack Deere, *Surprised by the Voice of God*, 50.

[2] Ibid., 51.

[3] Ibid., 62.

prophets if hearing the voice of God in private revelations is "simply normal New Testament Christianity."[4]

2. Receiving revelation is frequent and not at all extraordinary. We should expect divine direction for the common and mundane decisions in Acts. If God provides revelation for choosing Thanksgiving turkeys,[5] contractors,[6] and church names,[7] we should expect divine revelation for the same kinds of decisions in Acts.

3. The voice of God in Acts looks like the model promoted by HVG teachers. We should read about promptings, nudgings, the still small voice, putting out fleeces, sensing peace, signs, and "feeling led." We should expect to read of ordinary Christians tuning into God's frequency, listening for His voice, and waiting on His whispers. We can expect examples of God's people looking for agreement between various sources of God's voice as they read signs, seek confirmations, and watch for God to get "thematic" in His leading.[8] The book of Acts should put HVG theology and methodology on full display, if, that is, it is indeed a biblical, normal, New Testament Christian experience.

THE NATURE OF ACTS

Acts covers a period of 30 years (approx. 33 A.D. – 63 A.D.). Though other apostles are mentioned, Acts focuses on the ministries of two: Peter, the Apostle to the Jews (Acts 1-12) and Paul, the Apostle to the Gentiles (Act 13-28). Luke records the spread of the gospel from Jerusalem to Rome, roughly following Jesus' description in Acts 1:8: "But you will receive power when the Holy Spirit has come upon you; and you shall be My witnesses both in Jerusalem, and in all Judea and Samaria, and even to the remotest part of the earth."[9] The narrative history of Acts unfolds around the two most notable apostles and contains a high

---

[4] Ibid., 50.

[5] Charles Stanley claims God revealed a particular turkey for Thanksgiving dinner https://www.youtube.com/watch?v=V4ocm31RJ7g.

[6] Shirer, *Discerning the Voice of God*, 110.

[7] Morris, *Frequency*, 84.

[8] Shirer, *Discerning the Voice of God*, 82.

[9] Acts 1-12 centers around the ministry of Peter and events primarily in Jerusalem, Judea, and Samaria. Acts 13-28 centers around the ministry of Paul and his missionary endeavors to take the gospel "to the remotest part of the earth."

concentration of supernatural events, miracles, and divine guidance.

Acts should be appreciated for its "transitional nature." The 30 years was marked by a number of significant transitions. Luke records the end of religious life under the Old Covenant and the transition to life in the Church under the New Covenant. The Church changed from an exclusively Jewish group in Acts 2 to a multicultural, multiethnic Church of Jews and Gentiles by Acts 28. The transition from law to grace, synagogue to church, Jew to Gentile, and apostles to elders makes the book of Acts a quick-paced story of sweeping change. As John MacArthur says, "Acts, therefore, covers an extraordinary time in history. The transitions it records are never to be repeated."[10]

Ignoring the unique nature of Acts and the extraordinary time period it covers, HVG teachers assume the revelatory events are intended as normative for believers today. I don't deny there are examples of supernatural revelation and divine guidance in Acts. However, when we examine the nature and occasions of divine guidance in Acts, we don't find the modern HVG methodology for hearing God speak.

DIVINE GUIDANCE IN ACTS

Acts records fourteen instances of supernatural divine guidance. There are numerous other miracles as well, but only fourteen examples of God providing special directives to His people.[11]

---

[10] John F. MacArthur, Jr., *Charismatic Chaos*, (Grand Rapids: Zondervan Publishing House, 1992), 172. This undeniable fact has hermeneutical ramifications. Ignoring the transitional and unique nature of Acts and the time period it covers can be theologically disastrous. Thus, McArthur cautions that the "only teachings in the book of Acts that can be called normative for the church are those that are explicitly confirmed elsewhere in Scripture." If this principle is ignored and unique events are considered "normative," Acts inevitably becomes a jumble of convoluted teachings and contradictory models.

[11] Jack Deere claims that with "the exception of Chapter 17, every chapter of Acts contains an example of, or a reference to, supernatural revelatory communication from God to his servants" (Deere, *Surprised by the Voice of God*, 53-54). On pages 54-56 of that chapter, Deere cites every example of "supernatural revelatory communication from God" he found in the book of Acts. From Acts 3 Deere says, "The healing of the lame man at the temple gate called Beautiful revealed the glory of Christ (v. 13)." Stephen's miraculous signs and preaching are cited from Acts 6. The appearance of Christ to Paul on the Damascus Road gets counted three times (Acts 9, 22, 26). In Acts 28 Deere claims, "God supernaturally spoke through miracles." He includes miracles, sermons, and the use of spiritual gifts in the category of "supernatural revelatory communication" effectively broadening the definition of "supernatural communication" to include almost everything said and done in the book of Acts. Since he included Peter's sermon in Acts 4, one wonders why he left out Paul's sermon in Acts 17.

Here are the fourteen instances in chronological order.[12]

1. An angel rescued the apostles from prison and *told* them to preach the gospel (5:19-20).

2. Philip was *directed* to the Gaza road by an angel (8:26).

3. Philip was *directed* to the Ethiopian eunuch by the Spirit (8:29).

4. Saul was converted on the Damascus road and Jesus *audibly directed* him to Damascus (9:4-6).

5. Ananias had a vision in which the Lord *instructed* him to visit Saul (9:10-16).

6. Cornelius was *instructed* by an angel in a vision to send for Peter (10:3-6).

7. Peter was *instructed* by the Spirit to visit Cornelius (10:19-20).

8. Peter was *ordered* by an angel to follow him out of prison (12:7-8).

9. Paul and Barnabas were *sent out* by the Holy Spirit on their first missionary journey (13:2).

10. The Holy Spirit *forbid* Paul to preach the word in Asia (16:6-7).

11. Paul was *directed* through a vision to preach in Macedonia (16:9-10).

12. Jesus appeared to Paul in a vision and *told him* to continue preaching in Corinth (18:9-10).

---

[12] There are two examples of direct divine guidance before Pentecost. First, Jesus, physically present with the disciples, instructed them to wait for the promised Holy Spirit (Acts 1:4-5). Second, the apostles cast lots to choose a replacement for Judas (Acts 1:24-26). There are also five examples of supernatural revelations which predicted future events but provided no divine direction (Acts 11:27-30; 20:23; 21:11; 23:11; 27:22-26). The list includes instances of direct divine guidance, the very thing HVG teachers say is presently available to all Christians through promptings, signs, and still small voices.

13. Paul was *told* through prophecy not to enter Jerusalem (21:4).[13]

14. Jesus *told* Paul in a vision to get out of Jerusalem (22:18, 21).[14]

Fourteen times! That sounds like a lot. At first glance, it seems that direct divine guidance was given at every turn. A closer look at the details provides some perspective.

First, these 14 examples took place over a period of thirty years. That is about one every other year. Considering the aggressive spiritual nature of the book of Acts and that the events occurred during the lifetimes of the men (apostles) who were authors of divine revelation, fourteen doesn't seem all that impressive. Put another way, from the time of Pentecost, during the ministries of the apostles, we have only fourteen instances of direct divine guidance. Only fourteen![15]

Second, the fourteen examples can be combined together into a shorter list when grouped according to the occasion that warranted direction. Two pertain to Philip's gospel preaching near Gaza (8:26, 29) and they occurred close together. Two happened around Saul's conversion on the road to Damascus (Acts 9:4-6;

---

[13] I include this because it is part of the list composed by Greg Koukl (see the footnote below) which I am citing in its entirety. Acts 21:4 reads, "After looking up the disciples, we stayed there seven days; and they kept telling Paul through the Spirit not to set foot in Jerusalem." If we understand this as divine guidance given through the Holy Spirit, it raises a problem in the text. Paul disregarded this direction and continued his journey to Jerusalem (v. 5, 13). This would suggest that Paul disobeyed the clearly-revealed will of God. A better understanding of the text is that the Spirit revealed the sufferings that awaited Paul in Jerusalem (Acts 9:16; 20:23) which the believers at Tyre interpreted as a warning to "not set foot in Jerusalem." The believers understood the revelation as a prohibition and Paul understood it as a prediction of His sufferings. In other words, using what was revealed by the Spirit, they warned Paul not to go to Jerusalem. The prohibition came from the believers and not from the Holy Spirit. Though I don't regard this as an example of divine direction to Paul, I'll grant it here for the sake of argument.

[14] This list, as well as a few of the observations that follow, come from Greg Koukl of Stand To Reason (str.org). His assessment of divine guidance in the book of Acts can be found in two different articles: https://str.org/articles/divine-direction-decision-making-in-the-book-of-acts and https://str.org/publications/does-god-whisper-part-2. Koukl teaches on this in an audio series titled "Decision Making and the Will of God."

[15] An HVG proponent might argue that there were probably times when God gave special direction during this period not recorded by Luke. That is possible, but we cannot build theology on what we assume happened. We can only draw conclusions from what is written, not what we wish might have been written. There is nothing in Acts that would lead us to believe that what has been recorded is only a small representative sample.

9:10-16). Two are connected with Peter taking the gospel to Cornelius (Acts 10:3-6; 19-20). Two directed Paul to take the gospel to Macedonia (Acts 16:6-7; 16:9-10). Two pertain to Paul's time in Jerusalem and eventual arrival in Rome (Acts 21:4; 22:18,21). Thus, ten of the fourteen instances surrounded only 5 separate events. Of the remaining four, two are jailbreaks (Acts 5:19-20; 10:3-6), one started Paul's first missionary journey (Acts 13:2), and one directed Paul to stay in Corinth for gospel ministry (Acts 18:9-10). Grouped that way, we find only 9 separate occasions over a 30-year period when specific divine guidance was given.

Third, the means of divine guidance is not as varied as HVG teachers assume. Guidance came through a vision (5x), Spirit speaking (4x), angelic messenger (3x), prophecy (1x), and the voice of Jesus (1x). All these are undeniably supernatural.

Fourth, the recipients of divine revelation were not as widely varied as HVG theology suggests. Seven are from the life and ministry of Paul. Two are from the life and ministry of Peter. One was given to the apostles[16] (5:19-20). Apart from apostles, Philip accounts for two (one event) while Cornelius and Ananias each had one. We must note that the divine directions to Cornelius and Ananias were connected to Peter and Paul respectively. Cornelius's vision instigated Peter's ministry to Gentiles; Ananias's accompanied Paul's conversion. Outside the life and ministry of Peter and Paul, there is only *one person* who received direct divine guidance – Philip. He was closely associated with apostolic ministry in Jerusalem (Acts 6:1-6) and one of only three non-apostles to perform miraculous signs.[17] Philip was also a key part of the worldwide spread of the gospel in Acts.

Fifth, only one of the fourteen examples of divine revelation *isn't* directly and specifically related to the spread of the gospel. Only the angel's order to Peter to follow him out of the prison (12:7-8) *is not* explicitly tied to an immediate gospel ministry purpose. Yet, even in this instance, it was an apostle being directed and not an ordinary believer. It could be argued that Peter's freedom was necessary for the worldwide spread of gospel ministry. All the other instances of divine guidance explicitly directed the spread of gospel ministry "to the remotest parts of the earth."

---

[16] Peter was in that group as indicated when he addressed the council (5:21-29ff.)

[17] Only three people who were not apostles are said to have done miracles: Stephen (Acts 6:8), Philip (Acts 8:6-7), and Barnabas (Acts 14:3). Barnabas was a traveling companion of the Apostle Paul. Philip and Stephen were both closely associated with the apostolic ministry of Peter and John in Jerusalem (Acts 6:1-8).

We can reasonably conclude from the examples in the book of Acts that the direct divine guidance recorded in the New Testament after Pentecost was connected solely to the apostles and their ministry for the express purpose of directing the rapid worldwide growth of the Church in the first century through gospel preaching.

WHERE ARE THE SIMILARITIES?

Does the guidance promised by HVG teachers look anything like the examples in Acts?

The features of HVG methodology are glaringly absent from Acts. Missing are any examples or mention of nudgings, promptings, signs, or an inner sense of the voice of God. The only ones that could be shoehorned into the HVG construct are the four instances where divine guidance is attributed to the Holy Spirit (Acts 8:29; 10:19-20; 13:2; 16:6-7). Even then, there is no mention of a still small voice, internal peace, or a confirmation.[18] God didn't direct them through words of Scripture wrenched from their context and given subjective, personalized meanings. They weren't looking for signs. They weren't waiting for God to get "thematic" with them. The language and methods of HVG theology are nowhere found in the book of Acts. There isn't a single record of God giving direction or knowledge of His will through the subjective means promoted by HVG authors.

There is no indication that those who received divine guidance were seeking it at the time. In every instance, the revelation was an unexpected intervention. They weren't "listening" or trying to discern His voice. They didn't tune into God's frequency. They didn't need to quiet their hearts, rid their lives of distractions, or remove barriers to perceive His direction. They didn't ask for a sign, seek direction, or wait to hear from God. Nobody learned how to hear the voice of God. Nobody. Every practice that HVG proponents tell us is essential for hearing the voice of God is conspicuously absent from the very book (Acts) they claim is their pattern.

---

[18] The first two instances are likely a clear audible voice (Acts 8:29; 10:19-20) described as "the Spirit said." Paul's call to the mission field in Acts 13:2 is also described with "the Holy Spirit said" and could have been an audible voice through one of the prophets active in the Antiochan Church (Acts 13:1). The fourth instance is entirely unclear. The phrases "forbidden by the Holy Spirit" and "the Spirit of Jesus did not permit" could refer to divine revelation through a prophet, an audible voice, or even no form of revelatory guidance at all. It is possible that whatever resistance met with Paul and his traveling companions was attributed by Luke to the direction of the Holy Spirit. In other words, it might be that they met with difficult circumstances that kept them out of Asia and Bithynia, which providential circumstances Luke later attributes to the will and purposes of the Holy Spirit, especially in light of the vision Paul received immediately afterward directing him to Macedonia (Acts 16:9-10).

Also missing is any uncertainty among those who heard God speak. The apostles never said, "I feel led to . . .," "I believe the Lord is telling me. . .," or, "I am sensing the Lord wants me to . . ." In every instance the revelation was clear and unmistakable. It didn't need to be interpreted or confirmed. Nobody needed to check for false positives or confirm the voice.

When God gave direct divine guidance in Scripture it was clear. He made it clear because He expected it to be obeyed. He doesn't speak through signs, symbols, or stray thoughts that must be deciphered. God speaks with clarity so His Word can be understood and obeyed. There was never any doubt! Paul didn't get up from the Damascus road and say, "You know, I *sense* that the Lord wants me to be an apostle and stop persecuting Christians. I *think* that that is what the Lord is telling me, but I'm going to have to pray about it and see if I get a peace about this decision. Maybe I can confirm it through a fleece when I get to Damascus."

Finally, all the instances in Acts were of a supernatural nature. More than half (eight) were either visions or angelic visitations. Another five were the voices of Jesus or the Holy Spirit. One was a prophecy. These were all supernatural manifestations. They were not impressions, hunches, or random thoughts. They weren't billboards, song lyrics, or floating beer cans. In Acts, God spoke to unique men (apostles) through supernatural means to direct the rapid advance of the gospel. In HVG theology, God speaks through hunches and signs to direct us to the right plumber. The supernatural examples of the apostles in Acts are misused to support the teaching that God speaks through natural circumstances to everyone. The HVG Emperor has no clothes.

DECISIONS WITHOUT DIRECTIONS

Acts doesn't contain the "pattern" that some claim. The fourteen examples are exceptional events by every measure. They stand in stark contrast to the numerous decisions recorded in Acts that were *not* guided by a voice from God. Greg Koukl writes:

> For balance we must also note other important decisions in Acts clearly *not* directed by God. There are many times when the disciples make decisions marking significant events in the life of the early church that are the kind many think require a word from the Lord. They entail decisions about the how, when, where, why, and who of ministry. Yet there is no evidence of intervention from God, and no indication the disciples even sought it. They simply

weighed their options in light of circumstances, then chose a judicious course of action consistent with prior, general commands of the Lord.[19]

Koukl cites seventy instances in Acts where Christians, including the apostles, made life and ministry decisions without any mention of divine direction.[20] These include Peter preaching at the temple (3:12-26), the appointment of deacons in Jerusalem (6:1-6), Peter and John going to Samaria (8:14), and the appointing of elders in the new churches (Acts 14:23). Decisions about travel plans, preaching events, elders and deacons, traveling companions, financial expenditures, and doctrinal issues, were all decided without needing or hearing the voice of God. These are the same issues that HVG proponents claim require clear and fresh words from God. If Acts offers us a pattern for decision-making, it is found in the seventy ordinary events and not in the fourteen extraordinary ones.

WHAT WE LEARN FROM ACTS

Does the book of Acts lead us to expect supernatural communication from God? Nothing in Acts indicates that such events are "normal New Testament Christianity" as Jack Deere claims.

How does guidance for an apostle concerning gospel preaching prove that God will reveal which restaurant to choose for lunch? How is direction for Peter to take the gospel to Gentiles the same as God nudging you concerning which lawn care service to hire? How is the Lord's direction to Ananias to baptize an apostle the same as Beth Moore being "told" to comb the hair of a random stranger in an airport?[21] The "voice of God" methodology taught by HVG authors is nothing like what we find in Scripture. All their claims that it is "just like in Bible times" ring hollow.

Extraordinary, supernatural guidance was not given to every believer. The unique events revolved around the ministries of Peter and Paul. Philip was the *lone* exception and he is not far removed from the apostolic circle. Special guidance for gospel ministry is not the birthright of every believer. The Scriptures don't teach us to expect such guidance. We are not promised such revelations in

---

[19] https://www.str.org/publications/does-god-whisper-part-2.

[20] https://www.str.org/articles/divine-direction-decision-making-in-the-book-of-acts.

[21] Beth Moore recounts this bizarre story as an evidence of what it means to be filled with the fullness of Christ (https://www.youtube.com/watch?v=U088JkiQeDQ).

Scripture. We have no justification for taking a handful of exceptional instances and making them a model for all Christians.

Chapter 17

How to Make Decisions Without HVG

17

My goal is to convince you that God is not whispering a hidden and mysterious divine will through dreams, signs, and ever-changing circumstances. I have addressed the key passages HVG teachers cite to prove God speaks outside Scripture. We have examined the methods they employ, the formulas they promote, and the Scriptures they use. Their assumptions and methodologies are riddled with inconsistencies. I have demonstrated that HVG theology abuses Scripture by taking verses out of context and using them in a manner never intended by either the human or divine authors. This practice is neither taught nor modeled in Scripture.

It is not enough to merely dismantle a flawed paradigm. We have to know: "What is the biblical model for decision-making?" How should we make decisions - even the big ones - with confidence that God is involved in the process? Is there a model for decision-making that doesn't rely upon twisted Scripture, subjective impressions, and shifting circumstances? Is there a method that *is* both taught and modeled in Scripture?

Yes. The Wisdom Model.[1]

---

[1] I was first exposed to "The Wisdom Model" in a CD series entitled "Decision Making and the Will of God" by Greg Koukl (str.org). Koukl borrowed that language from a book by the same title by Garry Friesen. Koukl's teaching provides a concise presentation of The Wisdom Model. Friesen's book is the most thorough presentation of this subject matter I have found. I heartily recommend both resources. I have gleaned heavily from the works of Koukl and Friesen on this subject.

WHAT IS GOD'S WILL?

The Wisdom Model is contrasted with the Traditional Model.[2] The Traditional Model teaches that God has a personal, individual will for us in each decision we make. God wants to reveal His individual will so we can obey Him by making the right decisions. According to the traditional view, God reveals whom we should marry, where we should live, which job we should take, how many kids we should have, what we should name them, and which church to join. God's will in these areas and thousands of others, can be discerned by watching for His leading, following the clues, and hearing His voice.[3] The traditional view of the will of God is at the heart of HVG theology.

By contrast, the Wisdom Model teaches that *within the guidelines of God's Word (God's revelation of His moral will and wisdom), we are free to do what we want with God's blessing.* In the Wisdom Model, God has revealed His will for us in Scripture. Provided we are within the parameters of what Scripture reveals, we have freedom to choose any option without fear of being disobedient.

The Bible speaks of the "will of God" in two different ways. The Bible describes God's sovereign will and His moral will. They are different, and understanding the difference is essential to knowing and doing God's will.

First, God's sovereign will is accomplished by His total control over all events. The sovereign will of God includes His unchangeable purposes, His mysterious providence, and His eternal decrees. For the most part, God has not chosen to reveal His sovereign will (Ephesians 1:11; Romans 9:19; Daniel 4:35; Acts 2:23, 4:27-28). His sovereign will is accomplished in history through divine providence as He "upholds all things by the word of His power" (Hebrews 1:3), "works all things after the counsel of His will" (Ephesians 1:11), and accomplishes all His good pleasure (Isaiah 46:10). Some of God's sovereign will is revealed in prophecy. In the description of future events, we see the broad strokes of God's plan

---

[2] "Wisdom Model" and "Traditional Model" are designations used by Garry Friesen in *Decision Making and the Will of God*.

[3] As pointed out in Chapter 4, there can be no such thing as a "small" or "insignificant" decision. We have no way of knowing which decision could alter our lives forever. This is why Charles Stanley is perfectly consistent with the HVG theology and the Traditional Model when he claims that God revealed which Thanksgiving turkey to purchase. Priscilla Shirer says revelation is necessary for picking a contractor for a remodel. Batterson claims God revealed the name of a his church plant to him.

and purposes yet to transpire. In history, we see God's sovereign will in hindsight as the events included in His sovereign plan from eternity past take place in time. We are not morally responsible for obeying the elements of God's sovereign will, a will He has decreed but not revealed (Deuteronomy 29:29).

Second, God's moral will is revealed in Scripture through commands, ethical teachings, and illustrative examples, both positive and negative. For example, we are commanded to walk in light and wisdom, love our neighbors, serve others, flee immorality, be generous, hospitable, and kind.[4] Since His moral will is revealed in Scripture, we are responsible to obey it. The better we know the Word of God, the more familiar we will be with God's revealed moral will.[5]

If we believe God has provided "everything pertaining to life and godliness" (2 Peter 1:3) in Scripture, which is "profitable for teaching, for reproof, for correction, for training in righteousness; so that the man of God may be adequate, equipped for every good work" (2 Timothy 3:16-17), we must conclude that it contains *everything necessary for wise, moral, God-glorifying decisions.* Everything. We are fully supplied with all the information, revelation, and wisdom necessary to make any decision. God's wisdom and moral will are revealed in the statements, principles, and examples of Scripture. This perfect and complete revelation is more than sufficient.

HVG advocates note that the *specifics* of God's will are not mentioned in Scripture.[6] This is the glaring "defect" of the Word of God that HVG teachers claim their system rectifies. It is not a defect at all. It was God's design to reveal His moral will and wisdom and then *give us the freedom to make decisions within those parameters.* The lack of individual and personal direction is not an inadequacy. It is a glorious strength of Scripture's design. God intended for us to grow in wisdom and knowledge while we make decisions within the sphere of His revealed will (Scripture). Therefore, *within the guidelines of God's Word (His moral will and*

---

[4] 1 Thessalonians 4:3; 5:15-18; Ephesians 5:15-21; Romans 12&13.

[5] Garry Friesen (*Decision Making and the Will of God*) thoroughly refutes the HVG/Traditional Model which teaches that God has an "individual will" He reveals through subjective means and circumstances. His thorough treatment of the texts demonstrates that we are not required to learn God's hidden and secret will. God has not promised to reveal it and will not hold us accountable to obey what He has not revealed.

[6] By "specifics" HVG teachers mean the will of God for daily decision-making: which house to buy, which mechanic to hire, which restaurant to choose, etc.

wisdom), we are free to do what we want with God's blessing. In other words, as long as we don't disobey God's revealed moral will (Scripture) and apply biblical wisdom, we are free to choose any option without fear that we have disobeyed God or missed His will. This is the biblical model for decision-making. I'll illustrate how this works in practice and show that it is taught in Scripture and modeled by the apostles.[7]

APPLYING THE WISDOM MODEL

This simple model can guide us in decision-making, even in the biggest decisions we face. Let's put it to the test in two of the biggest and most consequential decisions we encounter: whom to marry and which career to choose.

Marriage is one of the most significant and life-altering decisions you could make. With all that Scripture says regarding marriage, we are never told to listen for the voice of God for guidance in choosing a spouse.

What guidance does God's moral will provide?

Scripture reveals the parameters of God's will on this question. You should marry:

1. Someone who is a Christian. 2 Corinthians 6:14 prohibits yoking yourself to an unbeliever: "Do not be bound together with unbelievers; for what partnership have righteousness and lawlessness, or what fellowship has light with darkness? Or what harmony has Christ with Belial, or what has a believer in common with an unbeliever?" A Christian is not free to marry a non-Christian.[8] This element of God's moral will narrows your options from 8 billion to something less than 1 billion people.

2. Someone of the opposite sex. Matthew 19:4-6 and 1 Corinthians 6:9-10 prohibit same-sex marriage. Jesus quoted God's ordinance for marriage found in Genesis 2:24: "For this reason a man shall leave his father and his mother, and be joined to his wife; and they shall become one flesh." God's revealed design for marriage, an institution He created, limits your choice to

---

[7] One of my main criticisms of HVG methodology has been the fact that the practices and assumptions are neither taught nor modeled in Scripture. I'll show here that this method of decision-making is both.

[8] This principle would rule out dating or courting an unbeliever since marriage is not an option in that relationship.

members of the opposite sex. That narrows it down by another 50%. We're making headway!

3. Someone who is biblically qualified to marry. 1 Corinthians 7 puts restrictions on who can marry and remarry.

4. Someone who is single. They can't already be married. Breaking up another marriage to facilitate yours would be a violation of the moral will of God (Matthew 19:3-9).

According to this brief survey of God's revealed moral will, you are free to marry someone who is a single, qualified, believer of the opposite sex. Though that narrows the field quite a bit, it doesn't eliminate everybody except "the one." God's moral will is not our *only* consideration. We are also commanded to use godly wisdom so that we will "live securely" and "be at ease from the dread of evil" (Proverbs 1:33).[9]

What guidance does wisdom provide?

1. Proverbs 21:9 says, "It is better to live in the corner of a roof than in a house shared with a contentious woman."[10] Wisdom cautions against marrying someone who is always trolling for a fight. If you want a house free from contention, don't marry someone who creates it. To avoid strife and quarrels (Proverbs 20:3) don't marry someone whose own convictions and interests will quarrel with yours. If you're a Calvinist and you're engaged to an Arminian, you're courting controversy. If you believe tongues no longer operate as they did in the New Testament era, you shouldn't marry someone who is going to use their "heavenly prayer language" to ask you to pass the salt at the dinner table.

2. Proverbs 11:22 says, "As a ring of gold in a swine's snout so is a beautiful woman who lacks discretion." Wisdom says: "don't marry strictly for beauty." It is foolish to marry a beautiful person and ignore their lack of discretion. You might get the ring of gold but you would have to live with the pig! At the same time, it wouldn't be wise to marry someone you are not physically attracted to since you have

---

[9] The first four chapters of Proverbs laud the blessings and benefits of heeding sound wisdom.

[10] The principles of Proverbs are equally applicable to a woman looking for a husband. Proverbs was written by Solomon to a son (1:8) so the wisdom is stated in terms addressed to him.

an obligation to meet the physical needs of a spouse in marriage (1 Cor. 7:1-7).

3. Wisdom tells you to avoid the lazy person (Prov. 10:26), the foolish person (Prov. 14:7), the contentious person (Prov. 27:15), and the immoral person (Prov. 5). A good and godly spouse is a gift from the Lord (Prov. 18:22). Knowing the wisdom revealed in Scripture and heeding its warnings will help you avoid the pitfalls of folly (Proverbs 8).

From this survey of God's moral will and biblical wisdom, we can see God has a lot to say about the kind of person we should be pursuing for marriage. As you'll notice, there is still a lot of freedom for you to decide, even between multiple options. Within the circumscribed boundaries of God's moral will, and in keeping with wisdom provided in Scripture, *you are free to marry whomever you wish.*

This is the exact method of decision-making Paul follows in 1 Corinthians 7, a chapter on the subject of marriage. He provides instruction on the moral will of God in marriage which include avoiding sexual immorality in marriage (7:1-7) and before marriage (7:8-9), commands regarding divorce (7:10-11), and instructions for living with an unbelieving spouse (7:12-16). Sprinkled throughout the chapter are bits of wisdom related to living in peace (7:15), the benefit of marriage (7:9, 32), its potential drawbacks (7:7-8, 26, 28, 33-34, 40), and the nobility of singleness (7:7, 25-40). Paul offers his own counsel, not in terms of God's moral will by command (7:25, 40), but by way of wisdom in light of present circumstances (7:26).

Ultimately, both the decision to marry as well as whom to marry is left up to the individual. Paul refrains from commanding anybody to either marry or remain single. After prescribing the boundaries of God's moral will concerning marriage, and providing wisdom in light of present circumstances, Paul left the decision up to the individual. Each one had freedom to marry or remain single in accordance with their own desires. As Garry Friesen notes, "At the outset, Paul established an important principle: One's decision about marriage is *regulated* by the moral will of God, but *not determined* by it. . . . The choice of whether to marry or remain single lies within the area of freedom."[11] The freedom to choose within the moral will and wisdom of God is evident in the following verses:

---

[11] Friesen and Maxson, *Decision Making and the Will of God,* 293-294.

1 Corinthians 7:25: "Now concerning virgins I have *no command of the Lord*, but *I give an opinion* as one who by the mercy of the Lord is trustworthy."

1 Corinthians 7:28: "But if you marry, you *have not sinned*, and if a virgin marries, she *has not sinned*. Yet such will have trouble in this life, and I am trying to spare you."

1 Corinthians 7:36: "But if any man thinks that he is acting unbecomingly toward his virgin daughter, if she is past her youth, and if it must be so, *let him do what he wishes, he does not sin*, let her marry."

1 Corinthians 7:39: "A wife is bound as long as her husband lives; but if her husband is dead, she is *free* to be married *to whom she wishes*, only in the Lord."

In 1 Corinthians 7, The Wisdom Model for decision-making is demonstrated. Paul tackles the biggest decision to face a believer: to marry or not to marry, and whom. Paul's answer: Heed to the revealed moral will of God, use sound wisdom, and do what you want. Marry or not. Marry whomever you want to marry. Do as you please.

Notice the *entire HVG paradigm* and methodology is completely absent from Paul's decision-making process. He doesn't say you need to get a fresh word from God. He doesn't advise us to read the signs, listen for a still small voice, tune into God's frequency, read tea leaves, ask for a dream, put out a fleece, seek a confirmation, or wait for a revelation. This is the exact place we would expect HVG theology to be put on full display. Here is where we should expect to see it taught and modeled. If HVG theology were biblical, Paul would say, "Don't make a decision this important without hearing from God. Wait for Him to reveal it to you through an impression, a quiet voice or a random Scripture passage plucked from its context. Of course, don't take just one of these to be God's voice unless you first confirm it with two or three other ways of hearing from Him. Once you think you have heard from God, once He gets thematic with you, confirm it with a fleece and look for some signs. God will make it clear if you listen carefully for His voice. Don't be distracted or He won't be able to get His messages to you."

Scripture tells you everything you need to know to make decisions. You don't need to hear another "voice." He has revealed all you need to make a good choice. Obey the moral will of God, apply wisdom, and choose what you want. No tea leaves. No fleeces. No still small voices. No inner promptings.

That is the biblical model for decision-making: *within the guidelines of God's Word (moral will and wisdom), we are free to do what we want with God's blessing.* If a private, personal word from God on a decision this important is not necessary, why is it necessary for any of a thousand lesser decisions?

CHOOSING A CAREER

Let's take another challenging example: careers. How do we apply the Wisdom Model for decision-making to deciding which job to choose?

What guidance does God's moral will provide?

God's moral will revealed in Scripture provides the parameters that guide our choices. Our first question is: "Of my options, do any violate God's moral will?" If the choices are plumber or prostitute, the decision is easy. One is clearly a violation of God's moral will.[12] Will the occupation be glorifying to God? Will you be forced to violate God's moral standards to perform your job? Does one option require you to sin or tempt others to sin? Will it put you in situations that tempt you to evil deeds (1 Thessalonians 5:22; Romans 13:14)? Options that violate God's moral will are not options at all.

What guidance does wisdom provide?

Proverbs has a lot to say about work. Would one choice join you to the conduct of fools (Proverbs 13:20)? Would it tempt you to immorality (Proverbs 5), lying (Proverbs 4:24), or laziness (Proverbs 6:6-10)?

If a vocation does not violate God's moral will and wisdom, you are *free to choose* whatever you wish with God's blessing. You can choose the job or occupation you enjoy. Your likes and dislikes should direct you in the decision. If you can't stand the sight of blood, don't pursue being a surgeon. If you hate animals, being a vet isn't for you. Would you prefer to work outside or inside, alone or as a team? Can you handle stress? Do you have the demands of a family or ministry that might influence the choice? These factors all come into play.

What if you have to choose between *two equal options?* Let's say two companies have offered identical jobs with identical benefits. One company is in Washington and the other in New York.

---

[12] I use this only for illustrative purposes. I have never met a plumber who could be a successful prostitute.

To further complicate the scenario, let's say neither choice is a violation of God's moral will or wisdom. Everything looks identical in every perceivable way. How do you choose? Do you wait for a word from God? Do you look for a sign, put out a fleece, wait for a peace and get a confirmation? No.

Make a choice. You are free to choose either option without fear you are missing God's best or disobeying His will. Scripture doesn't teach that you need a personal revelation to make a choice that honors Him. God has provided everything you need in Scripture. It is sufficient to equip you for every good work.

HVG theology assumes God has already determined which decision He wants us to make. Scripture doesn't teach that He makes our decisions for us. He is a good Father who trains His children in moral principles and wisdom. He expects us to make decisions using those guidelines. We grow "in the grace and knowledge of Christ" (2 Peter 3:18), in holiness - obedience to God's moral will (1 Peter 1:15), and in wisdom (Proverbs 4:5, 7). As we do, we will be fully equipped for every work (2 Timothy 3:17), walking in wisdom (Ephesians 5:15), and glorifying God (1 Corinthians 10:31). As we mature, we grow in our ability to make wise and moral decisions based on the revelation of truth and wisdom provided in the treasure of Scripture. He gives us the freedom to do so.

ANOTHER APOSTOLIC EXAMPLE

We don't see either the apostles or other Christians in the New Testament waiting to hear from God before making decisions, no matter how important. They didn't listen for voices, read signs, wait for promptings, examine their feelings, watch for themes, wait for a peace, or seek confirmations before acting. They lived in obedience to the revealed moral will of God in the Word and applied wisdom before making decisions. Paul's planned visit to Rome (Romans 1:9-15) is a great example.

Paul was obligated to take the gospel to Gentiles (1:14). That was God's moral will. He had a desire to visit the Christians in Rome (Romans 1:10) and it seemed, at long last, he had an opportunity to do so (Romans 15:22-24). He entrusted himself to God's sovereign will saying it would happen "if perhaps by the will of God" (Romans 1:10). Paul had received no "personal word" regarding his travel plans. He wasn't commanded to go, but he desired to go. His plan to visit Rome was in keeping with God's moral will and there was nothing unwise about it. He could choose to go or not go without fear of disobeying God either way. If you had asked Paul why he was planning a trip to Rome, he would have answered, "I *want* to see them and minister to them" (Romans 1:10). Paul made his plans as he desired with wisdom in keeping with the revealed, moral will of God. Paul didn't try and "spiritualize" the decision by claiming, "I feel the Lord is leading me. . . ," or, "I think the Lord is telling me to . . . ," or, "I sense the Lord getting thematic with me about Rome and I have put out a fleece for confirmation . . ."

Similarly, the apostles made a moral and wise decision regarding the feeding of Hellenistic widows in Acts 6. The apostles didn't want to neglect their duties and give their time to another task, as worthy and noble as it was. It was in keeping with the moral will of God for them to serve tables or appoint others to do so. It was wise to distribute the workload and find godly, spirit-filled, and trustworthy people to do the work. They apparently made the decision without a sign, a voice, a peace, an impression, or a confirmation. Scripture doesn't say they "sensed God's direction," "felt led" to do it, or even heard from God. They chose to appoint men, and further, they even chose which men to appoint, all without any special word from God.[13] They made a moral and wise decision.

Paul's instructions to Timothy for appointing elders is yet a third example. Paul didn't tell Timothy to put out a fleece, hear from God, or get a peace about choosing men for elders. He instructed Timothy in God's moral will (qualifications – 1 Timothy 3:1-7), and Timothy appointed and recognized elders on that basis. No still small voice. No internal peace. No confirmations. This method is both taught and practiced in Scripture. Know God's moral will. Apply wisdom. Choose as you wish. Trust God for the results.

WHERE IS GOD IN ALL THIS?

People object to this model by saying, "You've taken God out of the process! You aren't relying upon Him to tell you what to choose. In your model, God is distant and uninvolved in day-to-day decision-making."

Nothing is further from the truth! According to the Wisdom Model, God has meticulously orchestrated history to provide a perfect, infallible, and living Word. It is filled with the treasure of His truth for His people. It is His gracious provision of everything we

---

[13] This is one of over 70 similar decisions made in the book of Acts without any appeal to special divine revelation. See the previous chapter.

need to live life and glorify Him. It is a treasure trove of wisdom. He has sovereignly moved in history to provide and preserve it for us.

Additionally, God is sovereignly and providentially involved in all our decisions to accomplish His will! His mysterious and invisible hand of providence has promised to work everything out for our good and His glory (Romans 8:30). God is intimately involved in every detail of history so as to accomplish His will. Our choices cannot thwart His sovereign purposes (Daniel 4:34-45; Isaiah 46:10). He is working all things - including our choices and decisions - after the counsel of His will (Ephesians 1:11). We can rest in God's sovereignty and trust His providential direction of all the affairs of His people.

God is certainly involved! In fact, He is involved in a far more intimate way than HVG teachers would suggest. According to the HVG model, God is trying to speak to us. He is trying to communicate. If we don't cooperate by listening and receiving His messages, we forfeit His involvement in our lives. In HVG theology, God's involvement is reduced to desperate attempts to communicate to His people, most of which are frustrated by our inability to hear. He lays out the breadcrumbs in hopes we will pick up His signals and make the right choices.

In my view, God has spent millennia working in history to give us His Word. He has orchestrated all the events of our lives and through providence directs every last detail. The Wisdom Model requires that we spend time reading and studying Scripture so we might accurately handle the Word of Truth. By reading, knowing, and meditating on Scripture, we are sanctified in truth (John 17:17) and conformed to the image of Christ (2 Corinthians 3:18). We must seek and pray for wisdom, pursuing obedience to His commands with hearts of love and devotion. We trust Him fully for the outcome of decisions we make, resting in His sovereignty and promises. Far from removing God from the process, the Wisdom Model draws the believer near to God through His Word.

When I say we are free to choose what we desire without fear of missing God's will or being disobedient, some think I am suggesting that God *does not care* what I choose. That is not what I am saying. Rather, He is pleased with *either* choice. As Garry Friesen points out:

> I avoid saying "God doesn't care" about a non-commanded decision because that terminology implies indifference (though 1 Corinthians 7:19 and 8:8 come very close to that wording). I affirm with Scripture that God cares about every

aspect of the life of His child (Matthew 6:25-34; 1 Peter 5:7). But that concern doesn't require Him to dictate our decisions. The positive way to express it is to say that God is *equally pleased* with two options that equally conform to His moral will.[14]

NOT SPIRITUAL ENOUGH?

For some people, this method of decision-making is not "spiritual enough." They can't imagine how someone could decide whom to marry without a word from God on the matter. I did. You want to know why I married my wife? I didn't get a word from God, a sign, or an impression. I married her because I *wanted* to. It was allowable within the revealed moral will of God for me to have a wife. She exemplified the qualities wisdom required. I was and am attracted to her. I loved her and still do. I wanted to marry her. This doesn't sound pious enough though, does it? It sounds so much more spiritually mature to say, "God told me to marry Diedre and then confirmed it through a sign."

"Oh, but Jim, I got personal direction from God. I got an impression, I prayed about it, got a peace about it, and God confirmed it. He told me I was supposed to marry my wife."

It's quite the coincidence, isn't it, that *God told you* to do what you already had the desire to do anyway? I suspect that if God had told you to marry a woman with an annoying laugh and irritating personality, one you were not at all attracted to, you would have suddenly become a staunch defender of The Wisdom Model of decision-making: "Oh, I don't think it would be wise to marry her . . ." The one who follows the Wisdom Model and the one who thinks they heard from God both end up marrying the person they want to be with. It just sounds more *spiritual* to claim God's personal and direct leading. I can point to Scripture and say that I made a good, moral, and wise decision and trusted God for the outcome.

How did I choose the names for my children? I didn't need to hear from God on the matter. I didn't pray about it, get a peace, have it confirmed, or pull it out of a random Bible verse. I named my children what I wanted to name them. I liked the four names we chose.

How did I decide to live in Sandpoint, Idaho? I like it here. I don't want to live anywhere else. I didn't hear a voice. I don't need to hear a voice.

---

[14] Friesen and Maxson, *Decision Making*, 154.

How did I decide to become a pastor at Kootenai Community Church? The moral will of God tells me I have a biblical obligation to serve the Body of Christ and wisely steward the gifts and education God has given me. I was qualified according to the Word of God and I desired the work (1 Timothy 3:1-7).[15] A need arose, the opportunity was offered, and I wanted to do it. Applying wisdom and consulting with others wiser than I, I concluded I could best glorify God by serving Him in this capacity. I didn't hear from God. I didn't receive an impression. In His providence, He directed my steps and prepared me for this work. Though I received no special revelation for it, in hindsight I see His hand of blessing and providence.

Is it wrong to make plans and decisions this way? You probably think so if you have been taught that hearing the voice of God is essential for knowing and doing His will. Remember what Paul said concerning his plans to visit Rome: ". . . if perhaps now at last by the will of God I may succeed in coming to you. *For I long to see you*" (Romans 1:10).

Why should we believe a decision isn't directed by God unless we hear a voice? Why justify decisions by claiming God was "leading" us or "telling us" what to do? Can't we use Scripture to make good, moral, and wise decisions while trusting in God to sovereignly accomplish His purposes? We don't need to baptize our wants and desires with "I felt led to..." lingo. Scripture provides sufficient guidance for making wise, moral, God-honoring decisions. Therefore, *using the guidelines of God's Word (moral will and wisdom), we are free to do what we want with God's blessing.*

A CONSISTENT METHODOLOGY

In Chapter 4 I critiqued HVG methodology by showing that it can't be applied consistently. There is no way to determine which decisions are "big" and which are "inconsequential" since we can't always see the results of any one decision we make. It may turn out that the color of shirt I wear or the restaurant I choose have far-reaching eternal consequences. Do HVG practitioners wait to hear from God about the shirt they wear, the toothbrush they use, or how much cream to put in their coffee? To be consistent, they would have to apply their complex method of hearing voices, checking sources, and getting confirmations on every decision they make.

---

[15] It is often overlooked that Paul speaks of a man "aspiring" to that office and "desiring" to do the work of an elder.

The Wisdom Model doesn't suffer from this crippling inconsistency. I don't agonize over which shirt I choose each morning. I choose clothing I want to wear, so long as it doesn't violate God's moral standards or wisdom. I trust Him for the outcome, believing that by His sovereignty and providence, He will use my decision to accomplish all His good pleasure. I choose restaurants, shoes, meals, my route to work, drinks, the use of my time, vacations, books to read, and games to play the exact same way. We make thousands of decisions every day that are no less significant than my choice of whether or whom to marry. We don't need special revelation for any of them.

CONCLUSION

How do we make decisions without hearing the voice of God? It is quite easy. In fact, even those who think God speaks to them to direct their decisions make thousands of decisions every day without waiting to hear from Him. They must, otherwise they would be crippled by the indecision inherent in their unbiblical methodology.

HVG theology is burdensome. False doctrine always is. Their onerous and oppressive approach to decision-making saddles the Christian with fear they might miss God's best or disobey a command He hasn't made clear. They can only hope they have heard the right voice, confirmed it the right way, and not received a false positive. They can only wonder if they have applied the right methods and tuned into the right frequency. What if they missed His clues? What if they make a wrong decision because they didn't hear from God first? HVG theology is an albatross that cripples and vexes the decision-making process.

We can have confidence that having obeyed God's moral will and applied wisdom, God will work through our decisions to accomplish His sovereign will. We can rest in Him and trust Him to accomplish His purposes for His glory and our good.

Chapter 18

Answering Questions
and Objections

18

If you are working through the issues surrounding "hearing the voice of God," and you have managed to stick with me to this point, chances are good that you have some questions. I have endeavored to be thorough in handling the issues surrounding HVG theology. In spite of that, I'm sure that there are a few unanswered questions or lingering concerns. In this chapter I will try to answer some of those.

I'm going to make two assumptions about you, the reader. First, I assume you have questions. Likely, much of what I have written in previous chapters is new to you. It's a new way of thinking, an entirely new paradigm. You may have never had these practices challenged, but now you've been exposed to a new way of understanding Scripture, the will of God, and the way He guides us. Abandoning previous convictions is never easy. My own journey through these issues raised lots of questions, some of which are answered here.

Second, I'm going to assume you have read the previous chapters. I'll assume you didn't flip through the table of contents, find the Q&A section of the book, and turned here. Most of your questions should have been answered in previous chapters. If you haven't read the previous chapters, this Q&A section will be very unsatisfying. It will only raise more questions - questions answered in previous chapters.

This chapter will deal with a number of questions not intentionally answered previously. I've divided them into three categories: general theological questions, scriptural questions, and methodological questions.

GENERAL THEOLOGICAL QUESTIONS
1. Doesn't your view of divine guidance put God in a box?

Sometimes the question is raised as an accusation: "You're just putting God in a box!" Mark Batterson would charge us with handcuffing God saying, "To believe that God speaks *only* through the Bible is to handcuff the God of the Bible as the Bible has revealed Him to us."[1] He writes:

> I know there are those who believe that God speaks *only* through Scripture. It's a well-meaning mistake that's often perpetrated by those who hold a high view of Scripture, as I do. I certainly believe that the Bible is in a category by itself as the inspired Word of God and that the canon is closed. But we actually undermine Scripture's authority when we discredit God's ability to speak to us now in the same ways He did in the pages of the Bible.[2]

I'll offer three lines of response to this objection. First, the objection misses the point. My position doesn't discredit "God's ability" to do anything. I haven't said anything in these pages about God's *inability* to speak today the way He did in Scripture. The issue is not what *God can* do but what He *does do.* God *can* speak to me through a talking dog if He wants. I have no good reason to believe He will and a whole bunch of very good reasons to believe He won't. God could make a snowman in my yard speak to me - Frosty the Snowman style. I have no reason to expect He will.

We must base our beliefs about God and His works on Scripture and not on what we imagine might be possible for a sovereign God. God has revealed Himself in Scripture. We aren't taught to expect promptings, whispers, or mystical leadings. We aren't told that our thoughts are the voice of God. To point these things out doesn't put God in a box, rather, it affirms what God has revealed about Himself.

Second, it isn't artificially handcuffing God to let Scripture dictate what we believe and teach about Him. In Scripture, God has

---

[1] Batterson, *Whisper,* 55.

[2] Ibid., 39. HVG theology can offer no biblical theological defense of Scripture's uniqueness. When Batterson equates random thoughts with the voice of God, it is he, not his critics, that undermines the authority and uniqueness of Scripture. While affirming a "high view of Scripture," he promotes a theology entirely inconsistent with that view. He claims that the position advanced in this book undermines Scripture's authority. The opposite is the case. I affirm that Scripture alone is the revealed Word of God. Batterson adds a plethora of competing "voices" to Scripture as legitimate sources for hearing from God. It is HVG methodology that undermines the authority of Scripture.

put Himself in a box. He has revealed His nature, His works, and the way in which we relate to Him. Scripture defines the limits of our beliefs about God. We aren't free to teach anything just so we don't put God in a box. If our understanding of God is limited by Scripture, we aren't putting Him in a box. Limiting our teaching to what is revealed in Scripture is faithfulness to the Word of God.

Is it putting God in a box to say that God can't lie (Titus 1:2), deny Himself (2 Timothy 2:13), or break a promise (Hebrews 6:17-18)? Of course not. This is simply to affirm what God has revealed about Himself and His way of working. It's the same with this subject of hearing the voice of God. To say that God has spoken in Scripture and in His Son and isn't currently whispering directions in your random thoughts, doesn't slight God's omnipotence or defame His abilities. I am making a claim about what Scripture says concerning God's way of revealing Himself and directing His people.

Third, it's the HVG teacher that actually puts God in a box. In HVG theology, God can't get His messages through to us unless we are tuned in to His frequency. He can't speak clearly and unmistakably. His voice is easily lost in the cacophony of life's busyness and distractions. His ability to speak is limited by our willingness to hear. God is *trying* to speak. He is *trying* to get our attention. He *needs* to communicate outside Scripture to ensure that we do His will. The god of HVG theology is an impotent deity who needs our cooperation in order to be heard. By teaching falsehood about how God communicates, HVG teachers are the ones who artificially put God in a box.

2. If God is not speaking to us in the manner HVG teachers claim, then what is the role of the Holy Spirit? Doesn't your theology make our relationship with God cold and distant?

There are two kinds of people who ask this question: those who mistakenly label every activity of the Holy Spirit "the voice of God" and those with a very underdeveloped pneumatology.[3]

First, some mistakenly label every work of the Holy Spirit as "the voice of God." I don't deny that the Spirit of God is at work in our hearts, but not every subjective experience of God's work in our lives should be called "His voice."

---

[3] "Pneumatology" is a "theology of the Holy Spirit." For an excellent and concise theological outline of pneumatology, see MacArthur and Mayhue, *Biblical Doctrine*, 333-396.

The Spirit regenerates, fills, seals, sanctifies, convicts, comforts, gifts, encourages, enables, and strengthens us. He guides our prayers, gives us holy desires, testifies with our spirit that we are the children of God, and leads us into holy living. He illumines the Word of God, empowers believers for service, and produces fruit in our lives.[4] The Holy Spirit is very active in the lives of God's people. None of these works is the "voice of God." None of these involve "speaking." We experience God in very personal, profound, and emotionally powerful ways, but those experiences aren't the "voice of God."

When my wife hugs me, I feel loved and comforted. It would be right to say that "I felt love and comfort." It would be wrong to say, "My wife spoke to me and said, 'I love you.'" She didn't. She hugged me. When my wife speaks, there is propositional content. When she hugs, there is comfort. The two are entirely different.

Or let's say I am standing in the checkout line and see the *Sports Illustrated Swimsuit Issue*. Something inside (sin) wants to pick it up. That thought immediately brings conviction and I realize that I would be giving in to temptation. I remember the covenant Job made with his eyes (Job 31:1). A dozen more Scriptures flood my mind pertaining to purity, sin, and temptation. I turn my eyes away and find something else to occupy my mind.

Did the Spirit "speak" to me? Did God "tell" me not to look? No. He did not communicate new revelation. Rather He brought His Word to bear on my heart. I was convicted, not spoken to. There are times when the presence of the Holy Spirit is almost palpable, His encouragement so strong, His conviction so compelling, and His comfort so perceptible. This isn't the "voice of God." It is the work of the Holy Spirit taking the Word of God and applying it to the hearts of His people to sanctify us in truth (John 17:17).

When I say God isn't speaking today outside Scripture, some will hear me say, "The Holy Spirit isn't active in your life in any way today." This is because they wrongly regard every work of the Holy Spirit as the voice of God. At the very best, they are being imprecise in their description of the Spirit's work. This isn't mere semantics. We should use biblical language to describe biblical concepts. We need to learn to think, reason, and speak in biblical categories. In doing so, we honor the Word of God and represent Him in keeping with the way He has revealed Himself to us in Scripture.

---

[4] John 3:5-8; Ephesians 1:13-14; 5:18-21; 1 Corinthians 6:11; 12:7-11; John 14:16-31; 16:8-15; Acts 9:31; Romans 8:1-17; Galatians 5:16-26.

Second, some people have an underdeveloped theology of the Holy Spirit. They can't see how the Spirit of God could be at work apart from whispering to them in their thoughts and circumstances. Suggest that God isn't "speaking" in this way and they think you've denied every work of the Holy Spirit. I have been told that my theology leaves no room for the Holy Spirit to work. That is patently absurd. If I didn't believe the Spirit of God works in our hearts, I would never preach! Every time I step into a pulpit, I believe with every fiber of my being that the Spirit of God will be active in His people, convicting, encouraging, strengthening, edifying, exhorting, rebuking, convincing, comforting, and sanctifying the listeners through the exposition of His Word.

I don't believe God is distant, cold, and uninvolved simply because He isn't whispering to me in my thoughts. I believe God is sovereignly directing my steps and conforming me to the image of Christ, sanctifying me, and working in me both to will and to work for His good pleasure. I see Him answer my prayers, work in my family, and open opportunities for me to serve. He enables and gifts me for work He has given and strengthens me for the task. Daily His grace is sufficient as I trust in Him and rely upon His provision. I know God is at work in all those ways. Sometimes I sense it. Sometimes I don't. It doesn't require less faith to believe God is at work in *all things* than it does to only see Him in the miraculous and supernatural.

3. Aren't you just objecting to HVG theology because you're a cessationist?

No. I object to HVG theology because Scripture doesn't teach that God speaks in whispers, promptings, and signs. Scripture doesn't teach us to expect God to speak. It doesn't teach that hearing from God is an ability to be cultivated or a skill to be learned. Scripture doesn't teach that God has difficulty communicating with His people.

Though I am a cessationist, and my critique of HVG theology is compatible with my cessationist theology, a non-cessationist could share the same objections. In fact, many non-cessationists do. Greg Koukl isn't a cessationist. He writes:

> I am not a "cessationist," that is, I do not think the so-called "sign" gifts (tongues, prophecy, etc.) ceased in the first century. There may be bona fide prophetic words for the church in the fashion of prophets of old. Alleged prophets,

however, should be tested (1 Thess. 5:20-21), and the test is the same now as it's always been (Deut. 18:22).[5]

In fact, Koukl is open to the possibility that God could, in unique situations, give legitimate divine revelation today, just as in biblical times. Yet, he objects to the HVG methodology saying:

> What *is* at issue for me is whether the Bible teaches *everyone* can be a prophet of sorts, whether *each* Christian can expect to hear from God in the ways described above with private, personalized revelations, and whether this is a standard, ordinary part of the Christian life that can be taught and developed.[6]

Though I don't share Greg's openness to modern revelations, I do share his concerns and critiques of HVG theology. One doesn't have to be a cessationist to recognize that God hasn't promised to whisper to us outside Scripture or to see when Scripture is being abused to support an unbiblical methodology.[7]

4. What about "listening prayer"? Is this practice biblical?

The term "listening prayer" refers to being still and quiet during prayer in order to "hear" what the Lord says. Believers are encouraged to quiet themselves, remove distractions, and wait with expectation for God to speak in the quietness of their thoughts. Some listening prayer resources recommend writing down revelations, and praying about them.[8] This is how Sarah Young received the "revelations" she shares in her wildly popular book *Jesus Calling*. Its popularity is an evidence of how widely "listening

---

[5] https://www.str.org/w/does-god-whisper-part-1.

[6] Ibid.

[7] It is beyond the scope and intention of this work to offer a robust defense of cessationist theology. One doesn't need to be a "card-carrying cessationist" to object to the unbiblical paradigm promoted by HVG teachers. Their faulty assumptions and unbiblical gnostic practices should concern Christians on both sides of the cessationist/continuationist divide. Like Koukl, Garry Friesen strongly opposes the HVG methodology critiqued here and he isn't a cessationist. He says, "I am open to the possibility of the miraculous gifts being present in the church today" (*Decision Making*, 432-433). For a robust biblical defense of cessationism, I would recommend Samuel E. Waldron, *To Be Continued: Are the Miraculous Gifts for Today?* (Merrick: Calvary Press, 2007); Victor Budgen, *The Charismatics and the Word of God* (Darlington: Evangelical Press, 1989); and John F. MacArthur, Jr, *Charismatic Chaos* (Grand Rapids: Zondervan Publishing House, 1992).

[8] There is a glut of resources and websites on this subject. Seth Barnes claims that there "are hundreds and hundreds of examples of God speaking to people in the Bible. It's his modus operandi—and he gives detailed instructions for this in both the Old and New Testament" (https://artoflisteningprayer.com/listening-prayer-101/). The practice and promotion of listening prayer is spreading with concerning rapidity.

prayer" has become accepted in the mainstream of evangelicalism. In an interview with the Christian Broadcasting Network, Sarah Young described how she learned to "dialogue" with God. She said:

> My journey began with a devotional book (*God Calling*) written in the 1930s by two women who practiced waiting in God's Presence, writing the messages they received as they "listened." About a year after I started reading this book, I began to wonder if I too could receive messages during my times of communing with God. I had been writing in prayer journals for years, but this was one-way communication: "monologue." I knew that God communicates through the Bible (and I treasure His Word), but I wondered what He might say to me personally on a given day. So I decided to "listen" to God with pen in hand, writing down whatever I sensed He was saying. Of course, I wasn't listening for an audible voice; I was seeking the "still, small voice" of God in my mind/heart.[9]

Scripture doesn't describe or commend "listening prayer." We are commanded, encouraged, and motivated to pray. Prayer is talking to God and never described as "listening for God's voice" or "receiving a personal word from the Lord." There are no examples of this in Scripture. Examples of godly men and women praying in Scripture are prolific. None "listened" for a still small voice. Further, in all Jesus' teaching on this subject there is no mention of this practice. When the disciples requested that Jesus teach them to pray (Luke 11:1ff), Jesus didn't say anything about listening for God's voice. Proponents of listening prayer describe it as an essential practice, a necessary component of a real and vibrant relationship with the Lord. If that is the case, why did the Lord neglect to teach His disciples this vital discipline?

If God isn't speaking, you will not hear Him no matter how hard you listen or how quiet you become. If He is speaking, you can't miss it. Nobody in Scripture ever needed to be quiet in order to hear God speak. He doesn't need us to be quiet. He has no trouble ensuring He is heard.

---

[9] http://www.cbn.com/entertainment/books/jesuscallingqa.aspx. For a far more detailed critique of Sarah Young's theology and books, please see my review, "Jesus Calling – A Critical Theological Review," available for free at https://kootenaichurch.org/book-reviews/.

SCRIPTURE-RELATED QUESTIONS

5. What about New Testament passages that speak of using miraculous revelatory gifts (1 Thessalonians 5:20-22; 1 Corinthians 14:26)?[10]

There are passages in the New Testament that speak of revelatory gifts in operation in the first-century church. That is not surprising to one who believes those gifts are no longer given by the Holy Spirit. I would expect to find instructions for and references to those gifts during the time when the Holy Spirit was using those gifts to establish the church.

Those references have nothing to do with all Christians receiving private revelation for living today. Even if I were to concede that God still speaks through revelatory gifts in the church today, that is entirely different than *every Christian* receiving private revelations through impressions, voices, and signs. That God may uniquely gift some individuals as instruments of divine revelation doesn't mean that every Christian is promised regular whispers from the Shepherd.

6. How Does God speak through Scripture?

Scripture *is* the voice of God. As my friend Justin Peters has said, "If you want to hear God speak, read the Bible. If you want to hear Him speak audibly, read it out loud." Scripture isn't the "context" in which the Word of God comes, nor is it a description of times when God spoke. It is His Word. Scripture is the living, abiding, and enduring Word of God (Hebrews 4:12; 1 Peter 1:22-2:3). When we read Scripture, we are reading (hearing) the voice of God. It's in written form delivered centuries ago, but it's His Word nonetheless.

The *meaning of Scripture* is the Word of God. When God breathed out His Word (2 Timothy 3:16-17) He didn't leave us a mystical, subjective collection of words and phrases that can be massaged into whatever "meaning" best fits our desires. Every student of Scripture should work to discern the Author's intended meaning in the passage. The meaning isn't determined by the reader, but by the Author. Diligent study is necessary to make sure we aren't twisting the meaning of Scripture, taking verses out of context, or misrepresenting the Author. When we read Scripture and understand God's intended meaning, we hear God's voice.

---

[10] I recommend Garry Friesen, *Decision Making and the Will of God*, for an explanation of dozens of passages often pressed into service for HVG theology.

When the Word of God is accurately preached the voice of God is truly heard. When Scripture is misinterpreted or abused, the voice of the preacher is heard in place of God's, since His intended meaning was silenced by the mishandling of His Truth.

For example, say I tell my oldest daughter that for Mother's Day we are going out to dinner at our favorite Mexican restaurant. I explain we will meet at the restaurant at 6:00 p.m. where I have a table reserved. Then I ask that she communicate this simple plan to all her siblings and their families. Then let's imagine that my oldest child tells her siblings that for Mother's Day, Mom is going to cook Chinese food for the whole family and they need to all meet at my house at 4:00 p.m.

In that example, I communicated propositional truth. I had an intended meaning in mind when I spoke those words. The meaning wasn't dependent on the hearer but on what I intended. In relaying (or proclaiming) my words to her siblings, my daughter got the meaning and intentions entirely wrong. Did they hear "my voice" or the "voice" of their sister?

The meaning of Scripture *is* Scripture. The meaning is the message. The message is the voice of God. When the meaning of Scripture is rightly ascertained, the voice of God is heard. If we are at all serious about "hearing from God," then our chief concern shouldn't be "tuning into frequencies," being still to listen for whispers, or divining messages from circumstantial signs. We must be *consumed* with understanding the Word of God. Our obsession should be the accurate handling and proper representation of God's truth revealed in Scripture, for when we hear that truth with the ears, heart, and mind, we hear God speak.

It isn't my subjective impression of Scripture leaping off the page that is the voice of God (see Chapter 8). It's the meaning and truth conveyed by the words on the page that is the voice of God. The meaning of Scripture is the propositional, objective, revealed truth.

7. Is there one interpretation but many applications, or does God give us personal interpretations?

There is one true interpretation for any passage of Scripture.[11] That one meaning may have multiple applications which differ from

---

[11] This is not to deny that a prophetic passage may have multiple fulfillments or that an author may have more than one meaning intended (double entendre) for a passage. However, the multiple fulfillments and/or double meaning comprise the "one true interpretation" for that passage.

person to person. Any proper application must be derived from an accurate understanding of a passage in its context. When the author wrote the passage, he had an intended meaning. The intended meaning doesn't change with the culture or reader. A passage can never mean what it has never meant. Scripture doesn't teach that God gives personal, subjective meanings for passages of Scripture. If a passage of Scripture can mean *anything* at all, then it doesn't mean anything at all. If the meaning is not objective and fixed, then it can be twisted into any teaching that fits the fancy of the reader. If there isn't one fixed meaning to Scripture, then there can be no such thing as inaccurately handling the Word of Truth (2 Timothy 2:15). Scripture could never be abused or cited out of context since people could just claim that the Holy Spirit "revealed" a personal meaning.

Further, 2 Peter 1:20 teaches that "no prophecy of Scripture is a matter of one's own interpretation." Peter goes on to explain that Scripture was given by the Holy Spirit (v. 21) through men. Since Scripture is of divine origin, its meaning is fixed by divine intent.

Some people challenge the teaching of Scripture with a dismissive, "Well, that's *just your* interpretation." Intended to end any discussion about the meaning of a passage, this implies that the true meaning can't be known with any certainty. They assume there are various viable interpretations for a passage, all of which are subjective and personal. There are two ways of answering this charge.

First, you can respond, "You are right. This is how I interpret the passage. But the fact that this is how I interpret it isn't proof the interpretation is wrong. I *might be wrong* in my interpretation of the passage, but that's only possible if we admit that there is a right interpretation." Simply pointing out that it is *you* that holds that interpretation does nothing to invalidate it.

Second, point out that just because there is more than one possible interpretation of a passage doesn't mean that none of them is correct. Just because people disagree on a question doesn't mean there is no "right answer." That some people get a math problem wrong doesn't mean the answer can't be known. People disagree over the shape of the earth but that doesn't mean the truth can't be known. Similarly, just because more than one interpretation of a passage is offered doesn't mean that one of them isn't right or that the true interpretation can't be known.

8. There were many things Jesus said that aren't recorded in Scripture (John 21:25), so why would there be an issue with Him saying things today that aren't recorded in Scripture?

This objection assumes that if God spoke things not recorded in Scripture in the past, He might be doing the same today. It's true that not everything God has ever said is recorded in Scripture. God spoke through prophets in Elijah's day words not recorded and preserved in Scripture. We have no reason to believe everything God said to Adam, Eve, or Noah are recorded in Genesis. Certainly, not every word Jesus spoke is recorded and preserved.

However, these observations are irrelevant to the issue at hand. My claim isn't that every word God has ever spoken has been recorded and preserved in Scripture. My claim is that every word God intends for us to have has been recorded and preserved in Scripture. I'm not saying nothing more was ever said, but that nothing more *needs* to be said.

Furthermore, those words not recorded are just as infallible, inerrant, and authoritative as what is recorded in Scripture. The unrecorded words of God carried just as much authority as Scripture. The authority, inerrancy, and infallibility of Scripture is not derived from the fact that it is written down or from the piety of the human persons who recorded it. Scripture is authoritative because it's God's Word. Anytime God speaks, it's authoritative and infallible. It can't be otherwise.

This puts the lie to the HVG teaching that God still speaks today, just not in an inspired, infallible, inerrant and authoritative way. They say His voice today *isn't* on the same level as Scripture.[12] This is utter nonsense. How does God speak in an unauthoritative, errant, and fallible way? Such a god is not the God of Scripture.

METHODOLOGICAL QUESTIONS

9. Without personal guidance through HVG in decision-making, how can we be certain we are actually doing God's will? How can we move forward with any confidence that we are not being disobedient?

I've seen Christians paralyzed by decisions because they fear God's discipline for not hearing Him accurately. God holds us responsible to obey what is revealed in Scripture. He doesn't reveal a secret will through vague impressions and breadcrumbs and then

---

[12] At the same time they inconsistently insist that the voice of God today is exactly like it was in biblical times.

punish us for not deciphering the clues. If we make a decision that doesn't violate the will of God revealed in Scripture, we haven't sinned. We can know we're within the will of God if we're living in obedience to Scripture. God will not discipline us for not obeying something He hasn't revealed. All He intends for us to know and obey is revealed in Scripture. Scripture is sufficient.

10. What about hunches and intuitions? Aren't these evidences that God is speaking to us?

We've all had "hunches" from time to time. Some of them turn out to be nothing. Others are prescient and profound assessments of circumstances. Sometimes hunches warn us of danger. Sometimes they portend something good. Acting almost like a "sixth sense," a hunch might provide clear direction on an issue. Everyone has ignored a hunch only to regret it later. Likewise, we have all credited some good decision to an intuition: "I just had a hunch about it." In HVG circles, this is treated as the voice of God.

I don't deny that we have hunches, intuitions, or impressions that feel compelling at times. What I do deny is that these feelings are the voice of God. How do I know? Because unbelievers have hunches too! Unbelievers have impressions and intuitions. They sense inexplicable "premonitions" and foreboding misgivings. Unbelievers have inklings and senses that something might happen or has happened. If this happens to unbelievers, then I can know for certain that it is not the voice of God whispering in our ear. Remember, HVG teachers tell us that such whispers belong to "His sheep."

All we can say about "hunches," "impressions," and "premonitions" is that they are a common experience. We all have them. We can't know with certainty the cause or source of a hunch. As Garry Friesen rightly notes, "Impressions could be produced by any number of sources: God, Satan, an angel, a demon, human emotions (such as fear or ecstasy), hormonal imbalance, insomnia, medication, or an upset stomach."[13]

There is nothing in Scripture that tells me when a hunch comes from God or originates with the kingdom of darkness. A hunch might be from God. It might not. The Holy Spirit might give us such a strong "sense" about something as to direct us toward or away from that thing. That isn't divine revelation. It's not His voice. It might be His work, but not everything the Holy Spirit does should be labeled

---

[13] Friesen and Maxson, *Decision Making*, 93.

"the voice of God." Since I can't know for sure what is causing the strong feeling or "sixth sense," I can't with any certainty claim it's the Holy Spirit.

11. How should we properly describe God's works in our life?

Modern Evangelical vernacular is littered with the shrapnel of bad theology. Have you heard any of the following?

The Lord is teaching me . . .

The Lord showed me . . .

The Lord led me to . . .

The Lord told me to . . .

The Lord laid it on my heart to . . .

I felt the Lord was telling me to . . .

These phrases imply a kind of direct revelatory insight into the intention or work of God. Someone using these phrases *may not* intend to describe personal revelation. He may simply desire to give God credit for His providential work of illumining Scripture, guiding his steps, or comforting him. He may want to give God credit for some good thought or motive behind a kind action. In that case, the intention is noble, but the language is misleading. Others intend to claim that God is directing their steps by whispers, impressions, and authoritative promptings. This, as I have endeavored to show, is entirely unbiblical.

As a rule, I try to be as precise with my language as possible. If I feel a strong compulsion to pray for a person or ministry, I won't say, "The Lord was leading me to pray," or, "The Lord laid it on my heart." Instead, I will say that "I felt a burden to pray for you. You were on my mind," or, "You were on my heart." I wouldn't say it was "the voice of God" or even His prompting. I don't know for certain why my heart was burdened at that particular moment. It might be the Lord's doing, but I can't be sure of that.

If I learned something through a sermon or my study of a passage, I don't describe that as "The Lord is teaching me" or "The Lord revealed..." That kind of language suggests God is providing new revelation. Instead, it is entirely biblical and appropriate to say, "That sermon made me realize . . .," or, "I learned that . . ."

Consider the following phrases:

I felt convicted to...

I learned that...

I was encouraged by...

I was burdened in my heart with...

We should seek to describe biblical concepts in biblical language avoiding confusing and unclear jargon. It is a noble intention to credit God with good things that happen in our hearts and lives. We should describe those works accurately. When we use unbiblical, inaccurate, or imprecise language to describe biblical truth, we risk attributing to God things that may not be His doing. We don't want to mischaracterize God's Word and works.

12. How should I interpret others' stories of "hearing God's voice"?

The books I have critiqued are *loaded* with examples of "hearing from God." A counter-argument to the position I have advocated typically goes something like this: "I prayed about it and I felt a quiet whisper in my heart telling me what to do. I did it and it turned out well. How do you explain that?" Or stated a little differently, "How should we interpret the experiences of those who felt they heard God speak?" My typical response to this challenge seems a bit harsh at first glance: "I can't exegete your experience." Further, I'm not obliged to exegete an experience.

I can exegete Scripture. When I do, it's obvious that the passages cited by HVG advocates don't support the theology they promote. My concern is with Scripture's teaching, not someone's experience. No one is obligated to explain Scripture in light of an experience. We should always seek to explain our experiences in the light of Scripture. Scripture determines truth, not experience. We can't build doctrine on experience nor let it dictate our interpretation of Scripture.

This is a fair approach to the question since I don't expect HVG teachers to explain my experience. I said in an earlier chapter that my lack of hearing from God isn't necessarily proof that He isn't speaking. My experience of *not* hearing from God has no more bearing on truth than someone else's experience of hearing Him.

I'm not saying that people don't feel impressions, sense burdens, or have hunches. We all do. Thoughts pop into our heads suddenly. We get ideas, musings, impressions, senses, perceptions, and gut feelings. Names and places come to mind as if out of nowhere. Memories resurface in our mind's eye. We get inklings, intuitions, premonitions. We can become suspicious, have misgivings, and feel unexplainable apprehensions. Some are baseless. Others turn out to be reliable. I have those things too! I don't label them "the voice of God" and regard them as divine direction. Scripture doesn't say that our impressions, burdens, hunches, feelings, thoughts or senses are the voice of God. Since Scripture never encourages us to regard the thoughts of our hearts or the meanderings of our minds as a word from God, nobody is obligated to explain away your claims to the contrary.

MISCELLANEOUS QUESTIONS
13. Aren't you just arguing from silence?

I understand the weaknesses of an argument from silence, but I'm not making an argument from silence. I'm claiming that if something isn't taught and modeled in Scripture, we aren't free to assume it was practiced. Further, we aren't free to teach and practice whatever we want. Our theology must be defined and constrained by Scripture. HVG theology claims that God is speaking today *just like He did* in biblical times. Well, where is it? Where is this method in Acts? Where is this taught in the Epistles? Where does Scripture teach this complex system for hearing from God? If "hearing the voice of God" is vital to Christian maturity, obedience, and spiritual well-being, we should see it *clearly* and *unmistakably* taught in Scripture. HVG teachers shouldn't have to abuse Bible verses to make their case.

Either the modern notion of hearing the voice of God through private revelations is complete nonsense, or God has been utterly negligent to clearly reveal the method by which we can discern and hear His voice.

14. Are people who think they hear from God lying or being deceived? Are they making up stories or do they sincerely believe God is speaking to them?

Yes. I am sure there are people in all those categories. I know genuine believers who are convinced that God is whispering to them in their thoughts. They're sincere. But I believe they're sincerely wrong. I'm equally certain that there are numerous frauds, charlatans, and false teachers who spin their tales of personal revelations to mystify and impress a willingly gullible following for their own reputation, fame, and financial gain.

277

Chapter 19

The Bad Fruit of HVG Theology

19

I have aggressively argued that HVG teaching is a fundamentally flawed, man-made, and unbiblical theology of divine revelation. It's inherently contradictory, confusing, and subjective. Their method of hearing from God isn't found in Scripture, despite their insistence to the contrary. The passages they cite are, without exception, taken out of context, misrepresented, and misapplied. A close examination of their teachings has demonstrated that their method of hearing from God is neither taught nor modeled in Scripture.

False teaching is always dangerous and Scripture repeatedly warns us about false and demonic doctrines.[1] Entire books of the New Testament are devoted to exposing false teachers and warning the church of the threats they pose.[2] James warned those who desired to be teachers of the Word of the stricter judgment they face (James 3:1). God takes truth seriously, and so should we. He is jealous for His name and His Word. Our desire should be the glory of both (1 Timothy 1:17; 6:13-16).

All we say about God should be true and worthy of Him. All we say about His Word should be accurate and faithful to it. Truth about God is a serious thing and misrepresenting Him is a blasphemy against the great benevolent King of Heaven. It is my contention

---

[1] 1 Timothy 1:3,18-20; 4:1-5; 6:3-5; 2 Timothy 1:13-14; 2:14-19; 3:1-9; Titus 1:9-16; 2:1; 3:9-11.

[2] Galatians, Colossians, 2 Peter, and Jude. By my count, every book of the New Testament, except Philemon, contains a corrective of false teachers, false teaching, or false doctrines.

that HVG theology misrepresents the God of Heaven and the sacred Scriptures in which He is revealed.

It's time to examine the fruit of HVG theology. Ideas have consequences, but bad ideas have victims. False doctrine, misrepresentations of God, and distortions of His Word are libels against His good name. Does HVG theology accurately represent God? Are their claims and promises true to Scripture? Do they manifest a consistently high view of God and His Word that is worthy of both?

Following are 12 ways that HVG theology misrepresents the truth about God and Scripture:[3]

1. HVG theology habitually misinterprets and misapplies Scripture.[4]

If HVG theology were true, its advocates wouldn't need to misinterpret Scripture to make the case. They wouldn't need to take verses out of context. Yet, they consistently do so. Hebrews 1, John 10, 1 Samuel 3, 1 Kings 19, Colossians 3, and Judges 6 are just a few passages that suffer ritual abuse at the hands of HVG teachers. They routinely divorce words, phrases, and verses from their context and press them into service in support of a man-made theological system.

The practice of divining personal messages out of scriptural texts constitutes a corruption of Scripture that would make a Jehovah's Witness blush. Without consideration for the author's intention or context, HVG teachers twist Scripture to their own ends. HVG theology isn't concerned with "accurately handling the word of truth" (2 Timothy 2:15), but only with how Scripture can become the vehicle for a personal message. The intended meaning of Scripture is irrelevant in their theological system. This is why it is so consistently ignored in pursuit of a personal message.

2. HVG theology misrepresents the nature of Scripture.[5]

HVG teachers describe Scripture as one of many means through which the voice of God may come. It is impossible to defend that theology without denying the uniqueness of Scripture. Though HVG teachers describe Scripture as "inspired" and "infallible," they

---

[3] Nearly everything in this chapter has been mentioned or expanded upon earlier. This list serves as a summary of the problems and errors in HVG theology.

[4] See Chapters 4-6, 8.

[5] See Chapter 8.

treat it as if it is no more unique than a song lyric, billboard, fortune cookie, or Magic 8-Ball. If you believe you are as likely to hear God speak through a random thought, a floating beer can, or soaring eagle as you are in the written Word of God, you have forfeited any claim to the Bible's uniqueness.

For HVG advocates, Scripture isn't the Word of God but a vehicle or context through which the word of God (a personal revelation) might come. It isn't itself a revelation, but only a record of God's past revelations. Scripture isn't God speaking, but a description of God speaking. This is a misrepresentation of the true nature of Scripture which claims to be the Word of God.

3. HVG Theology is a denial of the sufficiency of Scripture.[6]

HVG teachers teach that Scripture is a good general revelation, but it lacks any specific and personal direction for the individual. Scripture isn't sufficient revelation of God's love, purposes, or nature. It isn't sufficient for decision-making. We need information and directions not provided in the Bible.

Their teaching that we need to hear from God as much as Moses, Noah, or Paul, presupposes that what is contained in the Scriptures is not enough. It is logically inconsistent to defend the sufficiency of Scripture and modern revelations at the same time. A modern revelation is only necessary if Scripture isn't sufficient. If Scripture is sufficient, then no further revelation is needed. All continuationists *must* argue for some lack or inadequacy in the written Word.

4. HVG Theology undermines the authority of Scripture.

HVG teachers claim Scripture is the inspired, authoritative voice of God and impressions are the uninspired and non-authoritative voice of God. But how can God speak authoritatively on one occasion and not another? They persistently claim the voice of God today is *just like it was in Bible times* and say the modern voice is neither authoritative nor inspired. By teaching that God can and does speak without authority or inspiration, they undermine Scripture's authority and claim to inspiration.

---

[6] See Chapters 4-6.

5. HVG Theology undermines the inspiration, inerrancy, and infallibility of Scripture.

If God can speak today but not guarantee the inerrancy and infallibility of His words, on what basis can we claim Scripture is inerrant and infallible? HVG advocates teach that while God is speaking today, we can misunderstand it, fail to hear it, or get the details wrong. They insist God's voice today is *just like in Bible times*. If that is true, how do we know that the authors of Scripture got it right?

How can God speak inerrantly on one occasion and errantly on another? If God guarantees the inerrancy of His own revelation, then everything He says must be inerrant and infallible. If God does not or is not able to guarantee the inerrancy of His own revelation, then how do we know Scripture is inerrant?

How can modern hearers of God's voice hear an "uninspired" word from Him? If God is the source, then, by definition, it is inspired. Inspiration is the act of God "breathing out" His Word. He cannot speak an uninspired word. Inspiration, authority, infallibility, and inerrancy are the qualities inherent in every word God speaks because they come from Him.

It is impossible to argue consistently for inspired, inerrant, infallible, and authoritative revelation in the past and uninspired, errant, fallible, and nonauthoritative revelation in the present. Thus, HVG theology undermines these precious doctrines.

6. HVG teaching undermines the uniqueness of Scripture.

In HVG theology, everyone is a prophet. Everyone gets personal words from God. Paul got direction for gospel preaching. We get direction for choosing a contractor or landscaper. Paul was told where to preach. We are told where to have lunch. Unique and special men chosen by God as vehicles for His revelatory and redemptive purposes become mere models for our own experiences. Every Christian can hear God's voice in HVG teaching. Moses, Joshua, and Elijah are not unique. They are examples of common men who knew how to tune in to God's frequency and hear His whispers.

If there is nothing special about those men and the "voice" they heard, why should I obey the whispers they received over my own private whispers? If God's voice to me is *just like* God's voice to them, why should I obey what they heard over what I heard? This is how HVG theology undermines the authority and uniqueness of Scripture.

Under the Old Covenant, not every Jew was a recipient of divine revelation. The God-fearing Jew got his instructions from the written Word of God delivered through the prophets. In the New Covenant, we see the same thing. Not every Christian receives divine revelation. Special men were called by God to give us the Scriptures. Just like the Old Testament Jew, the New Testament Christian relies upon the written Word of God delivered through the prophets and apostles.

7. HVG theology leads Christians *away* from Scripture.

There is no encouragement in the HVG paradigm for the diligent study of Scripture, since the meaning of a passage is unrelated to the message received through it. We are encouraged to listen for God's voice, quiet our hearts, meditate upon our own thoughts, read the signs, and exegete our circumstances. What God speaks in the moment is more important than what He said 3,000 years ago. That is the unavoidable conclusion of HVG teaching.

Why do I need Scripture if God will direct me through other means? Why study the Scriptures to see what God says about marriage if He will reveal through a sign which woman I should marry? It is a waste of time to study the Proverbs, Ephesians 5, 1 Corinthians 7, Colossians 3, and 1 Peter 3 for God's wisdom on choosing a spouse if I can expect to hear His personal direction outside Scripture.

It is easier to assign divine authority to stray thoughts than to diligently study Scripture. Why make effort to get the meaning of Scripture right if I can get private whispers that leap off the page with a message completely unrelated to the meaning of the text? In fact, I can keep my Bible closed altogether and wait to get an impression, put out a fleece, and receive a confirmation for any decision. The bottom line is this: *If God genuinely speaks as promoted by HVG teachers - then I don't need Scripture.* In practice, it carries no more authority in HVG methodology than a billboard next to the freeway.

8. HVG Theology denigrates the God of Scripture.

Behold the god of HVG theology: He was able to speak infallibly in the past but not in the present. He can't guarantee His voice will be heard clearly. He needs our help. We have to listen intently, remove distractions, and quiet our hearts. We have to learn to hear him, for if we don't, he won't be able to get his message to us. Even if he does manage to get a message through to us, there is no guarantee we have received it accurately. We could still mess it up or misunderstand him. He is difficult to hear, and even harder to understand. Because he doesn't speak clearly or unmistakably, we frequently get what he says wrong. He wants us to hear and hopes that we will, but he can't guarantee that his purposes for our lives will be accomplished. He is *trying* to get us a message. He *needs* to get us a message. Scripture isn't quite enough to adequately communicate his love or his will for us. Without a whispered word from him, we are stranded in a one-sided relationship with only our Bibles for guidance.

The god of HVG theology is a god of confusion, vague hints, and unclear directives. He is unable to clearly speak to anyone. Though we need him to tell us what to do, he can't reveal it in any clear fashion. Every ambiguous hint and unsettled stirring of the mind needs to be tested, checked and double checked, and confirmed before it can be trusted. Even after this cumbersome process, the voice is not authoritative or infallible in any meaningful sense. All we can do is stumble along life's path and hope to keep our errors to a minimum.

If only God were able to give us a "more sure word."

Does this sound like the God revealed in Scripture? Does this sound like the God who sits enthroned in Heaven Who does as He pleases (Psalm 115:3)? Is this the Sovereign God Who establishes all His purposes and accomplishes all His good pleasure (Isaiah 46:10)? It is not. Perhaps the most egregious error of HVG theology is its blasphemous portrayal of God and His ways.

9. HVG theology inevitably blames God for a lot of silly and foolish decisions.

In HVG theology, the blame for unwise decisions falls at the feet of God, who allegedly revealed His will through an impression or inner voice. In a bizarre teaching session, Beth Moore claims that God told her to walk up and brush the hair of a complete stranger in an airport.[7] She also claims that she built a snowman with God:

I heard the voice of God speak to my heart: "Come and play." I love that He said, "Come." Not, "Go." "Come." That meant He was already there.

---

[7] https://www.godvine.com/god-tells-beth-moore-to-brush-a-strangers-hair-10972.html.

I also love how I could tell by the sweet tone of the silent voice whispering to my spirit that He was smiling. . . . I could have outlined His expression with my finger.

Then she claims, "I built a snowman. . . . I laughed with God. He laughed with me. . . . I am so in love with Him. *I am so in love with Him.*"[8]

Matt Chandler told a ridiculous tale of encouraging someone with a vision he had of a pirate ship being chased by sharks. Though Chandler admitted that the vision was "weird," "crazy," and "didn't make any sense at all," he still attributed it to the Holy Spirit's prompting.[9] Further, he encouraged his congregation to consider their random thoughts and impulses - what they chalk up "to just stuff flowing through your head" - as something divine - God's "invitation to play." This kind of nonsense is inevitable when every stray thought is assumed to be a word from God. When the muddled meanderings of our minds are assigned divine authority and our musings are stamped with "The Lord told me . . .," God takes the blame for the foolishness that inevitably follows.

I went to Bible college with a kid who left the dorm at 8:00 p.m. one evening and hitchhiked to the nearest town (45 miles away) in the dead of winter because God "told him" to go to the coffee shop to witness all through the night. He disobeyed school policy, dorm rules, and missed class the next day. How do you reason with someone who "heard the voice of God" tell him to do such a thing? I know of a lady who justified her adultery by saying that "God told her" it was the right thing to do. I worked on a construction site with a young man who heard a different directive from God every week. "God's voice" in any given week would contradict the voice from the previous week.

Do you think this is uncommon? Twenty-four hours of programming on Trinity Broadcast Network will prove me right. Pick a day, any day.

10. HVG theology puts words in God's mouth.

As if misrepresenting what God has said is not bad enough, they misrepresent what He hasn't said. HVG practitioners attribute words to God with an alarming flippancy. They think nothing of

---

[8] Beth Moore, *When Godly People Do Ungodly Things* (Nashville: Broadman & Holman Publishers, 2002), 123-124.

[9] The entire message is available here: https://www.youtube.com/watch?v=n0aB1lolHn0. The pirate ship story begins around the 39:10 mark.

claiming "The Lord said...," "God told me to...," and, "I heard the Lord say..."

How do you, dear reader, like being misquoted? Have you ever had someone claim that you said something that *you did not say?* Have you ever been misrepresented? Has anyone put words in your mouth and attributed statements to you that you never uttered? Do you think God takes it lightly when He is misrepresented in that way? Read through the prophetic books (Isaiah-Malachi) and take note of the occasions where God condemned false prophets who spoke in His name when He did not send them. The wrath of God burned against them. That is a form of blasphemy. Misrepresenting God and His Word is a serious thing.

HVG teachers would have every right to be indignant if I misquoted them in this book. They would feel wronged if I were to misrepresent what they have said by taking their words out of context and claiming they teach something they don't, in fact, teach. Yet, they do this to God all the time. They don't afford Him the same dignity and respect that they would demand from others.

It is a serious thing to claim to speak for God. It is a grievous sin to put words in His mouth and claim divine fiat for your random thoughts.

11. HVG theology promotes a false view of Christian maturity.

In HVG circles, hearing the voice of God is a mark of maturity. The spiritual believer who walks closely with God will hear the Shepherd's voice. The health of one's spiritual life is not measured by his understanding of Scripture, his ability to handle it accurately, or his obedience to it. In HVG theology, hearing a fresh word from God is the measure of maturity. It is the *essential* component of healthy spirituality.[10]

True maturity isn't marked by an ability to hear God outside Scripture. It is growing in the grace and knowledge of Christ (2 Peter 1:2; 3:18), being sound in doctrine (Ephesians 4:11-16), and walking in a manner worthy of our high calling in Him (Ephesians 4:1).

---

[10] See Chapters 4-6.

12. HVG theology promotes a Gnostic view of the Christian life.

In the first century, a pagan notion of knowledge and enlightenment started making inroads into some Christian circles. It was later referred to as the "Gnostic Heresy." "Gnostic" comes from the Greek word *gnosis* which means "knowledge." Early gnostic doctrines threatened some churches. Paul and John addressed some early versions of gnostic teachings (Colossians, 1 John).[11]

The gnostics taught that some people belonged to an elite group with "special knowledge." They claimed a knowledge of God and spiritual realities unavailable to the common Christian. According to the gnostics, salvation came by a special enlightenment given to some, but not all.

The gnostic tendencies in HVG theology are apparent. Though they affirm God has communicated to us all in Scripture, only some have developed the discipline of hearing His voice. Those who have tuned in to God's frequency and learned to hear His whispers have a knowledge of God's will not available to all. They claim access to secrets God reveals to them alone.[12] This is a repackaged Gnosticism masquerading as intimacy with God.

This is the fruit of HVG theology. Their HVG view of God is wholly unworthy of Him. Their treatment of Scripture is inexcusable. Let the believer, zealous for God's honor, abandon every vestige of HVG teaching.

---

[11] For a clear and concise treatment of various early church heresies, see Justin S. Holcomb, *Know the Heretics* (Grand Rapids, Zondervan). I would also recommend a preaching series by Phil Johnson, the Executive Director of Grace to You, available at his website: https://www.thegracelifepulpit.com/sermons.aspx?code=PJ-CDA04.

[12] Beth Moore claims that God tells her secrets. She writes, "What little I know, I want others to know. Before God tells me a secret, He knows up front I'm going to tell it! By and large, that's our 'deal'" (Beth Moore, *Praying God's Word* [Nashville, B&H Publishing Group, 2009], 2.).

Conclusion

A Final Appeal

20

My own experience with hearing the voice of God - or more accurately, *not hearing the voice of God* - doesn't prove that God doesn't speak today outside Scripture. The same would be true if I had sensed some whisper during that crisis at college. If I had sensed the voice of God at that time, it wouldn't be proof that God does speak today outside Scripture. Our experience *proves* nothing. It might agree with truth. It might contradict truth. It does not determine truth. God's Word does.

I haven't attempted to present an argument from experience in this book. I've argued from the teaching of Scripture. HVG advocates claim their teachings are firmly rooted in God's Word citing passages in support. We have examined those passages in their context and compared them with the teachings of those who claim to hear from God. In case after case, the passages they cite do not support the weight of the teachings built upon them. The assumptions they make aren't taught in Scripture and the practices they promote aren't supported by the texts.

God doesn't *try* to communicate. He doesn't need to *try* because He doesn't lack the power to accomplish anything He does. He doesn't need our help. He isn't stymied by our inabilities. Rather than attempting to communicate in vague signs, confusing dreams, and unreliable impressions, God has given us an objective written revelation. It is sufficient and perfect. It's everything we need for life and godliness (2 Peter 1:3-4). It's "more sure" than even the most fantastic personal experiences (2 Peter 1:16-21). It equips us for every good work (2 Timothy 3:14-17).

If your relationship with God has revolved around the subjective experiences described in this book, you may feel a bit shaken by this point. Perhaps I have convinced you that HVG methodology is fraught with unbiblical assumptions, twisted Scripture, and spiritually dangerous practices. If you are rattled by this and unsure where to stand, I point you to Scripture. The "hearing from God" experiences you have stood on for all these years was an unsure and unsteady foundation. Scripture is the solid rock. You need nothing more.

With the Holy Spirit dwelling in you and the Word of God before you, you stand on a sure foundation. Scripture is the treasure trove of divine wisdom, truth, and knowledge of your God. Read it. Meditate upon it. Memorize it. Hear it preached. Study it. Love it. Obey it. It will take you a lifetime to familiarize yourself with it. You will never master it. You will never move beyond it. You will never need more.

> How firm a foundation, ye saints of the Lord,
> Is laid for your faith in His excellent word!
> What more can He say than to you He hath said,
> To you who for refuge to Jesus have fled?
> — John Rippon, "How Firm A Foundation"

"And now I commend you to God and to the word of His grace, which is able to build you up and to give you the inheritance among all those who are sanctified" (Acts 20:32).

Bibliography - HVG Authors

Batterson, Mark. *Whisper: How to Hear the Voice of God.* New York: Crown Publishing Group, 2017.

Blackaby, Henry T., and Claude V. King. *Experiencing God: How to Live the Full Adventure of Knowing and Doing the Will of God.* Nashville: Broadman & Holman Publishers, 1994.

Bolz, Shawn. *Translating God: Hearing God's Voice for Yourself and the World Around You.* Glendale: ICreate Productions, 2015.

Deere, Jack. *Surprised by the Power of the Spirit.* Grand Rapids: Zondervan Publishing House, 1993.

Deere, Jack. *Surprised by the Voice of God: How God Speaks Today Through Prophecies, Dreams, and Visions.* Grand Rapids: Zondervan Publishing House, 1996.

Doyle, Tom. *Dreams and Visions: Is Jesus Awakening the Muslim World?* Nashville: Thomas Nelson, 2012.

Eckhardt, John. *God Still Speaks: How to Hear and Receive Revelation from God for Your Family, Church and Community.* Lake Mary: Charisma House, 2009.

Eldredge, John. *Walking With God.* Nashville: Thomas Nelson, 2008.

Grudem, Wayne. *Christian Ethics: An Introduction to Biblical Moral Reasoning.* Wheaton: Crossway, 2018.

Grudem, Wayne. *Systematic Theology: An Introduction to Biblical Doctrine.* Grand Rapids: Zondervan, 1994.

Grudem, Wayne. *The Gift of Prophecy in the New Testament and Today.* Wheaton: Crossway Books, 2000.

Hybels, Bill. *The Power of a Whisper: Hearing God. Having the Guts to Respond.* Grand Rapids: Zondervan, 2010.

Jacobs, Cindy. *The Voice of God: How to Hear and Speak Words from God.* Minneapolis: Baker Publishing Group, 2016.

Meyer, Joyce. *How to Hear from God: Learn to Know His Voice and Make Right Decisions.* New York: Faith Words, 2003.

Moore, Beth. *Praying God's Word: Breaking Free from Spiritual Strongholds.* Nashville: Broadman & Holman Publishers, 2009.

Morris, Robert. *Frequency: Tune in. Hear God.* Nashville: Thomas Nelson, 2016.

Shirer, Priscilla. *Discerning the Voice of God: How to Recognize When God is Speaking.* Chicago: Moody Publishers, 2012.

Shirer, Priscilla. *He Speaks to Me: Preparing to Hear From God.* Chicago: Moody Publishers, 2006.

Stanley, Charles. *How to Listen to God.* Nashville: Thomas Nelson Publishers, 1985.

Storms, Sam. *Practicing The Power: Welcoming the Gifts of the Holy Spirit in Your Life.* Grand Rapids: Zondervan, 2017.

Willard, Dallas. *Hearing God: Developing a Conversational Relationship with God.* Downers Grove: IVP Books, 2012.

Qureshi, Nabeel. *Seeking Allah, Finding Jesus: A Devout Muslim Encounters Christianity.* Grand Rapids: Zondervan, 2018.

Bibliography - Recommended Resources

Budgen, Victor. *The Charismatics and the Word of God: A Biblical and Historical Perspective on the Charismatic Movement.* Llandrillo: Evangelical Press, 2001.

Ferguson, Sinclair B. *Discovering God's Will.* Edinburg: The Banner of Truth Trust, 2013.

Friesen, Garry and Robin Maxson. *Decision Making and the Will of God.* Sisters: Multnomah, 2004.

Hinn, Costi W., and Anthony G. Wood. *Defining Deception.* El Cajon: Southern California Seminary Press, 2018.

Jensen, Philip D., and Tony Payne. *Guidance and the Voice of God.* Sydney: Matthias Media, 1997.

Koukl, Gregory. *Decision Making and the Will of God.* Audio CD Series.

MacArthur, John. *Charismatic Chaos.* Grand Rapids: Zondervan, 1992.

MacArthur, John. *Final Word: Why We Need the Bible.* Orlando: Reformation Trust Publishing, 2019.

MacArthur, John. *The MacArthur New Testament Commentary: Acts 1-12*. Chicago: Moody Press, 1994.

MacArthur, John, and Mayhue, Richard, eds. *Biblical Doctrine: A Systematic Summary of Bible Truth*. Wheaton: Crossway, 2017.

Sproul, R.C., Voddie Baucham, Jack MacArthur, John MacArthur, Martyn Lloyd-Jones, Steven J. Lawson, Mark Dever, R. Albert Mohler, Jr., Conrad Mbewe, Nathan Busenitz, Justin Peters, Phil Johnson. *One Foundation: Essays on the Sufficiency of Scripture*. Valencia: Grace to You, 2019.

Swavely, Dave. *Decisions, Decisions: How (and How Not) to Make Them*. Phillipsburg: P&R Publishing, 2003.

Waldron, Samuel E. *To Be Continued: Are the Miraculous Gifts for Today?* Merrick: Calvary Press Publishing, 2005.

About the Author

Jim Osman was born in May of 1972 and has lived in Sandpoint, Idaho since he was three years old. He graduated from Sandpoint High School in 1990. Jim came to know Christ through the ministry of Cocolalla Lake Bible Camp in the summer of 1987. Kootenai Community Church has always been his home church, attending Sunday School, Vacation Bible School, and Youth Group.

After graduating from High School, Jim attended Millar College of the Bible in Pambrun, Saskatchewan. It was at Bible College that Jim met his wife-to-be, Diedre, who was also enrolled as a student. Jim graduated with a three-year diploma in April of 1993 and married Diedre in August of that same year. He returned to Millar to further his education in September of 1994 and graduated from the Fourth Year Internship Program with a Bachelor of Arts in Strategic Ministries in April of 1995. He was inducted into the Honor Society of the Association of Canadian Bible Colleges and appointed a member of Pi Alpha Mu.

Jim and Diedre returned to Sandpoint where Jim began working in construction as a roofer until he was asked to take over as the preaching elder of Kootenai Community Church in December of 1996. Now he counts it his greatest privilege to be involved in ministering in the church that ministered to him for so many years. He is the author of *Truth or Territory: A Biblical Approach to Spiritual Warfare*, *Selling the Stairway to Heaven: Critiquing the Claims of Heaven Tourists*, and *The Prosperity of the Wicked: A Study of Psalm 73*. You can follow his preaching at the Kootenai Community Church website and his writings at truthorterritory.com.

Jim loves to be outdoors, whether it is camping, hunting, or working in his garden. He enjoys bike riding and watching football, especially his favorite team, the San Francisco 49ers, for whom he has cheered since childhood. Jim and Diedre have four children: Taryn, Shepley, Ayden and Liam. They are all 49er fans! You can contact Jim through Kootenai Community Church (http://www.kootenaichurch.org) or by writing to him at jimcosman@truthorterritory.com.

Made in United States
Orlando, FL
10 July 2024

48835494R00190